Contemporary Architecture in Germany

Contemporary Architecture in Germany

Introduction by Ulrich Conrads · Text by Werner Marschall
Translated by James Palmes

Frederick A. Praeger, Publisher, New York

BOOKS THAT MATTER

Published in the United States of America in 1962
by Frederick A. Praeger, Inc., Publisher
64 University Place, New York 3, N.Y.
All rights reserved
© Verlag Gerd Hatje 1962
Library of Congress Catalog Card Number: 62–13860
Printed in Germany

Fundamental Aspects of German Post-war Architecture

If an accurate picture of the principal features of new German architecture is to be obtained, we must first turn to post-war building in Germany, to building as an operation judged by quantity, as a problem of statistics. In a country devastated by war, where, by comparison with 1939, one fifth of all dwellings were destroyed, in which a further two-and-a-half million homes for refugees from the Eastern Zone and central Germany did not exist and, in addition, a million young families of the new generation had nowhere to live – in a country such as this, architecture and the erection of buildings was no more, to begin with, than a question of arithmetic. With a shortage of 5,800,000 homes, town centres and public services of every kind destroyed or no longer able to function in what had been left to them, a state of dire need, of acute emergency, prevailed. Until the early fifties this condition could only be alleviated by improvisation.

It was the consequences of the currency reform of 1948 and – a year after in September 1949 – the establishment of the Federal Republic of Germany, which opened the floodgates to a spate of building activity. The Federal Republic was recognised as a sovereign state in 1955 and, in the same year, the stagnation of the early post-war years was transformed into a building boom, which far exceeded that of the late nineteenth century.

The boom continued and, five years later in 1960, measures were devised and introduced to stem the tide of building work. The Federal Minister of Housing found himself obliged to propose controls on the granting of building permission when a few months before he had allowed the ratification of the law transferring housing to the free market. It had been possible for this law to come into force because of the unprecedented quantitative achievements in housing construction since 1950, and it was passed in conjunction with the Federal Building Act of 20th May 1960, which henceforth provided a foundation and executive instrument for all building operations in the Federal Republic.

The attainment of state sovereignty and the ratification of the Federal Building Act define historically and chronologically the second five-year period of building in post-war Germany. The buildings of this time were planned and erected in five exuberant years of flood tide, of soaring prosperity, of an economic serenity which scarcely wavered.

But in creating the new framework of the Federal state, which was envisaged by the authors of the statute (the Parliamentary Council) as only an interim matter, the creation of new towns, which could not be achieved by provisional action, was left in the background. Except in the field of housing, the strictly federal structure of the building industry hindered the ratification of the far-reaching legislation which was needed. Opposition to every centralizing measure – a reaction to a decade of restrictions and controls – went much too far, and this was also true in the individual provinces of the Federation. One of the basic principles of the new state, independence, was practised to excess in just those matters in which the right of the other man to contribute is indispensable to an intelligent, independent, point of view – in all planning and building. In administrative and economic questions, an appropriate interpretation of self-determination was much more easily and logically found.

But in the reconstruction of towns a too narrow regard for the rights and duties of land and building ownership hampered constructive town planning developments. For reconstruction was a task for the community and, as such, linked with social progress. In common with all aspects of spatial and urban planning, it ought to have been from the start a reflection of the new society. But the metamorphosis of a war and post-war community into a democratic society was – and still is – a slow process. The individual's right to self-determination, so long missing and now implicit in all legislation, did not lead to an architectural representation of the newly emerging, free, society. In the second paragraph of article 14 of the constitution it is said: "Property implies responsibilities. It should be used to serve the community." Ten years have not been enough, however, to give concrete substance to these sentences, which are so decisively important for all building.

The following situation, therefore, arose. Except in housing, which inspired constant exertions, except in purely functional building for commerce and industry, except in the production of the basic necessities for living and working, there existed at first a kind of mental vacuum. All building which went beyond ensuring life remained unessential. This vacuum was filled in a rippling, and finally overflowing, tidal wave of unprecedented free-for-all competition, by government buildings, banks, insurance palaces, office blocks, stores, cinemas and hotels. Over night, so to speak, one was confronted by a mass of buildings which strove to ensure confidence not in a whole new way of life, but in themselves. These buildings were intended to represent the most secure, most efficient, most trustworthy, most impressive (or any other appropriate superlative) enterprise in an economically flourishing, but socially still only embryonic community. Thus post-war Germany had two forms of building: one which, under the most stringent financial and material restrictions, but protected from abuses by compulsory technical building regulations, produced from 1953 a yearly average of 550,000 homes; and another which, thanks to the boom, expended its surplus funds on a host of luxurious, or apparently luxurious, objects. From 1950 the architect in Germany was caught between two fires. In housing, he was compelled by strict regulations, upon which the granting of public resources inevitably depended, to abandon progressive ideas and experiments. He found himself tied to a very few house and housing types, which were considered to have special economic virtues. He could, it is true, design variants and work at improvements in the floor plan, but genuine alternatives, however convincingly presented, had little chance. Planning considerations, with a few exceptions, remained secondary, while the study of technical details and the rationalization of building methods were pursued with dogged perseverance.

On the other hand, the architect found himself confronted by tasks that demanded individuality, representative design and fashionable façades without ignoring economy and functionalism. He was asked to be different from the others, to have a distinctive style, yet at the same time to conform to all the latest trends. He was not expected to spend less than was legally permitted; on the contrary, he was supposed to get the greatest possible appropriations from the authorities. Not the architect with an artistic conscience was in demand, but the facile mass producer; and he soon found himself presiding over a large staff.

But before these problems – very roughly sketched here – became acute, the first post-war years were concerned with the marshalling of forces, sharply decimated by war and emigration, but fertile in points of view. These first discussions and meetings were full of exciting prospects.

Viewed very simply, there existed at this time three intellectual camps or, better, three schools of thought, which derived from the influence of the important architectural teachers of the twenties. The group around Bonatz and Schmitthenner was the most important, although its exponents were most reticent in public discussions. As far back as 1930 – despite the Bauhaus, the Berlin architects' "ring" and the influence of the "radicals" – this group had decided the essential features of so-called good average architecture: solid, earthbound stuff, relying on craftsmanship and with regional traits. They based their standards on either the provincial architecture of a particular region or a tenuous classicism. This was an architecture which looked for repose and harmony, with no surprises or violent contrasts, containing the seeds of a national style. National Socialism hailed it immediately and without difficulty as The German Architecture, and was able later to distort it into Hitler's architecture of might. It is hardly surprising that the architects of this school, even when they expressly disowned the Nazis, endured the era of the Third Reich with less molestation than colleagues imbued with the spirit of the Bauhaus and CIAM, who regarded the new architecture as an international affair.

This second group remained scattered during the first post-war years. The masters of the Bauhaus and their followers had, with a few exceptions, been forced to leave Germany by the early thirties, or had left of their own free will. The few who remained were scattered to the winds, and among them was no Gropius or Mies van der Rohe capable of rallying the stragglers.

The third school, and the most significant in the development of our post-war architecture, were those whom we can lump together as Poelzig's disciples. Most of them had found refuge during the bleak years in industrial building, or had been able to devote themselves to jobs of an essentially functional kind, in which modern solutions passed undetected. They came together, a phalanx of strong personalities with sometimes vastly different individual viewpoints, to trace the broad outlines of a new architecture in post-war Germany. They brought brains to their work and found their way to the empty academic chairs of the university colleges. Their position at that time, offering a point of departure, held great promise. To-day, twelve years later, this position is secure. But, does it still hold any promise?

We must remember that the last German building of international stature before the war was Mies van der Rohe's Barcelona pavilion of 1929. Mies had gone to the United States in 1938, like Gropius and others before him. Hans Poelzig, dismissed from his teaching post, was dead by 1936. Bereft of their teachers and masters, and deprived of their high critical standards, the second generation of modern architects faced a post-war task, which required not only courage and an unshakeable belief in their cause, but more than a reasonable share of artistic and intellectual gifts – in short, a spark of genius. The problem of building in devastated Germany far exceeded anything that could have been predicted.

At first, therefore, things moved along the well worn and tested, unequivocal, pretentious, track which had been drawn and laid in the twenties. In this conception a variety of influences were mingled, deriving from the new contacts which German architects were now able to make with other countries. From Switzerland, from new buildings in the U.S.A. and England, and from Scandinavian achievements, the new German architecture was shaping towards a more humane interpretation of its former "new practicality", to a less abstract architectural cubism, associated with comprehensive technical development in all the processes of building. Materials, construction, function, cubic solidity allied to transparency, the logical and flexible interrelationship of space – these were the principal things that mattered. Architecture had become tidier, more elegant, in conception.

But such a programme was hardly fitted to the two kinds of task which we outlined at the beginning. Its dogmatism was suited neither to the urgent problems of popular housing, nor was it acceptable to the opportunists, to whom everything in the young democracy which could be exploited was as grist to their mill. The determining factor, however, was that the decisive, incisive, idea was lacking. This new architecture was little more in spirit than a revival. The struggle to get back to work, to recover the leeway of more than ten barbarous years, to restore self-confidence and find security, immeasurably weakened initiative. Fresh risks were shunned.

The circumstances of the unwonted liberty of action of the middle class – that is to say the clients – failing, while a simultaneous condition of dire shortage and urgency existed, produced an architecture which rarely reflected the capabilities of those who had to practise it, and often practised it against their better judgment. That this reaction upon a timorous, uncertain clientèle was an essential feature of young and unfamiliar democratic freedom was of small consolation in its results.

Was there nobody, then, to work out new plans and a new architecture from the experience of Germany's self-destruction, no one who, confronted with the ruins, which were not merely on the surface, drew conclusions of deeper significance for building? Such men existed, but they remained isolated and without influence, then as now. Hugo Häring, who had once coined the term "neues Bauen (new building)", sat, old and alone with his thoughts, at Biberach. What he had to say, as an architect and thinker, went unheeded and therefore, without effect. Even Martin Mächler's broad perspectives had no influence. Both died in 1958.

In 1946 words were spoken which could have marked a beginning. The new town, said Hans Scharoun, as a planner of the new Berlin, "will have to be constantly recast by the evolving social pattern of its inhabitants. Otherwise it is they who will be cast in its mould. For there can be no ethical freedom without an imaginative system of orderly development for the new town." That was a step forward, and support came to him from every possible source – but to no purpose. Crisis and boom do not listen; or, as Max Frisch said, we were afraid to have ideas and, because we had no ideas, we were afraid. So the achievements of German post-war architecture, even those buildings of the past five years collected in this volume, stand in an empty space. Their standard of quality is on the whole of small consequence. Securing a livelihood, conventional reconstruction, spiritual regeneration, these things overshadowed and overshadow what ought to have initiated our new architecture after the war – the resolute foundation of a science for the human habitat from the mid-century onwards.

Even in university colleges, questions of a fundamental nature or structural problems concerning habitation were rarely tackled. The details of building, the handling of isolated architectural tasks, held pride of place. Only in exceptional cases were diploma studies and projects set as a broad survey. Where wider implications were indicated, they hardly ever went beyond housing schemes. In town-planning schools, too, there usually reigned a confusion of ideas about housing. There was an all too rigid

devotion to mere building matters in the tasks submitted to teachers. The method of working had its influence on theory and research. Functional and economic thinking, necessary as both were and are, restricted far too often the development of talent. Nevertheless, university colleges remained centres where contemporary problems were discussed soberly and intelligently. They continued to maintain their effectiveness during the fifties, especially where strong personalities formed "schools" which today influence the architectural scene in general.

By the middle fifties this contribution was quite appreciable. The third generation, born between 1920 and 1930, had left their studies and training behind them. Sceptical of their opportunities, critical of their teachers, these young architects brought firm principles and convictions from the schools to the world of architecture. Many succumbed quickly to the routine of the big offices; others accommodated themselves to the general trend of events in the hope of better things. But everywhere a few carried on with little concession or compromise. They faced the temptations of the building boom with patient and tenacious endeavour. They disciplined themselves on inconspicuous, often complicated, jobs. The particular qualities of these first works and buildings are achieving recognition. The young architects have had successes in competitions and come forward with solutions which often show far above average competence, dispelling with speed and encouraging finality any objections to entrusting big commissions to young people. The buildings of the third generation are beginning to be noticed in our townscape. In many instances they set the standard.

The third generation arrived without programme or manifesto. Their temperament is, so to speak, unimpassioned. It is unrevolutionary, extremely conscientious, expressing restraint, austerity and reserve rather than exuberance. Their dreams are practical, and amount to a rejection of individuality. To work like an "engineer" is regarded as a compliment. They are reluctant to expose themselves, and only do it when they are certain of their ground. They have no wish to court misunderstandings, and by no means do they like to appear young. Reason characterizes the arguments and buildings of this generation. Purpose, function, economy they regard as principles which can help them to sell architecture more easily. Good architecture is something slipped in through backdoors like these. For the rest they are "honest and of good appearance", helping each other, but no longer acting in combination, because they have learnt that good architecture cannot any more be presented and proclaimed, but must be quietly, firmly and subtly introduced. Able and adaptable, this generation of architects is submerged by a society, from which self-confidence is still missing and which continues to dissipate their capabilities in cautious and limited projects. Or in outright rejection of what it believes is beyond their powers.

On the whole, this young generation of architects sacrifices its youth. However salutary self-restraint may be amid the mistakes of the new architecture with which our towns are cluttered, it has a bitter reverse side. The discouragement of ideas, the suppression of creative imagination, the elimination of artistic values, the thwarting of ambitions – all these lead sooner or later either to a conventional dogmatism or to a silent, enduring resentment against our time and circumstances. In the end we give in. But anyone who kept his eyes and ears open must have noticed in the last few years that there has been less reticence in discussions. Responsibilities are recognized, interests aroused, opinions expressed, and chances taken. To the passive rights and duties of an executive are now added those of active participation. A fact particularly relevant to the third generation is that henceforth the architect is more of a politician than before. His artistic and technical qualifications are supplemented by a keen political judgment and a sense of our social interdependence. His part is to give form and substance to the problems of building in a democracy. In this respect the prospects are already encouraging, as indeed some of the buildings collected in this volume reveal.

German Architecture 1955–61

The most significant approaches to solutions, those which go well beyond the conventional and indeed the modern, are to be found among the unexecuted projects of the period covered here; but what is, in this context, the relevant part is constantly treated as secondary. The powers of discrimination of those who have had to decide on the merits or shortcomings of these projects, are still much prejudiced by considerations of form. If only a few of these designs are built, their feasibility can only in a few instances be tested.

For this reason, our selection of buildings actually erected during the last five years is hardly representative of the forces that are trying to break through. It can only show the quality of that which could be achieved under the social, economic and technological conditions of those years. Often enough, however, we are dealing with exceptions, made possible by the support of unusually perceptive and purposeful clients, or carried to fruition by the strongly held convictions of particular architects. Although our selection excludes projects, it is still not typical for architecture in Germany today. The examples were chosen only from the very best; they show the direction in which architects are trying to go. The sum total gives neither cause for special pride, nor for diffidence. One may fairly claim that the result is good, for good it undoubtedly is. But we ought not to be complacent.

This is above all true of housing, in spite of its variety of forms. All the exertions made during the period of this report have not succeeded in influencing to any extent the normal types of dwelling in post-war Germany – detached home, terrace house, 2- or 4-storey flats. As before, the conventional dwelling follows traditional patterns, the economic soundness of which seems to be established, but whose value as a place to live in lies far below its (often only ostensible) economic worth. It was probably a sign of this incongruous situation that Eduard Ludwig was permitted only to design a sparse flat for two people for the German section of the 1958 World's Fair in Brussels, and that the model flat in one of the German pavilions carefully avoided any definite architectural statement. Yet there is no dirth of such statements, whether they concern the influence of the landscape on architecture, the combination of an intimate, homey atmosphere with open spaces, or the spatial relationships of living areas. The architects of the third generation have very definite ideas; they are no longer concerned only with the purely formal aspects of building.

The garden courtyard house on the Durlacher Berg by Reinhard Gieselmann, Gottfried Böhm's home by the Rhine, the country residence in the Odenwald by Waldemar Lippert and the houses on the Taunus foothills by Wilfried Beck-Erlang and Eugen Söder – all these are thoroughly considered attempts to make home life a full life and not just a departmentalized process. That here and there features are to be seen, details perhaps, which derive from the preconceived cubic form of the building's mass, and have little to do with the amenities of living, indicates the particular viewpoint from which the problem has to be visualized. It is still an open question whether the traditional cubic form of houses can offer new possibilities and new ways of living modes. For there are not only differences informal conception (compare, for instance, Gerhard Schwab's Studio house with the house at Brunswick by Friedrich Wilhelm Kraemer and those at Lörbach and Königstein already mentioned), but also astonishing differences in the character of houses, in the interpretation of val-

8

ues, as the attractive "bungalows", which are everywhere super-seding the "villa", most convincingly show.

Two detached houses, one in Brunswick by Kraemer and the other (with two self-contained flats and office) by Oswald Mathias Ungers at Köln-Müngersdorf, illustrate the extremes in concep-tion, between which German domestic architecture has hovered in recent years. In the first instance, emphasis is laid on enclosed and rigidly defined cubic figures. The carefully modelled façade owes its appeal to the materials and not least to the contradic-tion that the "enclosed" form is in fact invitingly open on all sides. In the other, the house in Cologne (Köln) is a multipartite composition of plastic shapes; a contrasting interplay of positives and negatives characterizes the whole design, which is almost uncompromisingly introvert, and yet, in its mass, is even more closely related to the site and adjoining buildings, in short to its environment. In both cases we must not allow ourselves to be deceived by formal resemblances. Kraemer's house has no more connection with Mies van der Rohe's prototype than has the house by Ungers with the "Neoplasticists". In both cases a thorough study of the plans is necessary to form an impartial judgment.

The aims pursued by Ungers become somewhat clearer in the block of flats on the Hansaring in Cologne: a plastic structure, specifically developed from the site conditions and the require-ments of the building programme (in this instance, filling a gap in a busy street, in which the South is the road side). Ungers' logical and by no means merely formal considerations contain important ideas for the renewal of old residential sections – something that cannot be accomplished by the usual, con-ventional methods of popular housing.

Still unheard are Hans Scharoun's ideas on the home and the processes of living, and on all those values connected with, and essential to, these processes. The architectural homeopathy, with which Scharoun opposes slick and unscrupulous solutions, must by its nature appear obscure. In "Romeo" and "Juliet", his tower blocks of flats at Stuttgart-Zuffenhausen, however, we now have tangible exemplars. One thing is clear about these two buildings, whatever their individual assets may be. The large block of flats can contribute a character and urbanity to town design of a kind which nobody until now has suggested. Decid-edly, Le Corbusier's "Unité d'Habitation" or the "Ville Radieuse" – even in the context of the South Hansa quarter of Berlin – as it is often still thought of to-day, is no longer the only alternative to the popular housing of the past decade.

It is a pity that, in comparison with other examples of housing blocks, the Berlin "Unité d'Habitation" is bound to come out badly, because Le Corbusier's conception (demonstrated in the "Unités" of Marseilles and Nantes) has been truncated. In Berlin, rejecting the Modulor measurement (about 8'4''), a room height

of approximately 9'2'' was stipulated; the two-storey type flats, occupying the full depth of the building, were transformed into flats on one level; all the intermediate floors were extended, so that in the whole block there were no longer any rooms of double height. As a result the "Unité" has become a folly. The open, load-bearing, ground floor is virtually closed by the building's private heating plant and by shops. To rescue the proportions, Le Corbusier has indulged in a piecemeal, rather trivial, colour scheme for the façades. For such expedients even the virtue of a site, which is outstanding from a town-planning point of view, can be small comfort.

The buildings of the South Hansa quarter of Berlin, which – in their various stages of construction – formed the central feature of the 1957 Interbau exhibition, had also to submit to regulations that had, in certain respects, long become nonsensical. But the ideas of the architects invited (19 of them foreigners) proved extremely well adapted and flexible. Above all, the 8- and 10-storey blocks by Alvar Aalto and Jaenecke/Samuelson, despite the lim-itations inherent in the brief, are in the first rank of European domestic architecture, both for the skilful development of the plans of the flats, and for the way in which these are arranged in each building. The same is true of the 4-storey structures by Kay Fisker, Wassili Luckhardt and Hubert Hoffmann. Of the five tower blocks bordering the railway, only the one by Van den Broek/Bakema has any exceptional merit. The high block by Gustav Hassenpflug, assembled out of storey-high, prefabricat-ed stanchions and hollow wall components, also prefabricated, deserves mention. One of the outstanding achievements in the Hansa quarter is Otto Senn's 4-storey point block, which ought to have been built as a tower in place of another high block near by. As a result Senn's unassuming building has not enjoyed the attention it deserves.

In the layout as a whole, and in the siting and relationship of individual buildings within the general scheme, the new Berlin Hansa quarter has not become the model for central urban area re-construction that might have been expected, in view of the exhaus-tive preliminaries, the replotting operations and the combined efforts of all the participating architects. The leadership was clear-ly unequal to the boldness of the enterprise. In overall conception the lure of pattern planning was too strong. This is apparent not only in the physically inappropriate juxtaposition of high and low buildings (including Arne Jacobsen's "atrium" terrace hous-es) and the very questionable alignment of high blocks along the railway, but also in obvious inconsistencies in the dimensions of external areas. All these practices have, it is true, more than re-paid the risks, but the inspired nature and dynamic conception of this reconstruction of a ruined central residential district has remained without wider influence. The entire scheme lacked cohesion, despite all the excellent individual solutions.

It is characteristic of the architectural situation towards the end of the fifties that significant steps can be recorded wherever the building programme is closely linked with function. The hospital is a case in point. A comparison of the floor plans of the district hospitals at Riedlingen by Johannes Krahn, and at Obernburg-am-Main by Köhler/Kässens, shows a development which proceeds from the conventional solution of an I- or T-shaped ground plan to apparently loosely organized but, in practice, strictly functional conceptions; to a conspicuous concentration of the treatment departments and administration sections on the lower floors, and also to a tight grouping of the ward units in close and logical relationship with the layout as a whole. The discipline of the internal organization, as our examples show, leads more and more to the featureless, objective, exterior. "Clinical" is becoming an architectural expression.

A similar trend is noticeable in restaurants and hotels, the running of which also demands a smooth and highly efficient deployment of services. An extreme example of concentration is the welfare building of a machine plant at Mainz by Hans-Joachim Lenz: a "feeding and washing contrivance" encased in an elegant steel structure. The particular architectural quality of this building makes obvious how easily good architecture can become a parody of its purpose. The "Buschmühle" Restaurant, in the Westfalenpark at Dortmund, has a very different function and task; but here, too, for the 1959 National Garden Show large-scale organization and quick service were needed. The idea of social service has in this instance been interpreted by Groth/Lehmann/Schlote with far greater freedom and humanity, but with equal attention to detail and to the architecture of the whole. In any case the huge, unfriendly, dining hall is no longer architecturally appropriate to the brief half hour, when the employee is released from his workaday routine and has the chance to become a person. It seems likely that the so-called canteen will gradually come to resemble a club-house with its less formal arrangement of rooms and adjoining space. That such welfare buildings may not have the amenities of site and surroundings of, for example, the Municipal Park Restaurant at Nürnberg, by Friedrich Seegy, or even the Tennis Club house at Berlin-Grunewald, by Paul Baumgarten, is self-evident.

As a building type, the hotel is also having to be reconsidered from the viewpoint of a harmonious system of associated functions and of spatial freedom of movement. The Hotel "Berlin" on the Lützowplatz by Schwebes/Schoszberger has a few contributions to make in this respect, as the completion of the remaining stages will make still clearer.

During the second half of the fifties interesting developments in school architecture took place. The act of protest symbolized in the widely expanding pavilion school, the first and much disputed answer to the old and not yet extinct scholastic barracks, has given place to more progressive proposals. And here we must once again place at the top the ideas of Hans Scharoun, crystallized in 1951 in his scheme for a primary school at Darmstadt. After his construction of the girls' high school at Lünen, his theory of a building aiming at every possible quality, academic and structural, every virtue arising from landscape and surroundings, began to find adherents. Above all, the treatment of light, its harnessing and adjustment to age and educational levels is now conceived as a constituent element of the design. It is recognized that, from this "informal" architecture results occur, or may occur, which differ essentially from those obtained when formal types of building are accepted or adapted. Scharoun creates not only diversity of space for a new school environment, but for him architecture itself lies close to teaching in the sense of providing a "nursery garden for growing minds".

Even if the architectural design of a group of school buildings is more abstract, the development is similar and tends towards the creation of a town-planning nucleus, in which the combination and contrast of the wide and narrow, the open and closed, the horizontal and vertical, are juxtaposed in a variety of relationships. The school grows in status both as an institution and as a part of the to townscape.

Whoever inquires nowadays about the best buildings in Dortmund, for example, will most certainly be directed to the Gymnasium by Friedrich Wilhelm Kraemer. The town of Offenbach is esteemed not only for its leather industry, but for a succession of outstanding school buildings, like the Rudolf-Koch-Gymnasium by Adolf Bayer or Steinmeyer/Nowotny's Humboldt School.

We have fortunately been preserved from deciding too rapidly about certain types of school building. This, it is true, was often the reason for economic disadvantages and has given us many false trails, but it proved on the whole a by no means valueless process of selection. It has undoubtedly been beneficial both to our architecture and in equal measure to the, still fluid, evolution of our school system. Thus on architectural matters the discussion continues to be open. One need only set a design by Scharoun next to a school by Dieter Oesterlen. Finding qualities in one or the other, we can learn and progress, and extend in tranquillity the architectural field of the province of education. We can enrich it with special forms, each of which can have and keep its particular quality. For an Arts Training Centre, like the one overlooking the Wupper valley near Remscheid; a college building, like that of the Faculty of Architecture of the Technical High School at Stuttgart, or the buildings of some public academy are all broadly concerned with the education and training of vital, intelligent, responsible human beings.

But here a note of criticism must be struck. We still approach the building of educational establishments with too many reservations. Many buildings are dead because their personality has been suppressed; plenty appear coldly insensitive. Must an arts school in a glorious setting be a group of austere cubes? Even the skill, with which Werner and Grete Wirsing have placed these buildings on a sloping site, does not detract from their bleak reticence. And isn't the extreme objective functionalism of that Stuttgart college building by Gutbrod/Siegel/Wilhelm, all too constricting, all too stern and uncompromisingly "adult" in its effect upon impressionable students? On the other hand, so many architectural critics have castigated Werner Düttmann's Berlin Academy of Arts as muddled and inconsistent. And yet how lively and fresh it is, and how freely we can circulate through and about it, although it has certainly not been poured from a single mould! Here the defects and shortcomings become creative architectural material for those who can exploit them. From them we learn that a building, which inspires and makes possible an interesting solution, is more important fundamentally than a perfect piece of architecture. The Berlin Academy, for example, possesses the most beautiful studio theatre in Germany, but whoever judges the interior of this theatre from the outside without knowing it is utterly deceived. The slightly asymmetrical auditorium, with its small and large range of stalls and stage between, lies diagonally to the longitudinal axis of the sloping roof.

The "little houses" of the two new theatre buildings at Mannheim and Gelsenkirchen also make it possible to stage plays between two rising banks of stalls–in the middle of the auditorium. Gerhard Weber's National Theatre at Mannheim combines a large and a small house (similar to the competition scheme by Mies van der Rohe) under one roof; in the Gelsenkirchen municipal theatre of Ruhnau/Rave/von Hausen, the "little house" forms a special wing adjoining the glass cube of the large theatre. The large houses of both theatres, however, are conventionally equipped with picture-frame stages, and if, in both cases, the clumsiness of the stage technical equipment is alarming, the spaciousness of the foyer and public rooms is delightful. But neither at Mannheim, nor at Gelsenkirchen, has the architectural problem been tackled resolutely in the sense of "theatre". The old institution of the municipal playhouse has simply been disguised as a modern, functional, public building. Added to which, the work of the mural painters and sculptors does not always seem to have been competent in every respect. That the Mannheim and Gelsenkirchen theatres had nevertheless to be included in our selection, and indeed they are well above average buildings, is a sign of a strange reluctance to experiment, and also, perhaps, of apathy on the part of the theatre people and clients.

In our approach to the problem of the Concert Hall, on the other hand, better progress has been made. Technically less exacting, richer in opportunities for spatial ingenuity, and above all less burdened with unavoidable expedients and compulsory precautions, it has been possible to put ideas into practice in this

field, which are profoundly influencing new designs for municipal halls, community centres and similar buildings. The "Liederhalle" at Stuttgart by Abel/Gutbrod and the Beethoven hall at Bonn by Siegfried Wolske have set the standard, their merit resting to no great extent on formal composition or on fitness for purpose, but principally upon a new sort of public appeal, which such buildings make possible. We ought surely to give credit to these experiments in our homeland, even if they lack perhaps the positive quality of the Festival Hall of 1951 in London.

The trend that was started at Stuttgart and Bonn – and will be continued with Scharoun's Berlin Philharmonic building – undoubtedly offers more possibilities than the architectonic and structural tour-de-force of the Congress Hall by Hugh Stubbins in Berlin between the Spree and the Tiergarten. The brilliance of his building was the subject of many long discussions, and has contributed enormously towards defining a position for our architecture between daring and temerity on the one hand and dullness and timidity on the other.

On the German side a prominent participant in these discussions was Frei Otto, whose tent structures and light buildings are among the few achievements of our post-war architecture to have roused a strong echo, even beyond our own borders. It is a pity that we still consider anything that is light and seemingly insubstantial as trivial and temporary. Misguided caution has restricted these light buildings to the field of exhibition architecture – surely a much too narrow field. Can we wonder that a splendid three-dimensional figure like the Great Hall of "Interbau", dedicated to the "Town of To-morrow", has been without effect. At any rate this building by Karl Otto/Günter Günschel/Frei Otto has had no successors so far.

Possibly not the most impressive, but the most conspicuous, German exhibition building of recent years was the group of pavilions designed by Eiermann/Ruf for the Brussels International Exhibition of 1958. The conception of eight linked pavilions was based on those well established principles which we at home are inclined to consider advanced. It represented, nearly thirty years after Mies van der Rohe's Barcelona pavilion, a piece of calculated modesty, and it did us much credit at this festival of the grandiose. Once again, if in another sense than in Barcelona, here was pure architecture. The exhibits and equipment were secondary – and that was just as well, if we compare what had been devised for exhibition. But we must not forget that the pavilions were far from typical of architecture in Germany – of the average standard. They did us proud.

In contrast to the deliberate self-consciousness of the Brussels pavilions, the exhibition building of Hameln Art Club by Oesterlen was designed to display its contents, in this case works of art. Abjuring publicity, it turns its back on the outside world. The exhibits are preserved in a serene architectural setting. Like Düttmann's exhibition gallery for the Berlin Academy of Arts, the qualities of this building lie in the interesting possibilities and spatial freedom offered by the interior.

In the commercial and office building such freedom is only permissible in sections used for prestige purposes. In many cases, as in the Frankfurt business house by Otto Apel, for instance, or the Mannesmann tower block by Schneider-Esleben/Knothe and the one for Phoenix-Rheinrohr by Hentrich/Petschnigg at Düsseldorf, a large and commanding entrance hall, with staircases and galleries, has assumed the rôle of impressing the customer. For the rest, this building type is exclusively concerned with the rational organization of work, which dictates not only the dimensions of individual areas, but also the overall proportions of useful space, e. g., the extremely important ratio of office to circulation areas.

Modern utilitarian buildings are essentially a problem of structural and technical skills. The flexibility in space allocation, which the organization specialists demand, can only be achieved by the skeleton frame. It is axiomatic that everything not strictly essential should be eliminated. The long accepted consequence is separation into supporting and filling elements, into load-bearing construction and skin, skeleton and curtain wall. This problem is now being exhaustively studied and technically perfected in Germany. Our selection shows some first rate examples.

In commissions of this sort, design – apart from problems of technical efficiency – is a matter of mass and proportions. Even under the strict discipline of fitting floor plan to elevation, opportunities occur for expressing an architect's individuality. Even buildings resembling each other as closely in type as those at Duisburg-Hamborn by Gerhard Weber and at Cologne (for the Rheinland Provincial Union) by Schulze-Fielitz/von Rudloff will not be confused even by laymen. The restful, uniformly substantial, nature of Otto Apel's business house at Frankfurt has a completely different appearance from the equally solid, but disciplined, elegance exemplified by Kraemer's offices at Goslar. The German meteorological service building at Offenbach by Karlfriedrich Posenenske, with its rugged exterior (and unusual construction) is as individual architecturally as the fresh and polished Lotteries house at Münster by Harald Deilmann. The reduction to simple components in Paul Baumgarten's Ruhr Coal Building is fundamentally unlike a similar experiment with the insurance building by Novotny/Hoschak at Gross-Gerau.

All these buildings are excellent achievements in their particular location, where they often supply an orderly element in a context of town-planning confusion. This is especially true, for example, of Egon Eiermann's headquarters for the Essen Coal Mines Group. The dimensions of this building are calculated for visual effect on the proportions of the small ceramic tiles (designed to look like anthracite), with which the building is faced throughout. All measurements are therefore related to a deliberately small squared pattern. But this organization of – or based upon – the smallest element has produced a building, which is the dominating feature amid the chaos of reconstruction in central Essen, although it is dwarfed in height by other buildings. A similar achievement is represented by the much smaller and, in appearance, far more elegant office building for a steel construction firm at Offenburg. Here Eiermann has tried to carry a stage further the theories which guided him in the Brussels pavilions. But, that the uninhibited business building can also undermine town-planning standards, and destroy urban coherence, is shown – notwithstanding its special structural quality – by the Düsseldorf Rheinrohr tower. In these days the view is growing that good architecture cannot be really effective, unless it is fully related to its environment. Willy Kreuer's unconventional ADAC building in Berlin, filling a bomb gap and providing a corner feature for a principal traffic artery, shows what this means, and the kind of opportunities open to architecture when it exploits its site. There are also of course examples of the industrial complex, in which the brief entails such involved problems of dimensions and layout that a prodigious effort is needed to relate and adjust the conflicting individual requirements to the whole. In the rather monumental "packing machine", which Egon Eiermann has built for a Frankfurt mail-order firm, this interrelationship of the parts with each other and within the whole programme has been done with striking success.

There is no doubt, however, that the architectural quality of administrative, commercial and industrial buildings is far superior to that of central area housing. Even in the country, in the provinces, this type of construction tends more and more to set a standard of leadership. A building which is adapted with such care and sensitivity to the landscape as the Blomberg factory by Schulze-Fielitz/von Altenstadt/von Rudloff is hard to match in Lippe. The structures on Heidelberg's industrial estates, which include the quite outstanding meat-processing plant by Lothar Götz, provides a far pleasanter example of local development than the new housing schemes in the Neuenheimer Feld. The small gramophone-record factory at Langenargen by Hans and Traudl Maurer, or the production shops for optical precision instruments at Brunswick by Friedrich Wilhelm Kraemer, contrast sharply with the suburban landscape of these towns. Even such a discreet creation as the Parkhaus Breuninger at Stuttgart by Gerd Wiegand supplies a criterion for a central district, which is still uncoordinated.

That in our townscape there is no alternative to these functional blocks but grotesque caricatures, no other form of architecture, nothing which puts this kind of utilitarian building in its right place in the picture as a whole, – all this is a measure of our intellectual and ethical poverty. The protests with which an "objective", matter-of-fact, architecture, with which the already far from youthful "Neue Sachlichkeit", is assailed, are not basically directed against objectivity itself, but against the poverty of ideas by which the town as a place to live in has been degraded. The pictorial quality, the essential graphic flair, are lacking! The town is still formless. After the destruction of the war it is not yet, as it once was, comprehensible.

Rudolf Schwarz must have sensed this, for in the last years of his life he constantly spoke of the pictorial rôle of architecture, which in his particular work, church-building, meant its sacred symbolism. And not only spoke; he composed as well. The church of the Holy Cross at Bottrop exemplifies a haven from the storms of the world; St. Mary the Queen at Saarbrücken is the Chalice and mystic Rose; St. Anna at Düren gathers the worshippers in a mantle of protection. But what opposition Rudolf Schwarz had to face! Fear of poetry, of a literary architecture, of succumbing to irrelevant influences, of lowering the rigid guard of the profession – these things had preserved the ideal of a purely formal conception of building from a liberation long overdue. But, especially in church architecture, where it is logical and appropriate, instances are multiplying of conceptions based on spiritual values: the sheltering air of Maria in den Benden at Düsseldorf by

Steffann/Rosiny, St. Albertus Magnus at Leverkus Holy Cross at Düsseldorf by Josef Lehmbrock; the open, ing, air of the church on the Lietzensee in Berlin by Paul garten; or the mystical serenity of Christchurch at Bochum Dieter Oesterlen. Air, fire, water, earth – the elements are a living realities in the architectural imagery of these churches. And why should not such symbols be used? Literary allusions do not create a literary architecture. Far from it. Poetry has never done architecture any harm. Signs are increasing that some prejudices are being overcome.

Structure and form – from these two concepts the lessons of architecture and planning must be learnt in the second half of the century. From the housing scheme and the dormitory town to the city and great metropolis, from the individual building to the ordering of our landscape, we are continually and actively confronted with providing the human habitat in its broad sense, of which we spoke earlier. In future, therefore, architecture must mean an acute recognition of the structure of our lives and of our interdependence, of the structure of country and town, and of the structure of business and labour, so that a form may be devised which will reconcile incompatibles and bring life to the all too static and inert. For this no ideology is needed, but an alert, clear-headed, perceptive, awareness – an awareness of ourselves, in the deeper meaning of the words.

Grundzüge deutscher Nachkriegsarchitektur

Wenn Grundzüge neuer deutscher Architektur nachgezeichnet werden sollen, muß zuvor der Blick auf das Bauen im Nachkriegsdeutschland schlechthin gehen, auf das Bauen als quantitativ meßbare Tätigkeit, als Sache statistischer Erhebungen. In einem vom Krieg verwüsteten Land, in dem, gemessen am Bestand von 1939, ein Fünftel aller Wohnungen zerstört war, in dem weitere zweieinhalb Millionen Wohnungen für Flüchtlinge aus den Ostgebieten und aus Mitteldeutschland fehlten, in dem zusätzlich eine Million Wohnungen für neugegründete Haushalte nötig wurde – in einem solchen Land können Architektur und bauliche Leistung fürs erste nicht anders denn quantitativ gemessen werden. Wo 5,8 Millionen Wohnungen fehlen, Stadtkerne und öffentliche Einrichtungen aller Art zerstört sind oder in ihren Resten nicht mehr funktionieren, da ist Not, herrscht Ausnahmezustand. Dieser Zustand konnte bis zum Beginn der fünfziger Jahre nur durch improvisierte Behelfe gelindert werden.

Erst mit den Konsequenzen der Währungsreform des Jahres 1948 und – ein Jahr darauf, im September 1949 – mit der Konstituierung der Bundesrepublik Deutschland lockerten sich die vielfältigen Beschränkungen einer Neubautätigkeit. 1955 wurde die Bundesrepublik als souveräner Staat anerkannt. Im gleichen Jahr war die Stagnation der Bautätigkeit in den ersten Nachkriegsjahren bereits in einen Bauboom umgeschlagen, der den der Gründerzeit bei weitem übertraf. Der Boom hielt an: fünf Jahre später, 1960, werden Maßnahmen zur Dämpfung der Baukonjunktur erwogen und eingeleitet. Der Bundeswohnungsbauminister sieht sich gezwungen, die dirigistische Maßnahme eines Baugenehmigungsstopps vorzuschlagen, nachdem er wenige Monate zuvor das Gesetz zur Überführung der Wohnungswirtschaft in die freie Marktwirtschaft hat verabschieden lassen. Dieses Gesetz konnte in Kraft treten angesichts der unerhörten quantitativen Leistungen des Wohnungsbaus seit 1950 und wird verabschiedet im Zusammenhang mit dem Bundesbaugesetz vom 20. Mai 1960, das künftig für die gesamte Bautätigkeit in der Bundesrepublik Grundlegung und Ausführungsinstrument darstellt.

Die Erlangung der Souveränität unseres Staatswesens und die Verabschiedung des Bundesbaugesetzes umgrenzen als geschichtliche Daten das zweite Jahrfünft des Bauens im Nachkriegsdeutschland. Die Bauten dieses Zeitraums sind entworfen und gebaut worden in Jahren der Hochkonjunktur, in fünf fetten Jahren, in Jahren sprunghaft steigenden Wohlstands, in Jahren eines nur selten gefährdeten wirtschaftlichen Gleichgewichts.

Aber über dem Neubau des bundesdeutschen Staatswesens, das vom Verfasser des Grundgesetzes, dem Parlamentarischen Rat, nur als zeitlich begrenztes Provisorium konzipiert war, geriet ins Hintertreffen, was sich nicht von provisorischen Plänen leiten lassen kann: der Neubau der Städte. Die mit Ausnahme des Wohnungsbaus streng föderative Struktur des Bauwesens hinderte die Verabschiedung der notwendigen übergreifenden Gesetze. Der Widerstand gegen jegliche zentralistischen Maßnahmen schoß – als Reaktion auf ein Jahrzehnt der Unfreiheit und Bevormundung – weit übers Ziel hinaus; auch innerhalb der einzelnen Bundesländer. Eine der Grundfesten des neuen Staates, die Selbstverwaltung, wurde ausgerechnet da in übersteigerter Weise praktiziert, wo das Mitspracherecht des anderen, des Nachbarn, zur Selbstbestimmung und Selbsteinordnung unerläßlich ist: bei allem Planen und Bauen. In administrativen und wirtschaftlichen Fragen wurde die angemessene Interpretation der Selbstbestimmung sehr viel leichter und aus der Sache heraus gefunden. Für den Neubau der Städte aber fehlten Urteilsmöglichkeiten. Eine zu enge Wertschätzung der Besitzrechte und Besitzverpflichtungen an Bau und Boden hemmten eine gesunde städtebauliche Entwicklung. Denn der Wiederaufbau war ja eine gemeinschaftliche Aufgabe und als solche verknüpft mit der gesellschaftlichen Entwicklung. Und Wiederaufbau, Neubau, Städtebau und Raumordnung hätten von Beginn an Selbstdarstellung der neuen Gesellschaft sein müssen. Aber die Wandlung der Kriegs- und Nachkriegs-Notgemeinschaft in eine demokratische Gesellschaft war – und ist noch! – ein langsamer Prozeß. Die Selbstbestimmung des einzelnen, lang entbehrt und nun in alle Rechte eingesetzt, ließ es zur baulichen Selbstdarstellung der neu sich bildenden, freien Gesellschaft nicht kommen. Wohl sagt das Grundgesetz im zweiten Absatz des Artikels 14: ›Eigentum verpflichtet. Sein Gebrauch soll zugleich dem Wohl der Allgemeinheit dienen‹, aber zehn Jahre reichten nicht, diesen für alles Bauen so entscheidenden Sätzen konkreten Inhalt zu geben.

So ergab sich folgende Situation: Neben dem Wohnungsbau, der die Kräfte zu immer neuen Anstrengungen trieb, neben dem rein funktionellen Bauen für Industrie und Handel, neben der Herstellung der unabdingbaren Folgeeinrichtungen für das Wohnen und Arbeiten verblieb vorerst ein geistiges Vakuum. Alles Bauen, das über die Sicherung der Existenz hinausging, blieb unverbindlich oder höchstens selbstbezogen. Dieses geistige Vakuum füllte sich bei beginnender und dann blühender Konjunktur mit einer nie zuvor beobachteten Konkurrenz des Maßstablosen: Behördenbauten, Banken, Versicherungspaläste, Verwaltungs- und Bürobauten, Kaufhäusern, Kinos, Hotels. Sozusagen über Nacht stand man einer Unzahl gebauter Positionen gegenüber, die Vertrauen nicht für ein neues Ganzes, sondern erst einmal für sich selbst zu sichern suchten. Diese Bauten suchten vorzustellen: die sichersten, leistungsfähigsten, vertrauenswürdigsten, attraktivsten (und was solcher Superlative mehr sind) Unternehmen und Einrichtungen eines wirtschaftlich aufblühenden, gesellschaftlich aber eben erst keimenden Gemeinwesens. Damit hatte das Nachkriegsdeutschland zweierlei Bauwesen: eines, das unter äußerster Beschränkung finanzieller und materieller Mittel, gegen groben Mißbrauch jedoch abgesichert durch verbindliche technische Baubestimmungen, seit 1953 im Durchschnitt jährlich 550.000 Wohnungen herstellte; und ein anderes, das die dank der Konjunktur abschöpfbaren Werte in einer Unzahl luxuriöser oder doch luxuriös scheinender Objekte verbaute.

Der Architekt sah sich in Deutschland von 1950 an zwischen diesen beiden Fronten: Beim Sozialen Wohnungsbau mußte er unter dem Zwang der engen Bestimmungen, von denen die Gewährung der öffentlichen Mittel abhängig gemacht war, auf weiterführende Ideen und Versuche verzichten. Er sah sich auf nur wenige Haus- und Wohnungstypen festgelegt, die für besonders wirtschaftlich gehalten wurden. Er konnte zwar Varianten entwerfen und an der Verbesserung der Grundrisse arbeiten, echte Alternativen aber hatten, so überzeugend sie auch vorgestellt wurden, wenig Chancen. Die planerischen Gesichtspunkte blieben, von Ausnahmen abgesehen, sekundär. Lediglich die Ausbildung der technischen Details und die Rationalisierung der Bauausführung wurden mit Zähigkeit betrieben.

Auf der anderen Seite stand der Architekt vor Bauaufgaben, die von ihm verlangten, daß er Visitenkarten entwerfe, repräsentative Einfälle habe und schicke Fassaden zeichne, trotzdem aber Wirtschaftlichkeit und Funktion nicht als Nebensächlichkeit abtue. Man verlangte von ihm, daß er es anders als andere mache, daß er Handschrift beweise, trotzdem aber sich der über Nacht herausgebildeten Konvention angleiche. Nicht zuletzt sah man darauf, daß er dabei die Grenze der gesetzlich erlaubten Nutzung nicht unterschreite, sondern im Gegenteil den Behörden lukrative Dispense abhandele. Nicht der Baumeister mit künstlerischem Gewissen, sondern der einfallsreiche Konfektionär war gefragt. Und der saß dann bald in einem Mammutbüro.

Bevor aber diese – hier sehr grob umrissenen – Aufgaben akut wurden, sammelten sich in den ersten Nachkriegsjahren die Kräfte, stark dezimiert zwar durch Emigration und Krieg, doch profiliert in ihren Anschauungen. Diese ersten Gespräche, diese ersten Treffen waren voll verheißender Perspektiven.

Sehr vereinfacht gesehen, gab es damals drei geistige Lager oder besser: drei Schulrichtungen, die im Wirken bedeutender Architekturlehrer der zwanziger Jahre gründen. Weitaus das größte Gewicht, bei aller Zurückhaltung in den öffentlichen Diskussionen, besaß die Richtung, die mit den Namen Bonatz und Schmitthenner umschrieben ist. Sie hatte ja bereits um 1930 – trotz Bauhaus, Berliner Architekten-›Ring‹ und den im Lande wirkenden ›Radikalen‹ – das Gesicht des sogenannten guten Durchschnitts wesentlich bestimmt: eine bodenständig sein

sollende, sich auf das Handwerk stützende Architektur mit regionalen Nuancen. Sie leitete ihre Maßstäbe entweder von der ländlichen Architektur der jeweiligen Region oder von einem nachlebenden dünnen Klassizismus her. Eine Architektur, die auf ein ruhiges, harmonisches Maß zielte, ohne Spannungen und harte Kontraste. Diese Architektur war in ihrem Wesen auf eine Manifestation des nationalen Stils angelegt. Der Nationalsozialismus hat sie sofort und ohne Umschweife als ›die‹ deutsche Architektur apostrophieren und später dann zu Hitlers Machtarchitektur verzerren können. Es nimmt nicht wunder, daß die Architekten dieser Richtung, auch wenn sie sich von den Nazis ausdrücklich distanzierten, weit weniger angefochten die Ära des Dritten Reiches überstanden als die Kollegen, die im Sinne des Bauhauses und der Kongresse für moderne Architektur (CIAM) neues Bauen als weltweite Sache betrachteten.

Diese zweite Gruppe blieb auch im Deutschland der ersten Nachkriegsjahre sozusagen in der Diaspora. Die Meister des Bauhauses und ihre Weggenossen hatten, von wenigen Ausnahmen abgesehen, Deutschland bereits Anfang der dreißiger Jahre verlassen müssen oder waren freiwillig gegangen. Die wenigen, die blieben, waren in alle Winde zerstreut; und unter ihnen war kein Gropius, kein Mies van der Rohe, der die Versprengten hätte sammeln können.

Die dritte und für die Entwicklung unserer Nachkriegsarchitektur wichtigste Gruppe bildeten diejenigen, die man, sehr pauschal, Poelzig-Schüler nennen kann. Die Mehrzahl von ihnen hatte während der dunklen Jahre im Industriebau Unterschlupf finden oder sich solchen Bauaufgaben widmen können, deren starke funktionelle Bindung moderne Lösungen unverdächtig machte. Sie trafen sich als eine Phalanx von eigenwilligen Temperamenten mit zum Teil recht unterschiedlicher persönlicher Zielsetzung, um Leitlinien und Perspektiven für ein neues Bauen im Nachkriegsdeutschland abzustecken. Sie brachten die Geister in Bewegung und fanden nun ihrerseits den Weg auf die verwaisten Lehrstühle der Technischen Hochschulen. Ihre damalige Position – eine Ausgangsposition – mußte als großes Versprechen gelten. Heute, zwölf Jahre später, ist diese Position gefestigt. Aber ist sie noch immer ein Versprechen?

Man muß sich ins Gedächtnis rufen, daß der letzte deutsche Bau, dem vor dem Krieg internationale Geltung zukam, Mies van der Rohes Barcelona-Pavillon von 1929 war. Mies war 1938, wie vorher Gropius und andere, in die Vereinigten Staaten gegangen. Hans Poelzig starb, aus seinem Lehramt gejagt, bereits 1936. Der Lehrer und Meister – und mit ihnen auch der Kritik und der gültigen Maßstäbe – beraubt, stand nach dem Krieg die zweite Architektengeneration der Moderne vor einer Aufgabe, die zu durchdenken nicht nur Mut und ungebrochenen Glauben an die Sache, sondern ganz einfach künstlerisches und geistiges Übermaß, nennen wir es Genialität, voraussetzte. Die Aufgabe des Bauens im verwüsteten Deutschland stand jenseits aller vorauszusehenden und abzumessenden Größen.

So steuerten die Dinge vorerst auf das durchdachte, bewährte, unmißverständliche und anspruchsvolle Gleis, das in den zwanziger Jahren definiert und angelegt worden war. In diese Konzeptionen mischte sich eine Vielzahl von Einflüssen; in der Reihenfolge, wie deutschen Architekten andere Länder wieder zugänglich wurden. Von der Schweiz her, von neuen Bauten in den USA und England, von den skandinavischen Leistungen her formte sich neues deutsches Bauen zu einer Humanisierung ehemals ›Neuer Sachlichkeit‹, zu einer ›Säkularisierung‹ des baulichen Kubismus, verbunden mit einer durchgreifenden Technisierung des gesamten Bauvorgangs. Material, Konstruktion, Funktion, kubische Körperlichkeit bei gleichzeitiger Transparenz, sich durchdringender und in Fluß gebrachter Raum – das waren Hauptbegriffe dieses Bauens. Architektur wurde konzipiert als sauberer Vortrag.

Aber solcher Vortrag taugte nur wenig für die beiden Aufgabenbereiche, die wir eingangs darstellten. Er paßte mit seinen festumrissenen Ansprüchen weder ins Notkonzept des Sozialen Wohnungsbaus, noch eignete er sich für die Repräsentation von Pseudo-Instanzen, die alles zu ihrem Terrain erklärten, was in der jungen Demokratie noch brach lag. Entscheidender aber war, daß die umgreifende, ausrichtende Idee fehlte. Dieses neue Bauen war, geistig gesehen, nur wenig mehr als eine Wiederaufnahme. Die Anstrengung, wiederanzuknüpfen, eine Rückverbindung zu gewinnen über mehr als ein Jahrzehnt der Barbarei hinweg, dieses Sich-vergewissern und Sich-versichern schwächte Eigenes oft bis zur Unkenntlichkeit. Man scheute neue Risiken.

Da die noch ungeübte Selbstverwaltung der Bürger – will sagen: der Bauherr – versagte, gleichzeitig aber Not war und Bedarf über alles bislang gekannte Maß, erzwang eine solche Situation ein Bauen, das nur selten den Fähigkeiten derer entsprach, die es zu praktizieren hatten; und die es, oft wider besseres Wissen, auch praktizierten. Daß dieses Eingehen auf eine wenig selbstbewußte, ja oft sich selbst verleugnende Bauherrschaft notwendiger Teilaspekt einer jungen und noch ungewohnten demokratischen Freiheit ist, stimmt angesichts der Ergebnisse wenig tröstlich.

Gab es niemanden, der neues Planen und neues Bauen vom Ereignis der Selbstzerstörung Deutschlands her bedachte, niemanden, der angesichts der Trümmer, die ja nicht nur äußere waren, tiefere Folgerungen auch für das Bauen zog? Es gab solche Stimmen, doch sie blieben – vereinzelt – damals wie heute ohne Wirkung. Hugo Häring, der einmal den Begriff ›neues bauen‹ geprägt hatte, saß, alt geworden und einsam mit seinen Gedanken, in Biberach. Was er als Architekt und Denker zu sagen hatte, blieb ungehört und darum fruchtlos. Auch Martin

Mächlers weite Perspektiven blieben ohne Einfluß. Beide starben 1958.

1946 wurden im damals noch nicht gesprengten Berliner Stadtschloß Worte gesprochen, die Initial hätten sein können: Die neue Stadt – so sagte damals Hans Scharoun als Planer eines neuen Berlin – ›wird von der Kultur ihrer Bewohner geprägt werden müssen, immer aufs neue, sonst wird sie die Prägeform für die Bewohner. Dann gäbe es keine sittliche Freiheit, ohne die das geistige Ordnungsprinzip der neuen Stadt nicht entwickelt werden kann‹.

Das war ein Anlauf. Von allen möglichen Seiten kamen ihm stützende Kräfte zu. Und doch ging es ins Leere. Not und Konjunktur haben keine Ohren; oder, wie Max Frisch sagt, man hatte Angst, Ideen zu haben, und weil man keine Ideen hatte, hatte man Angst. So stehen die Leistungen der deutschen Nachkriegsarchitektur, auch die in diesem Band versammelten Bauten der letzten fünf Jahre, in einem geistigen Vakuum. Ihr qualitativer Rang ist aufs Ganze gesehen von geringem Belang, Existenzsicherung, konventioneller Wiederaufbau, Restauration überschatteten und überschatten dasjenige, was unser neues Bauen nach dem Krieg hätte leiten müssen: die entschlossenen Anfänge einer Wissenschaft vom Wohnen nach der Mitte des Jahrhunderts.

Auch an den Hochschulen wurden die Fragen einer übergreifenden Ordnung, wurden die mit dem Wohnen verbundenen Strukturfragen nur selten aufgegriffen. Das punktuelle Bauen, die Behandlung der einzelnen Bauaufgabe, hatte bei weitem den Vorrang. Nur in Ausnahmefällen wurden Entwurfs- und Diplomthemata aus einer Überschau heraus gestellt. Wo Zusammenhänge angedeutet wurden, gingen sie kaum über den Siedlungsbau hinaus. Auch an den Lehrstühlen für Städtebau blieb man zumeist unter Verwechslung der Begriffe im Siedlungsbau befangen. Allzu eng blieb die Bindung an Bauaufgaben, die den Lehrern angetragen sind. Die Methode ihrer Bewältigung färbt ab auf Lehre und Forschung. Zweckdenken und ökonomisches Denken, so notwendig beides war und ist, beengten allzuoft die Entfaltung der Kräfte.

Trotzdem blieben die Hochschulen Zentren nüchterner Auseinandersetzung mit den Wirkkräften der Gegenwart. Sie behielten auch in den fünfziger Jahren ihre ausstrahlende Kraft, besonders da, wo fest umrissene Persönlichkeiten ›Schulen‹ bildeten, die heute hinauswirken in das allgemeine Baugeschehen.

Um die Mitte der fünfziger Jahre wird dieser Beitrag ganz konkret: Die dritte Generation, die der zwischen 1920 und 1930 Geborenen, hat ihre Studien- und Lehrzeit hinter sich. Skeptisch gegenüber ihren Wirkungsmöglichkeiten, kritisch gegenüber ihren Lehrern, fügen sich die jungen Architekten in das Baugeschehen ein. Sie kommen mit festen Grundsätzen und Überzeugungen von den Hochschulen. Viele resignieren schon bald im

Alltag der großen Büros; andere passen sich um der besseren Existenz willen schnell an die allgemeinen Trends an. Überall aber setzen sich einige wenige von ihnen ohne größere Kompromisse durch. Sie begegnen den Verführungen der Baukonjunktur mit geduldiger und zäher Arbeit. Sie schulen sich an bescheidenen, zum Teil schwierigen Aufgaben. Die besonderen Qualitäten dieser ersten Arbeiten und Bauten bleiben nicht unbeachtet. Die jungen Architekten haben Erfolge in Wettbewerben und warten mit Leistungen auf, die oft weit über dem Durchschnitt stehen und die die Bedenken, jüngeren Leuten große Aufgaben anzuvertrauen, schnell und hoffentlich endgültig zerstreuen. Die Bauten der dritten Generation beginnen, das Bild der Städte mitzubestimmen. In vielen Fällen setzen sie Maßstäbe.

Die dritte Generation kam ohne Programme und Manifeste. Ihr Temperament ist sozusagen unterkühlt. Sie ist nicht revolutionär, sondern eher übertrieben gewissenhaft; sie äußert sich verhalten; Härte und Sprödigkeit liegen ihr mehr als Frische; ihre Phantasie ist sachlich; sie reduziert bis zur Verleugnung alles Eigenen: wie ein ›Maschinenbauer‹ zu arbeiten, gilt als Auszeichnung. Man exponiert sich nur ungern; und wenn man es tut, geschieht es nur da, wo man sicher ist; man will keine Chance geben, mißverstanden zu werden; und man will am allerwenigsten jung erscheinen.

Diese Generation argumentiert und baut ›vernünftig‹. Zweck, Funktion, Ökonomie entdeckt sie als Begriffe, mit deren Hilfe man Architektur leichter verkaufen kann. Gute Architektur schleust man quasi durch diese Hintertüren. Im übrigen ist man brav und gut angezogen und gibt sich zwar Schützenhilfe, tritt aber nicht mehr gemeinsam auf, weil man gelernt hat, daß gute Architektur nicht mehr vorgestellt und proklamiert werden kann, sondern

still und entschlossen infiltriert werden muß. Geschickt und anpassungsfähig, unterläuft diese Architektengeneration eine Gesellschaft, der das Selbstbewußtsein noch abgeht und die ihre Kräfte zu großen Teilen vorläufig noch verausgabt im Absichern und Abgrenzen. Oder gar in krasser Ablehnung dessen, was sie sich nicht zumuten zu können glaubt.

Das Verhalten der jungen Architektengeneration ist insgesamt ein Opfer ihrer Jugend. So heilsam ihre Selbstbeschränkung sein mag inmitten der Mißverständnisse neuen Bauens, mit denen unsere Städte vollgestopft sind – sie hat ihre bittere Kehrseite. Die Reduktion der Ideen, die Beschneidung der schöpferischen Phantasie, das Abkappen des Künstlerischen, das Verbergen der Ambitionen – alles dies führt über kurz oder lang entweder zu einer Gewohnheitsdogmatik oder zu einer stillschweigenden, dauernden Anklage der Verhältnisse und Zeitläufte. Am Ende steht die Resignation.

Aber wer zugehört und zugesehen hat in den letzten Jahren, hat bemerken können, daß die Gespräche wieder offener werden. Man erkennt Zusammenhänge und engagiert sich, man nimmt Partei und geht Wagnisse ein. Zu den passiven Rechten und Pflichten eines Ausführenden nimmt man sich nun auch das aktive Mitspracherecht. Es wird Sache vor allem dieser dritten Generation, daß der Architekt in Zukunft mehr als bisher auch politischer Mensch ist. Zu seiner künstlerischen und technischen Qualifikation werden die Schärfe eines politischen Urteils und der Sinn für gesellschaftliche Zusammenhänge treten. Der Frage des Bauens in der Demokratie wird er zu seinem Teil Umriß und Inhalt geben. Wir haben in diesem Hinblick schon manches Versprechen, auch unter den Bauten, die in diesem Band zusammengetragen sind.

Deutsche Architektur 1955–61

Die wesentlichsten Ansätze zu Lösungen, die über die Konventionen, auch die modernen, hinaus- und weiterführen, finden sich naturgemäß in den unausgeführten Projekten des hier erfaßten Zeitraums; vor allem in solchen, die von landschaftlichen Räumen, wirtschaftlichen Strukturen und bestimmten wesensmäßigen Konstellationen her entwickelt sind. Aber das in diesem Sinn Verbindliche wird immer wieder als nebensächlich abgetan; das Unterscheidungsvermögen derer, die über Wert oder Unwert dieser Projekte zu befinden hatten, ist noch allzusehr in formalen Maßstäben befangen. So gewinnen nur wenige dieser Entwürfe Gestalt, wird nur weniges nachvollziehbar und nachprüfbar.

Unsere Auswahl von Bauten der letzten fünf Jahre ist darum kaum stellvertretend für die Kräfte, die zur Entfaltung drängen, sondern zeigt die Qualitäten dessen, was sich unter den gesellschaftlichen, wirtschaftlichen und technischen Voraussetzungen dieser Jahre realisieren ließ. Oft genug aber handelt es sich auch da um Ausnahmen, ermöglicht nur durch den Beistand einer besonders bewußten und entschlossenen Bauherrschaft; oder auch durchgesetzt mit der zähen Überzeugungskraft der jeweiligen Architekten. Unsere Auswahl ist also, wenngleich sie auf Projekte verzichtet, keineswegs gültig für die Situation des Bauens in Deutschland schlechthin. Im Gegenteil, die ausgewählten Bauten sind sozusagen dessen oberste Grenzwerte; sie sind symptomatisch für die Richtungen, in die die Anstrengungen gehen. Die Quersumme gibt weder Anlaß zu besonderem Stolz, noch zu einem understatement. Man mag gerechterweise sagen, das Ergebnis sei gut. Es ist gut. Aber es sollte uns nicht gut genug sein.

Das gilt vor allem für den Wohnungsbau, ungeachtet seiner verschiedenen Formen. Alle Anstrengungen im Zeitraum dieses Berichtes haben es nicht vermocht, die landläufigen Wohnformen im Nachkriegsdeutschland – Einfamilienhaus, Reihenhaus, 3- oder 4geschossiges Miethaus – merklich zu beeinflussen. Nach wie vor folgt der allgemeine Wohnungsbau herkömmlichen Rezepten, deren Wirtschaftlichkeit erwiesen scheint, deren Wohnwert aber hinter der (oft nur scheinbaren) Ökonomie um Längen zurückbleibt. War es ein Zeichen dieses Mißverhältnisses, daß Eduard Ludwig für die deutsche Abteilung der Brüsseler Weltausstellung 1958 gerade nur eben ein Existenzminimum für zwei Personen entwerfen durfte und daß die Modellwohnung in einem der deutschen Pavillons jeder verbindlichen Aussage über das Wohnen aus dem Weg ging? Dabei fehlt es keineswegs an solchen Aussagen, mögen sie nun die bauliche Bestimmung eines landschaftlichen Ortes, die Verklammerung von häuslicher Intimsphäre und Freiraum oder die räumliche Durchdringung der Wohnbereiche betreffen. Da warten vor allem die Architekten der dritten Generation mit ganz klaren Vorstellungen auf, die nun nicht mehr ausschließlich nur die formale Seite des Hausbaus betreffen.

Das Gartenhofhaus am Durlacher Berg von Reinhard Gieselmann, das eigene Wohnhaus von Gottfried Böhm am Rheinufer, das ländliche Wohnhaus im Odenwald von Waldemar Lippert und die Wohnhäuser an den Abhängen des Taunus von Wilfried Beck-Erlang und Eugen Söder – alle diese Häuser sind gründlich durchgearbeitete Versuche, Wohnen im Sinne eines Vollzugs und nicht nur als bloße gegliederte Funktion zu ermöglichen. Daß hier und da noch Additives zu erkennen ist, Gliederungen etwa, die sich aus der vorgefaßten kubischen Form der Baukörper ergeben und mit dem Wohnvorgang nur wenig zu tun haben, deutet an, nach welcher Seite hin die Aufgabe zu präzisieren ist. Die Frage, ob vom strengen geschlossenen Kubus her noch weitere Nuancierungen der Wohnvorgänge zu erreichen sind, ist noch durchaus offen. Denn es gibt auch da ja nicht nur Unterschiede der formalen Auffassung (vergleiche dazu etwa das Studiohaus von Gerhard Schwab mit dem Braunschweiger Haus von Friedrich Wilhelm Kraemer und die schon genannten Häuser in Lörbach und Königstein), sondern auch erstaunliche Qualitätsunterschiede. Darüber können die feschen ›Bungalows‹, die zur Zeit überall die ›Villa‹ ablösen, sehr eindringlich belehren.

Zwei Einfamilienhäuser, das Haus in Braunschweig von Kraemer und das Haus (mit zwei Einliegerwohnungen und Büro) von Oswald Mathias Ungers in Köln-Müngersdorf, zeigen die extremen Auffassungen, zwischen denen sich der Hausbau in Deutschland während der letzten Jahre bewegte. Einmal ist da die Entscheidung zum geschlossenen und sehr streng gegliederten kubischen Körper; die sorgfältig ausgebildete Fassade nimmt ihren Reiz von den Materialien und nicht zuletzt von dem Widerspruch, daß die geschlossene Form nach allen Seiten offen und einladend ist. Demgegenüber ist das Haus in Köln eine vielfältig gegliederte Komposition plastischer Körper; positive und negative Formen wechseln im Widerspiel des Ganzen, das sich nach außen fast rigoros abschließt, dennoch aber in seiner Körperlichkeit weit mehr auf den Ort, die Nachbarbebauung, kurz, auf das Ambiente bezogen ist. In beiden Fällen darf man sich durch formale Anklänge nicht täuschen lassen: das Haus von Kraemer folgt so wenig dem Vorbild Mies van der Rohes wie das eigene Haus von Ungers dem der Neoplastizisten. In beiden Fällen bedarf es eines genauen Studiums der Grundrisse, um sich vor einem Vorurteil zu bewahren.

Die Ziele, die Ungers verfolgt, werden fast noch deutlicher in dem Miethaus am Kölner Hansaring: ein plastisches Bauen, jeweils entwickelt aus den örtlichen Gegebenheiten und den Forderungen des Bauprogramms (in unserem Beispiel war an einer lauten Hauptverkehrsstraße eine Baulücke zu füllen, wobei die Südseite Straßenseite ist). In den von Ungers angestellten sehr konsequenten und keineswegs nur formalen Überlegungen verbergen sich äußerst fruchtbare Ansätze für die Sanierung überalterter Wohngebiete, die erwiesenermaßen mit den Rezepten des landläufigen Sozialen Wohnungsbaus nicht zu bewältigen ist.

Noch immer ungehört sind Hans Scharouns Gedanken zum Wohnen, zu den Wohnvorgängen, zu allen mit diesen Vorgängen verbundenen oder unabdingbaren Qualitäten. Die bauliche Homöopathie, die Scharoun den unbedenklich-flotten Lösungen entgegensetzt, muß von ihrer Natur her esoterisch wirken. In den Wohntürmen ›Romeo‹ und ›Julia‹ in Stuttgart-Zuffenhausen aber haben wir nun die greifbare Probe aufs Exempel. An diesen beiden Bauten wird – wie immer auch die Wertungen im einzelnen sein mögen – eines deutlich: daß das große Mietwohnhaus städtebauliche Qualitäten und urbane Wirkungen haben kann, über die uns bisher noch niemand belehrt hat. Bestimmt ist Le Corbusiers Wohneinheit nun nicht mehr die einzige Alternative zum Sozialen Mietwohnungsbau der letzten zehn Jahre, als die die ›Strahlende Stadt‹ – auch angesichts der Wohnbauten des südlichen Hansaviertels in Berlin – noch heute oft eingeschätzt wird.

Wir müssen bedauern, daß bei einem wertenden Vergleich mit anderen Lösungen des Miethausbaus die Berliner ›Unité d'Habitation‹ schon deshalb schlecht abschneiden muß, weil Le Corbusiers (den Wohneinheiten in Marseille und Nantes entsprechende) Konzeption in entscheidenden Punkten beschnitten wurde: in Berlin wurde in Ablehnung des Modulor-Maßes von 2.26 m eine Raumhöhe von 2.50 m verlangt; die zweigeschossigen, die ganze Tiefe des Baukörpers beanspruchenden Wohnungstypen wurden in Appartements und Zweizimmerwohnungen umgewandelt; sämtliche Zwischendecken wurden durchgezogen, so daß es im ganzen Haus keinen Raum mehr mit doppelter Höhe gibt. Zu großen Teilen ist die Wohneinheit damit zu einer ganz unsinnigen zweibündigen Anlage geworden. Das freie Stützengeschoß wurde mit einem hauseigenen Heizkraftwerk und mit Läden so gut wie geschlossen. Um die Proportionen zu retten, ließ sich Le Corbusier zu einer zersplitterten, kleinlichen Farbgebung der Fassaden hinreißen. Über diesen ›halben‹ Le Corbusier kann auch die städtebaulich ganz hervorragende Wahl des Bauplatzes nicht hinwegtrösten.

Auch die Bauten des südlichen Hansaviertels in Berlin, die – in ihren verschiedenen Baustadien – den Mittelpunkt der ›Interbau‹ 1957 bildeten, mußten sich die Reglementierung durch eine zu Teilen längst unsinnig gewordene Bauordnung gefallen lassen. Doch erwiesen sich hier die Vorstellungen der eingeladenen Architekten (darunter 19 Ausländer) als weitaus elastischer und anpassungsfähiger. Zumal die 8- und 10geschossigen Wohnhäuser von Alvar Aalto und Jaenecke/Samuelson gehören trotz der gegebenen Beschränkung durchaus in die erste Reihe europäischer Wohnarchitektur, und zwar sowohl von der Entwicklung der Wohnungsgrundrisse her als auch von deren Disposition innerhalb der Baukörper. Ein Gleiches gilt für die 4geschossigen Wohnhäuser von Kay Fisker oder Wassili Luckhardt und Hubert Hoffmann. Unter den fünf Turmhäusern entlang der S-Bahn hat das von Van den Broek/Bakema ganz besonderen Rang. Das Wohnhochhaus von Gustav Hassenpflug ist als Montagebau aus geschoßhohen, vorgefertigten Stützen und ebenfalls vorgefertigten zweischaligen Wandplatten zu nennen. Eine der überragenden Leistungen im Hansaviertel ist das 4geschossige Wohnhaus von Otto Senn, ein Punkthaus, das man anstelle eines anderen Wohnturmes ganz in der Nähe als Hochhaus hätte ausführen sollen. So hat der bescheidene Bau von Senn leider nicht die Aufmerksamkeit gefunden, die er verdient.

In der Gesamtanlage und in der Einordnung und Bindung der einzelnen Bauten in den ganzen Bezirk ist das neue Berliner Hansaviertel nicht jenes Muster für einen innerstädtischen Wiederaufbau geworden, das man angesichts der umfangreichen Vorbereitungen, der Umlegungsverfahren und der gesammelten Anstrengung aller beteiligten Architekten erwarten mußte. Dem mutigen Unternehmen fehlte offensichtlich der führende Kopf. Zu sehr ließ man sich bei der Gesamtplanung von Planspiel-Gesichtspunkten leiten. Das verraten nicht nur das strukturell unbewältigte Nebeneinander von Hoch- und Flachbau (mit der Atriumhausreihe von Arne Jacobsen) und die sehr anfechtbare

Reihung der Hochhauskörper entlang der S-Bahn, sondern nicht zuletzt auch die spürbare Unsicherheit in der Bemessung der Außenräume. Alle diese Erfahrungen haben zwar das Risiko mehr als belohnt, doch blieben Art und Intensität, Idee und Anstrengung dieses Neubaus eines zerstörten innerstädtischen Wohngebietes ohne weitere Wirkung. Dazu war die Gesamtkonzeption zu unverbindlich; trotz aller hervorragenden Einzellösungen.

Es wirft ein bezeichnendes Licht auf die Situation des Bauens gegen Ende der fünfziger Jahre, daß einschneidende Schritte gerade dort zu verzeichnen sind, wo das Bauen von der Aufgabenstellung her streng an Funktionen gebunden ist. Hervorragendes Beispiel ist der Krankenhausbau. Ein Vergleich der Grundrisse des Kreiskrankenhauses in Riedlingen von Johannes Krahn und des Kreiskrankenhauses in Obernburg am Main von Köhler/Kässens deutet eine Entwicklung an, die von der konventionellen Lösung eines I- oder T-Grundrisses zu scheinbar aufgelösten, in Wirklichkeit aber streng funktionellen Konzeptionen führt: zu äußerster Verdichtung der Behandlungsabteilungen und des Wirtschaftsteils in den unteren Geschossen, zu einer Konzentrierung auch der Pflegeeinheiten in rationellster Verklammerung mit der Gesamtanlage. Die Strenge des inneren Gefüges führt, wie unsere Beispiele zeigen, mehr und mehr zur akzentlosen, sachlichen Fassade. Das ›Klinische‹ wird zum architektonischen Ausdruck.

Ein ähnlicher Trend läßt sich auch bei Gaststätten und Hotels beobachten, deren Betrieb ja ebenfalls äußerste Wirtschaftlichkeit und reibungsloses Funktionieren aller Dienste verlangt. Extremes Beispiel für Konzentration ist das Sozialgebäude einer Maschinenfabrik bei Mainz von Hans-Joachim Lenz: eine ›Verpflegungs- und Bade-Apparatur‹ in Form eines noblen Stahlbaus. Gerade die besondere architektonische Qualität dieses Gebäudes macht sinnfällig, wie leicht auch gute Architektur zur Parodie einer Aufgabe werden kann. Das Restaurant ›Buschmühle‹ im Dortmunder Westfalenpark hat eine ganz andere Funktion und Aufgabe; aber auch hier ging es ja im Rahmen der Bundesgartenschau 1959 um Massenbetrieb und schnelle Abfertigung. Der Gedanke des sozialen Dienstes ist hier von Groth/Lehmann/Schlote weit menschlicher und freier definiert worden; und wohlgemerkt bei gleicher Sorgfalt für die architektonische Ausbildung und das Detail. Der ungegliederte große Speisesaal jedenfalls kann nicht mehr bauliche Form sein für jene knappe halbe Stunde, in der der Arbeiter, aus dem Arbeitsablauf gelöst, die Chance hat, Person zu sein. Wenn nicht alles täuscht, wird sich die sogenannte Kantine allmählich der Gestalt eines Club-Hauses mit dessen relativ freier Verfügbarkeit über Räume und Raumzusammenhänge nähern. Daß ein solches Sozialgebäude nicht die von der Landschaft und vom Ort her entwickelte Ordnung haben kann wie etwa das Stadtpark-Restaurant in Nürnberg von Friedrich Seegy oder gar das Tennis-Club-haus in Berlin-Grunewald von Paul Baumgarten, versteht sich. Auch die Bauaufgabe ›Hotel‹ wird von einer wohlabgewogenen Disposition funktioneller Bindungen und räumlicher Freizügig-keit her neu definiert werden müssen. Das Hotel ›Berlin‹ am Berliner Lützowplatz von Schwebes/Schoszberger hat einige Ansätze dazu. Nach Fertigstellung der restlichen Bauabschnitte wird das noch deutlicher werden.

Der Schulbau zeigt in der zweiten Hälfte der fünfziger Jahre eine sehr lebendige Entwicklung. Die ›Protestaktion‹ der reinen, weit auseinandergezogenen Pavillonschule, die eine erste, sehr um-strittene Antwort auf die alte, immer noch nicht ausgestorbene Schulkaserne war, hat nuancierteren Entwurfsgedanken Platz gemacht. Hier sind wiederum an erster Stelle die Überlegungen von Hans Scharoun zu nennen, die er schon 1951 im Entwurf für die Volksschule in Darmstadt fixierte. Nachdem er nun das Mäd-chen-Gymnasium in Lünen hat bauen können, beginnen diese Gedanken eines auf alle möglichen Qualitäten – auf pädagogi-sche, strukturelle, landschafts- und ortsgebundene Qualitäten – abzielenden Baus Schule zu machen. Zumal die Behandlung des Lichts, seine Führung und seine Zuordnung zu den Alters- und Lernstufen werden nun als konstituierendes Element des Entwurfs begriffen. Es bestätigt sich, daß von diesem ›informel-len‹ Bauen Wirkungen ausgehen, ausgehen können, die sich von der Übernahme oder Adaption formaler Typen wesentlich unterscheiden. Scharoun schafft nicht nur vielgegliederten Raum für eine neue Pädagogische Provinz, sondern ihm ist Bauen selbst pädagogisches Anliegen, ganz im Sinne einer ›Pflanzstätte für Geister‹.

Auch da, wo bei der baulichen Ordnung eines Schulkomplexes abstrakter verfahren wird, geht die Entwicklung ähnliche Wege und zielt auf eine städtebauliche Kernzelle, in der Weite und Enge, Offenes und Abgeschlossenes, Flaches und Hohes, Sich-einfügen und Sich-exponieren miteinander in Wechselbezie-hung stehen. Die Schule gewinnt nicht nur als Institution, son-dern auch als öffentliches Bauwerk zusehends wieder Rang. Wer heute etwa nach den besten Bauten in Dortmund fragt, wird ganz sicher auch auf das Aufbau-Gymnasium von Fried-rich Wilhelm Kraemer verwiesen; die Stadt Offenbach bezieht ihre Geltung nicht nur von der Lederindustrie, sondern auch von einer Reihe ausgezeichneter Schulbauten wie etwa dem Rudolf-Koch-Gymnasium von Adolf Bayer oder der Humboldt-Schule von Steinmeyer/Novotny.

Wir sind glücklicherweise im Schulbau vor einer allzu schnellen Festlegung auf bestimmte Typen bewahrt geblieben. Das war zwar oft von wirtschaftlichem Nachteil und hat uns manche Fehlentwicklung beschert, war aber, aufs Ganze gesehen, ein in seinem Wert kaum abzuschätzender Ausleseprozeß. Er ist ganz zweifellos nicht nur unserer Architektur, sondern im glei-

chen Maß der immer noch nicht gefestigten Entwicklung unse-res Schulwesens zugute gekommen. So ist auch vom Baulichen her die Diskussion nach wie vor offen. Dazu braucht man nur einen Schulentwurf von Scharoun neben eine Schule von Dieter Oesterlen zu stellen: Wo man auf Qualität hier wie da trifft, können wir lernen und wachsen und mit sehr viel Ruhe weiterbauen an der Pädagogischen Provinz. Wir können sie anreichern mit Son-derformen, deren jede ihr Gesicht haben und wahren kann. Denn auch eine Musische Bildungsstätte wie die über dem Tal der Wupper bei Remscheid, ein Kollegiengebäude wie das der Ar-chitektur-Fakultät der Technischen Hochschule Stuttgart oder auch die Bauten einer freien Akademie gehören in den großen Zusammenhang der Erziehung und Bildung des wachen, mün-digen, sich verantwortenden Menschen.

Doch auch hier bedarf es eines kritischen Wortes: Noch verfah-ren wir beim Bau unserer Bildungsstätten mit allzuviel Zurück-haltung. Manche Bauten ersterben geradezu in der Drosselung des Temperaments; vieles wirkt mehr als unterkühlt. Muß etwa eine musische Schule in einer prachtvollen Landschaft eine Gruppierung harter Kuben sein? Auch das Geschick, mit dem Werner und Grete Wirsing diese Baukörper auf den abfallenden Hang setzten, nimmt dem Bau nicht die klanglose Spröde. Und wirkt die äußerste Sachlichkeit, mit der das Stuttgarter Kollegien-gebäude von Gutbrod/Siegel/Wilhelm auf- und ausgeführt wur-de, nicht allzu lähmend, allzu ernsthaft und ganz und gar ›erwachsen‹ auf noch bildsame Studenten? Durch Werner Dütt-manns Berliner Akademie der Künste hingegen wird so mancher Architekturkritiker mit dickem Rotstift gehen, um Unstimmiges und Inkonsequentes anzukreiden. Aber wie lebendig ist dieser Bau, welch freien Atem hat er, wie frei kann man mit ihm und in ihm umgehen, obwohl er wahrlich nicht aus einem Guß ist. Da wird das Unvollkommene, Nicht-zu-Ende-geführte zum bildsamen räumlichen Stoff derer, die ihn benutzen. Wir lernen daran, daß ein Bau, der lebendige Vollzüge ermöglicht oder gar provoziert, wichtiger, ja wesentlicher sein kann als ein makelloses Architek-turstück. So besitzt die Berliner Akademie zum Beispiel das schönste Studio-Theater in Deutschland; wer aber vom Äußeren dieses Theaterbaus auf dessen Inneres schließt, ohne es zu ken-nen, sieht sich genarrt: der leicht asymmetrische Theatersaal mit dem kleinen und großen Parkett und der Bühne dazwischen liegt quer zur Längsrichtung des abgefalteten Daches.

Die Möglichkeit, zwischen zwei ansteigenden Parketts, also in-mitten der Zuschauer zu spielen, geben auch die Kleinen Häu-ser der beiden Theater-Neubauten in Mannheim und in Gelsen-kirchen. Das National-Theater in Mannheim von Gerhard Weber vereint Großes und Kleines Haus (analog der Wettbewerbskon-zeption von Mies van der Rohe) unter einem Dach; beim Gelsen-kirchener Stadttheater von Ruhnau/Rave/von Hausen ist das Kleine Haus als besonderer Baukörper neben den gläsernen

Kubus des Großen Hauses gesetzt. Die Großen Häuser beider Theater aber sind durchaus konventionell als Guckkastenbühnen ausgebildet. Erschreckend ist in beiden Fällen die Hypertrophie des bühnentechnischen Apparats, erfreulich die Ausweitung des Foyers und der Gesellschaftsräume. Die Bauaufgabe selbst aber, die da ›Theater‹ heißt, ist weder in Mannheim noch in Gelsenkirchen entschieden definiert. Die alte Institution des Stadttheaters wurde in den Mantel eines modernen öffentlichen Zweckbaus gesteckt. Darüber kann auch die zu Teilen nicht immer qualifizierte Mitarbeit von Malern und Bildhauern hinwegtäuschen. Daß das Mannheimer und das Gelsenkirchener Theater gleichwohl Platz in unserer Auswahl finden mußten, und zwar als durchaus überdurchschnittliche Bauten, ist Zeichen einer seltsamen Experimentierunlust, vielleicht aber auch von Resignation auf seiten der Theaterleute und Bauherren.

In der Durchdringung der Bauaufgabe ›Konzertsaal‹ sind wir hingegen ein gutes Stück weiter. Technisch weniger angestrengt, freier in den räumlichen Dispositionsmöglichkeiten, vor allem weniger belastet mit unabdingbaren Abläufen und Zwangsvorkehrungen, konnten Ideen realisiert werden, die nun sehr intensiv weiterwirken in neueren Entwürfen für Stadthallen, Kulturzentren und ähnlichem. Mit der Liederhalle in Stuttgart von Abel/Gutbrod und der Bonner Beethovenhalle von Siegfried Wolske sind, was selten genug vorkommt, Leitbilder gesetzt worden. Man möge dieses Urteil nicht so sehr auf die formale Ausbildung dieser Konzerthäuser beziehen, auch nicht nur auf deren Zweckdienlichkeit, sondern vor allem auf die neuen Formen der Öffentlichkeit, die diese Bauten ermöglichen. Schon erste tastende Versuche in dieser Richtung sollten wir hierzulande hochloben, auch wenn ihnen noch die sichere Kraft etwa der Londoner Konzerthalle von 1951 abgeht.

Der in Stuttgart und Bonn eingeschlagene Weg – demnächst wird sich Scharouns Berliner Philharmonie-Gebäude hinzugesellen –, dieser Weg ist zweifellos weitaus fruchtbarer als die architektonische und konstruktive tour-de-force von Hugh A. Stubbins bei seiner Kongreßhalle in Berlin zwischen Spree und Tiergarten. Die Heraldik dieses Baus war Gegenstand vieler und langer Diskussionen und hat zu einer Standortbestimmung unseres Bauens zwischen Unbedenklichkeit und Wagnis einerseits, Phantasielosigkeit und ängstlichem Zögern andererseits außerordentlich viel beigetragen.

Von deutscher Seite war an dieser Diskussion vor allem Frei Otto beteiligt, dessen Zeltbauten und leichte Konstruktionen zu dem wenigen gehören, was von unserem Nachkriegsbauen ein starkes Echo auch jenseits unserer Grenzen auslöste. Zu bedauern ist, daß das Leichte und scheinbar Unsolide bei uns immer noch mit Spielerei oder Provisorium gleichgesetzt werden. Die bisherige Domäne dieser Leichtbauten, der Ausstellungsbau, ist wahrhaftig ein aus ahnungsloser Vorsicht viel zu eng bemesse-

nes Feld. Was Wunder, daß da auch eine so prachtvolle Raumfigur wie die Große Halle der ›Interbau‹, die der ›stadt von morgen‹ gewidmet war, ohne Wirkung blieb. Jedenfalls hat dieser Bau von Karl Otto, Günter Günschel und Frei Otto bislang kaum Nachfolge.

Vielleicht nicht der eindrücklichste, dafür aber exponierteste deutsche Ausstellungsbau der letzten Jahre war die Pavillon-Gruppe, die Eiermann/Ruf für die Weltausstellung in Brüssel 1958 entwarfen. Die Konzeption der acht zusammenhängenden Pavillons stützte sich auf das zuverlässige technische Niveau, in dem wir hierzulande Spitzenniveau zu sehen gewohnt sind. Das war, fast dreißig Jahre nach Mies van der Rohes Barcelona-Pavillon, eine bewußte Selbstbescheidung. Sie hat uns gut getan auf diesem Festival der Superlative. Wiederum hatten wir, wenn auch in einem anderen Sinn als damals in Barcelona, so etwas wie absolute Architektur vor uns: die Ausstellungsobjekte, die Einbauten wurden zur Nebensache. Das war, gemessen an dem, was da an Ausstellung erdacht und realisiert war, durchaus in der Ordnung. Und nicht zu vergessen: die Pavillons waren für das Bauen in Deutschland, für das Durchschnittsniveau dieses Bauens, in keiner Weise repräsentativ. Sie haben uns würdig vertreten.

Gegenüber der Selbstherrlichkeit der Brüsseler Pavillons ist das Ausstellungsgebäude des Kunstkreises Hameln von Oesterlen ganz auf die Präsentation eines Inhalts, hier von Kunstwerken, konzipiert. Es dient nicht dem Spektakulären, sondern schließt die Außenwelt aus. Die Kunstwerke sind geborgen in einer klaren architektonischen Form. Wie Düttmanns Ausstellungshaus der Berliner Akademie der Künste lebt dieser Bau ganz aus den lebendigen Möglichkeiten und der räumlichen Freizügigkeit des Innern.

Dem Geschäfts- und Bürohausbau ist solche Freizügigkeit nur in den Repräsentationstrakten oder -geschossen gestattet. In vielen Fällen, wie zum Beispiel dem Geschäftshaus in Frankfurt von Otto Apel, dem Mannesmann-Hochhaus von Schneider-Esleben/Knothe und dem Hochhaus der Phoenix-Rheinrohr von Hentrich/Petschnigg in Düsseldorf, hat eine große, oft überhöhte und mit Aufgängen und Galerien verbundene Eingangshalle diese Rolle des Repräsentativen übernommen. Im übrigen ist diese Bauaufgabe ausschließlich von einem rationellen Arbeitsablauf her bestimmt. Danach richten sich nicht nur die räumlichen Abmessungen im einzelnen, sondern auch sämtliche Nutzflächenverhältnisse, etwa das überaus wichtige Verhältnis der Bürofläche zur Verkehrsfläche.

Der moderne Zweckbau ist im wesentlichen eine Aufgabe der konstruktiven und technischen Ausbildung. Die Variabilität der Raumaufteilung, die von den Organisationsfachleuten gefordert wird, kann nur der reine Skelettbau ermöglichen. Es geht darum, alle störenden Festlegungen – außer den unabdingbaren Windverbänden – zu eliminieren. Die längst bekannte Konsequenz ist die Trennung in Tragendes und Füllendes oder in Tragkonstruktion und Haut, in Skelett und vorgehängte Fassade. Diese Aufgabe wird nun auch in Deutschland gründlicher erarbeitet und technisch bewältigt. Unsere Auswahl zeigt einige vorzügliche Beispiele.

Bei solcher Aufgabenstellung konzentriert sich die Gestaltung – abgesehen von Problemen der technischen Ausbildung – auf die Frage der körperlichen Gliederung und der Proportionen. Auch unter der strengen Bindung eines Grundriß- oder Fassadenrasters bleiben Differenzierungsmöglichkeiten, durch die sich Temperamente ausdrücken können. Selbst einander in der Machart so nahestehende Bauten wie etwa das Betriebsgebäude in Duisburg-Hamborn von Gerhard Weber und das Verwaltungsgebäude des Landschaftsverbandes Rheinland in Köln von Schulze-Fielitz/von Rudloff sind auch dem Laien unverwechselbar. Die ruhige Körperlichkeit des Frankfurter Geschäftshauses von Apel hat ein völlig anderes Gesicht als die ebenfalls körperhafte straffe Eleganz, die den Verwaltungsbau von Kraemer in Goslar auszeichnet. Das Gebäude des Deutschen Wetterdienstes in Offenbach von Karlfriedrich Posenenske ist mit seiner rauhen Schale (und seiner besonderen Konstruktion) so gut bauliches Individuum wie das kühle und glatte Zahlenlotto-Haus in Münster von Harald Deilmann. Die Reduktion auf einfache Elemente bei Paul Baumgartens Ruhrkohle-Haus in Berlin unterscheidet sich wesentlich vom gleichen Versuch bei der Ortskrankenkasse in Groß-Gerau von Novotny/Hoschak.

Alle diese Bauten sind jeweils überragende Leistungen an ihrem Ort, wo sie oft als raumordnende Elemente in konfusen städtebaulichen Zusammenhängen stehen. In besonderem Maß gilt das zum Beispiel für Egon Eiermanns Verwaltungsgebäude der Essener Steinkohlenbergwerke AG. Die Abmessungen dieses Baus richten sich für den Augenschein nach den Maßen der anthrazit wirkenden kleinen Keramikplatten, mit denen die Fassaden durchgängig verkleidet sind; alle Maße beziehen sich also auf einen denkbar kleinen Raster. Aber diese Ordnung vom kleinsten Element her – oder auf dieses Element hin – ließ einen Bau gelingen, der im Wiederaufbau-Chaos der Essener Innenstadt durchaus dominiert, obwohl er von anderen Bauten in der Höhe weit überragt wird. Ähnliches läßt sich auch von dem viel kleineren, in seiner Erscheinung sehr viel eleganter wirkenden Bürohaus eines Stahlbau-Unternehmens in Offenburg sagen. Hier versuchte Eiermann Baugedanken weiterzuführen, die ihn bereits bei den Brüssel-Pavillons leiteten. Daß aber gerade Geschäfts- und Bürohäuser auch städtebauliche Maßstäbe sprengen oder städtebauliche Zusammenhänge zerreißen können, zeigt – einmal ungeachtet seiner besonderen konstruktiven Qualität – das Düsseldorfer Rheinrohr-Hochhaus. Mehr und mehr bildet sich in diesen Jahren das Urteil heraus, daß gute Architektur nicht

taugen kann, solange sie nicht aus einer Sicht auf größere Zusammenhänge entwickelt ist. Der unkonventionelle Bau des ADAC-Hauses in Berlin von Willy Kreuer, Füllung einer Bombenlücke und neue Ecklösung an einer Hauptverkehrsader, zeigt, wie das gemeint ist und welche Chancen ein vom Ort her entwickeltes Bauen haben kann.

Fest aber steht, daß die architektonische Qualität des Bauens für Verwaltung, Handel und Industrie der Qualität unseres innerstädtischen Wohnungsbaues weit voraus ist. Auch auf dem Land, in der Landschaft, setzt dieses Bauen mehr und mehr maßgebliche Akzente. Einen Bau, der mit soviel Sorgfalt und Fingerspitzengefühl in die Landschaft eingefügt ist wie die Fabrik in Blomberg von Schulze-Fielitz/von Altenstadt/von Rudloff kann man im Lippischen lange suchen. Bauten auf dem kleinen Heidelberger Industriegelände, darunter das ganz hervorragende Haus der Fleischerei-Innung von Lothar Götz und Gerhard Hauss, sind eine weitaus erfreulichere Ortserweiterung als die neuen Wohnsiedlungen im Neuenheimer Feld. Die kleine Schallplattenfabrik in Langenargen von Hans und Traudl Maurer oder das neue Werkstattgebäude für die Herstellung optischer Hochleistungsinstrumente in Braunschweig von Friedrich Wilhelm Kraemer stechen krass ab in den Vorstadt-Landschaften dieser Städte. Und selbst eine so nüchterne Einrichtung wie das Stuttgarter Parkhaus Breuninger von Gerd Wiegand gibt für einen noch ungeordneten innerstädtischen Bezirk bereits einen Maßstab ab. Daneben gibt es allerdings auch Industrieanlagen, die von der Bauaufgabe her solche Abmessungen und Ausdehnungen gewinnen, daß es aller Anstrengung bedarf, das auseinanderstrebende Einzelne auf das Ganze zu beziehen und es einzubinden. Bei der geradezu monumentalen ›Verpackungsmaschine‹, die Egon Eiermann für ein Frankfurter Versandhaus baute, ist diese Inbezugsetzung des Einzelnen untereinander und zum Ganzen in besonders augenfälliger Weise geglückt.

Daß im Stadtbild allen diesen funktionsbedingten Bauten nur deren aufgeputzte Karikaturen antworten, daß diesen Zweckbauten kein anders geartetes Bauwesen gegenübersteht, nichts, was diesem auf Materialien, Vorgängen, Organisationen bezogenen Bauen seinen richtigen Ort in einem Ganzen zuweist, – darin bekundet sich unsere geistig-sittliche Armut. Die Proteste, mit denen immer wieder gegen ein sachliches Bauen, gegen die nun schon alte ›Neue Sachlichkeit‹ Sturm gelaufen wird, richten sich im Grunde ja nicht gegen diese Sachlichkeit selbst, sondern gegen die Ideenarmut, mit der die Stadt als Ort des Wohnens mißhandelt wird. Die Bildhaftigkeit, der Inbegriff fehlen! Die Stadt ist noch ohne Gestalt; nach den Zerstörungen des Krieges ist sie nicht mehr und noch nicht wieder lesbar.

Rudolf Schwarz muß das empfunden haben, wenn er in seinen letzten Lebensjahren immer wieder von ›Architektur als Bild‹ – für seine Arbeit, den Kirchenbau: als heiligem Bild – sprach. Und nicht nur sprach; er hat das Bild ja gebaut: Heilig-Kreuz in Bottrop ist der gebaute Welthafen, die Bucht vor dem Offenen; Maria Königin in Saarbrücken ist Kelch und mystische Rose; St. Anna in Düren umfängt die Beter wie ein großer Schutzmantel. Aber welchem Widerstand begegnete Rudolf Schwarz mit solchen Deutungen! Die Furcht, sich literarisch zu gerieren, Literatur zu bauen, die Konturen des Metiers zu verwässern, diese Furchtsamkeit vor Wirkkräften, die aus anderen Bereichen kommen, – sie haben das Ideal des ›reinen‹ formal bestimmten Bauens vor einer längst überfälligen Ablösung bewahrt. Doch mehren sich, zumal im Kirchenbau, wo es allerdings naheliegt, die geistigen, im Geistigen begründeten Vorstellungen: der ›bergende‹ Raum (Maria in den Benden in Düsseldorf von Steffann/Rosiny, St. Albertus Magnus in Leverkusen und Heilig-Kreuz in Düsseldorf von Josef Lehmbrock); der helle ›sich öffnende‹ Raum (Kirche am Lietzensee in Berlin von Paul Baumgarten); der ›mystisch-klare‹ Raum (Christuskirche in Bochum von Dieter Oesterlen). Luft, Feuer, Wasser, Erde – die Elemente sind als Lebenswirklichkeiten hineingenommen ins architektonische Bild dieser Kirchen. Warum sollten wir nicht wieder

umgehen mit diesen Kräften? Daß man literarisch deuten und umschreiben kann, macht noch längst keine literarische Architektur! Läßt sich nicht im Gegenteil behaupten: Poesie hat zu keiner Zeit der Architektur Abbruch getan! Die Zeichen mehren sich, daß einige falsche Gewissensfragen abgebaut werden.

Struktur und Gestalt – in diesen beiden Begriffen sind die Aufgaben des Bauens und Planens nach der Jahrhundertmitte enthalten. Von der Siedlung über die Wohnstadt zur City der Großstadt und Weltstadt, vom einzelnen Bau bis zur Ordnung landschaftlicher Räume – immer begegnen wir lebendigen Vollzügen menschlichen Wohnens in seinem weiten Sinn, von dem wir eingangs sprachen. So wird Bauen künftig auch heißen müssen: die Strukturen unseres Lebens und Zusammenlebens, die Strukturen des Landes und der Orte, die Strukturen des Handelns und Arbeitens sehen und erkennen, um so die Gestalt zu entwerfen, die das Widerstrebende bindet und das allzu Verfestigte in Bewegung bringt. Es bedarf dazu keiner Ideologie, sondern eines hellen, wachen und nüchternen Bewußtseins. Es bedarf – in des Wortes tieferer Bedeutung – des Selbst-Bewußtseins.

Das auf dem Gelände des Deutschen Pavillons errichtete erdgeschossige Haus wurde für einen Zwei-Personenhaushalt entworfen. Eine zwei Meter hohe, unverputzte Klinkermauer umschließt als gewinkelte Spirale die kleine Wohnung von 53 qm und einen Wohnhof von 106 qm, der in eine mit Platten belegte Terrasse und eine größere Rasenfläche unterteilt ist. Küche und Bad, an eine gemeinsame Installationswand angeschlossen, sind im Mittelpunkt des Hauses zu einer Naßzelle zusammengefaßt. Schiebetüren trennen sie von Wohnraum und Schlafraum. Ein auf drei Seiten zwischen dem abgehobenen, von Flußstahlrohren getragenen Flachdach und der Klinkerwand umlaufendes Fensterband und die wandhoch verglaste Gartenfront öffnen die Räume zum Licht und ermöglichen die geringe Raumhöhe von 2,35 m. Die Inneneinrichtung und die Kamingruppe im Garten sind nach Entwürfen des Architekten ausgeführt. Auf Heizung wurde verzichtet, weil das Haus nach Ausstellungsende wieder abgebrochen wurde.

The single-storey house, built on the site of the German Pavilion at the Brussels Exhibition, was designed for a household of two. A seven-foot wall of exposed brick encloses, in a rectangular "spiral", the 500-square-foot home and 1,000-square-foot courtyard, comprising a paved terrace and a larger area of lawn. Kitchen and bath, sharing a service wall, form a core in the middle of the house. Sliding doors separate the living and bed rooms. A continuous ribbon window on three sides, set between the brick wall and the flat roof carried on steel stanchions, and the completely glazed wall of the garden front, provide light and make it possible to limit the internal height to less than 9'. The interior furnishings and the fireplace in the garden were made to the architect's designs. No heating was installed, as the house was demolished when the exhibition closed.

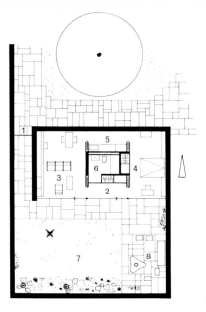

Grundriß / Ground plan
1 Zugang / Entrance
2 Windfang, Garderobe / Way-in, cloak room
3 Wohnraum / Living room
4 Schlafraum / Bedroom
5 Küche / Kitchen
6 Bad / Bath
7 Gartenhof / Garden
8 Kamin / Fireplace

1 Blick vom Schlafraum in den Wohnhof mit offenem Kamin.
  View from the bedroom into the garden with its open fireplace.
2 Eingangsseite.
  Entrance front.
3 Blick vom Wohnhof auf die verglaste Südfront des Hauses.
  View from the garden of the glazed South front of the house.
4 Wohnraum.
  Living room.

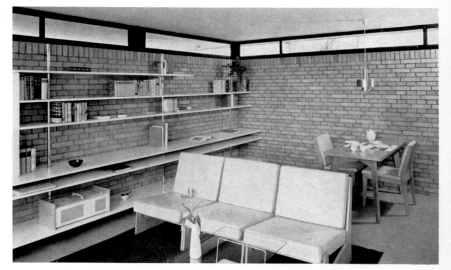

Gartenhofhaus in Karlsruhe-Durlach – 1959
Architekt: Reinhard Gieselmann, Karlsruhe

Garden house, Karlsruhe-Durlach – 1959
Architect: Reinhard Gieselmann, Karlsruhe

Schnitt / Section

Das Grundstück steigt nach Südwesten an. Das Wohngeschoß ist auf die Ebene des südlich vorge-lagerten Gartens gehoben. Der Keller auf der Nordseite ist direkt belichtet. Von der Straße führt eine schmale Treppe an der Garage vorbei zum Eingangsvorplatz. Ein nach Süden offener Gartenhof, die überdeckte Terrasse, das Zimmer des Hausherrn und der zentrale Wohnraum bilden den Wohn-bereich. Die Schlafzimmer sind in einem nach Südosten orientierten Flügel zusammengefaßt. Nach Nordwesten liegt anschließend an die Küche eine Einliegerwohnung mit eigenem Eingang. Auch sie hat Anteil am Garten, ohne den Wohnbereich der Hauptwohnung zu stören. Der offene Kamin und ein Wasserbecken markieren den Übergang zu Rasenflächen und Obstgarten. Von der Diele gelangt man über eine Treppe zur Tischtennishalle im Keller. Die bestimmenden Materialien des Baues sind der Wandputz, das unverputzte Klinkermauerwerk der Kamine und Sichtbeton an der Schürze des Flach-daches.

The site rises towards the South-West. The living room floor is raised to the level of the garden, which extends South. The cellar on the North side has direct lighting. A narrow flight of steps leads past the garage to the entrance. A garden-court opening to the South, a covered terrace, the owner's room and the central sitting room form the principal living space. The bedrooms are grouped in a South-East wing. On the North-West side, adjoining the kitchen, is a self-contained flat, having its own entrance and sharing the garden, but without interfering with the life of the main part of the house. An open fire-place and a tiny pool mark the frontier of the lawn and orchard. Stairs lead from the hall to a table-tennis room in the cellar. Distinctive features of the building are the wall-finishes, the unrendered brickwork of the fire-place, and the exposed concrete purlins of the flat roof.

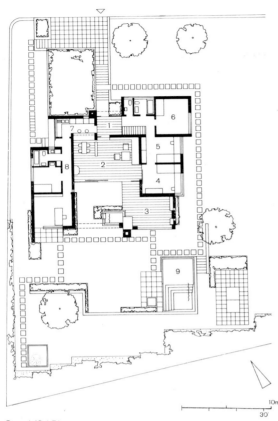

Grundriß / Plan
1 Diele / Entrance
2 Wohnraum / Living (sitting) room
3 Gedeckte Terrasse / Covered terrace
4 Zimmer des Hausherrn / Bedroom (owner)
5 Zimmer der Dame des Hauses / Bedroom (owner's wife)
6 Kinderzimmer / Children's room
7 Küche / Kitchen
8 Einliegerwohnung / Separate flat
9 Schwimmbecken / Swimming pool

1 Eingangsseite von Nordosten.
  Entrance front from the North-East.
2 Südansicht vom Garten her.
  South view from the garden.
3 Blick aus dem Wohnraum in den inneren Gartenhof und die
  überdeckte Terrasse.
  View from the sitting room towards the inner garden-court
  and covered terrace.
4 Blick vom Wohnraum zum Zimmer des Hausherrn.
  Looking from the sitting room into the owner's bedroom.

Wohnhaus in Köln-Weiss – 1955
Architekt: Gottfried Böhm, Köln

House at Cologne-Weiss – 1955
Architect: Gottfried Böhm, Cologne

Alle Räume des erdgeschossigen, auf drei Seiten von nahezu fensterlosen Ziegelmauern umschlossenen Hauses sind um einen geräumigen Innenhof gruppiert. Diese Anordnung schützt die Bewohner vor dem Einblick aus den Nachbargrundstücken. Nur die zum Rhein gerichtete Südfront des Wohnzimmers ist wandhoch verglast. Vom Eingang her, der mit einer kleinen Diele verbunden ist, gelangt man im Ostflügel vorbei an Küche und Eßplatz zur Bibliotheksecke des Wohnraumes. Auf der Westseite des Innenhofes liegen die Schlafräume mit einem Bad. Sie können vom Flur durch Vorhänge abgetrennt werden und haben je ein kleines Fenster nach Westen. Die Kinderschlafräume sind an die Diele, das Elternzimmer an den Wohnraum angeschlossen. Die Außenwände wurden mit Ytongsteinen gemauert und mit roten Backsteinen verblendet. Rings um den Innenhof und an der Südfront ruht das Stahlbetondach auf frei vor der Glasfläche stehenden Vierkantrohren.

All the rooms of this single-storey house, enclosed on three sides by almost windowless brick-walls are grouped about a spacious internal court. This arrangement protects the occupants from being overlooked by their neighbours. Only the South face of the living room is glazed, to the full height and width of the house. From the front door, which opens on to a small hall, we enter the East wing, proceeding past the kitchen and dining space to the library corner of the living room. The bedrooms and bathroom are placed on the West side of the internal court. They can be curtained off from the passage, and each has a small window in the West wall. The children's bedroom is connected to the hall; the parents' room is next to the living room. The external walls are ytong blocks faced with red bricks. Along the South front and about the internal court the reinforced concrete roof is carried on free-standing piers rectangular in section, set in front of the glass.

1 Die geschlossene Eingangsfront.
  The closed entrance front.
2 Die verglaste Südwand des Wohnraumes.
  The glazed South wall of the living room.
3 Der Blick geht von der Diele durch Innenhof und
  Wohnraum bis zum Flußufer.
  View from the entrance hall through the inner court and
  living room to the river bank.

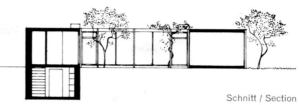

Schnitt / Section

Grundriß / Plan
 1 Windfang, Garderobe
   Entrance, cloak room
 2 WC
 3 Diele / Hall
 4 Küche / Kitchen
 5 Eßplatz / Dining space
 6 Wohnraum / Living room
 7 Arbeitsplatz / Study
 8 Innenhof / Internal court
 9 Eltern / Parents
10 Bad / Bath
11 Gast / Guest room
12 Kinder / Children

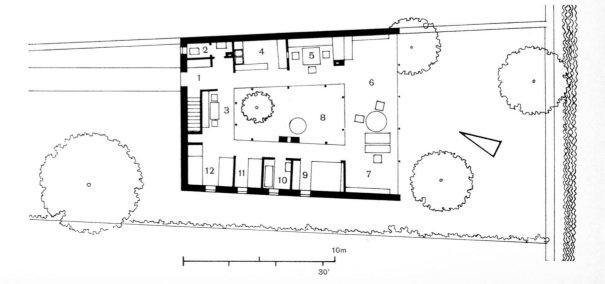

10m
30'

Studiowohnhaus in Stuttgart – 1957
Architekt: Gerhard Schwab, Stuttgart

Studio-house at Stuttgart – 1957
Architect: Gerhard Schwab, Stuttgart

Die Gestaltung des Grundrisses wurde bestimmt von der Hanglage des Grundstückes, das nach Nordosten zum Teil eine weite Aussicht bietet, und von der Forderung des Bauherrn, das Haus in mehreren Bauabschnitten zu errichten. Der Bauteil A, der Kern der Anlage, ist zweigeschossig und enthält im Untergeschoß den vorläufigen Eingang, die Installationsräume und einen Schlafraum. Eine Wendeltreppe führt zum großen Studio-Wohnraum im Erdgeschoß. Das breite Nordostfenster ist durch die Aussichtsrichtung bedingt, ein Glasbaustein-Fensterband in der Südwestwand läßt Sonnenlicht ein. Im Westen liegt vor dem Wohnraum eine Terrasse, unter der im Bauabschnitt B ein größerer Schlafraum ausgebaut werden soll. Gleichzeitig wird die Küche mit einem Eßplatz an die Stelle des kleinen Schlafraumes treten. Im Bauabschnitt C wird der Haupteingang ins Erdgeschoß verlegt, das noch um einen kleinen Arbeitsraum erweitert wird. Zuletzt kommt im Südwesten eine Garage hinzu.

The plan was dictated by the sloping site, which offers an extensive view to the North-East, and by the requirements of the client, who wanted the house to be built in several stages. Stage A, the main part of the scheme, is on two floors and contains, on the lower level, the temporary entrance, a kitchen and service rooms and a bedroom. A spiral staircase leads to the large studio-living room above. The big North-East window was determined by the view; a glass brick ribbon window in the South-West wall provides sun light. On the West side there is a terrace, beneath which, in Stage B, a larger bedroom will be constructed. At the same time the kitchen and dining space will occupy the place of the small bedroom. In the third stage, the main entrance will be moved to the upper floor, which will be expanded to include a small study. Ultimately, a garage will be added to the South-West of the house.

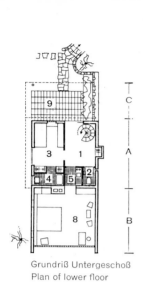

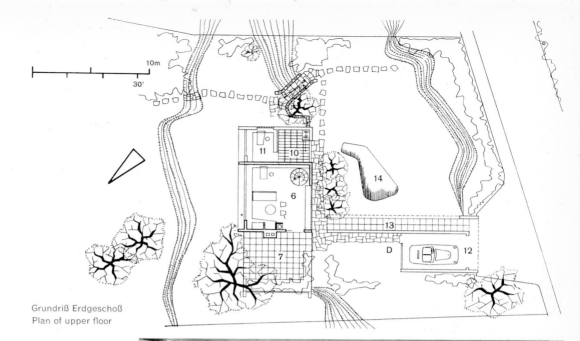

Grundriß Untergeschoß
Plan of lower floor

Grundriß Erdgeschoß
Plan of upper floor

Bauabschnitt A / Stage A:
1 Diele / Hall
2 WC
3 Schlafraum / Bedroom
4 Dusche / Shower
5 Küche / Kitchen
6 Wohnraum, Studio / Studio living room
7 Terrasse / Terrace
Bauabschnitt B / Stage B:
3 Eßplatz mit Kücheneinbau / Dining space and kitchen
5 Schrankraum / Storage
8 Schlafraum / Bedroom
Bauabschnitt C / Stage C:
9 Überdeckter Sitzplatz / Covered sitting space
10 Windfang, Garderobe / Entrance, cloak room
11 Arbeitszimmer / Study
Bauabschnitt D / Stage D:
12 Garage
13 Bildwand / Screen
14 Wasserbecken / Pool

1 Nordostansicht. Über dem geschlossenen Untergeschoß der
   Wohnraum mit dem großen Fenster. Rechts die Terrasse.
   North-East view. The living room with the large window, contrasting with the almost unbroken wall of the floor below.
   Terrace on the right.
2 Wohnraum mit großem Aussichtsfenster.
   The living room with its big window and fine view.
3 Die Terrasse, ebenerdig auf der Bergseite, auf der Talseite
   vom Astwerk eines Obstbaumes eingerahmt.
   The terrace, flush with the side of the hill, framed on the valley
   side by the boughs of a large fruit tree.

Wohnhaus in Lörbach, Odenwald – 1957–58
Architekt: Waldemar Lippert, Weinheim

House at Lörbach, Odenwald – 1957–58
Architect: Waldemar Lippert, Weinheim

Das an einem Westhang gelegene Haus bietet einen weiten Blick über die Vorberge des Odenwaldes bis zur Rheinebene. Eingang, Wohnraum, Küche und Eßplatz liegen im Obergeschoß, die Schlafräume und ein kleines Arbeitszimmer im sockelartigen Untergeschoß, das zum Schutz gegen Bergwasser als Grundwasserwanne ausgebildet ist. Die Mauern des Untergeschosses und der Terrasse sind in rauh geschaltem Beton mit eingelegten Porphyrsteinen hergestellt. Auf ihnen ist die Stahlkonstruktion des Wohngeschosses mit seinem zweischaligen Flachdach aufgesetzt. Der Wohnraum öffnet sich nach Westen und Süden zum Tal und zur Aussicht. Das weit vorspringende Dach vor den Glasflächen schützt gegen die Sonne. Der so entstandene überdeckte Sitzplatz kann durch Schiebetüren geschlossen werden, die sich in geöffnetem Zustand hinter der Außenwand der Küche und des Abstellraumes befinden. Die fensterlose Eingangsseite ist mit Holz verschalt.

Lying on a Western slope, the house enjoys a wide view across the foothills of the Odenwald to the plain of the Rhine. Entrance, living room, kitchen and dining room are placed above, with the bedrooms and a small study in a basement-like lower floor, which is constructed as a groundwater "caisson" to counteract seepage from springs. The walls of the lower storey and of the terrace are in rough exposed concrete with inlaid porphyry blocks, from which the steel frame of the living room storey rises with its flat, hollow-ceilinged, roof. The living room opens to the South and West, the valley and the view. The deep projecting roof in front of the windows provides sun protection. The resulting covered sitting space can be enclosed by sliding panels which, when open, disappear behind the outside walls of the kitchen and storage room. The windowless entrance front is faced with timber.

32

1 Ansicht von Westen. Über dem sockelartigen Untergeschoß der leichte Aufbau der Wohnräume.
  View from the West. Above the solid lower storey stands the light superstructure of the living rooms.
2 Betonierte Freitreppe zur Terrasse.
  Open-air concrete staircase to the terrace.
3 Ansicht von Süden mit Terrasse.
  View from the South, showing the terrace.
4 Der durchgehende Fußboden aus grauen Solnhofener Platten verbindet den Wohnraum mit dem überdachten Sitzplatz.
  The floor, from the living room to the covered sitting area, is paved throughout with grey "Solnhofen" slabs.
5 Sitzgruppe im Wohnraum. Wandflächen und Einbaumöbel aus Teakholz.
  Sitting space in the living room. Wall surfaces and built-in furniture are teak.

Grundriß Obergeschoß
Upper storey plan

10m
30
Grundriß Untergeschoß
Lower storey plan

1 Garderobe / Entrance and cloaks
2 Eßplatz / Dining room
3 Küche / Kitchen
4 Wohnraum / Living room
5 Überdeckter Sitzplatz / Covered sitting area
6 Abstellraum für Gartenmöbel / Storage closet for garden furniture
7 Terrasse / Terrace
8 WC
9 Gästezimmer / Guest room
10 Kleines Arbeitszimmer / Small study
11 Bad / Bath
12 Schlafzimmer / Bedroom
13 Vorräte / Storage
14 Heizung / Heating

Einfamilienhaus in Königstein/Taunus – 1955–56
Architekt: Eugen Söder, Buchschlag bei Frankfurt am Main

House at Königstein/Taunus – 1955–56
Architect: Eugen Söder, Buchschlag near Frankfurt-on-Main

Das zweigeschossige Haus ist so in den alten Baumbestand des von der Straße nach Süden fallenden Grundstückes eingefügt, daß die Wohnräume im Erdgeschoß einen weiten Blick über die Ausläufer des Taunus bis zur Mainebene gestatten, während die Schlafräume im Untergeschoß direkte Ausgänge in den Garten haben. Ein Steg führt von der Straße über einen kleinen Bach zum Eingang im Erdgeschoß. Der Wohnbereich wird durch eine auf drei Seiten von Mauern umschlossene, zum Teil überdachte Terrasse – darunter befindet sich die Garage – ergänzt. Eine Freitreppe verbindet ihn mit dem Garten. Die ursprünglich geplante Erweiterung des Wohnbereiches und die Hinzufügung eines Studios im östlichen Bauteil wurde im zweiten Bauabschnitt durch den Einbau einer Einliegerwohnung für die Eltern des Bauherrn ersetzt. Die Schräge des Welleternit-Grabendaches ist in die Räume einbezogen, die Untersicht mit Lärchenriemen verschalt.

The two-storey house, which stands among old trees on a site sloping South from the roadway, is so placed that the ground-floor living rooms enjoy a wide view over the lower spurs of the Taunus to the plain of the Main, while the bedrooms underneath have direct access to the garden. A footbridge leads from the road over a small stream to the entrance on the ground floor. The living area is completed by a terrace (over the garage), which is enclosed by walls on three sides, partly covered in, and connected to the garden by an open-air staircase. The original proposal to increase the living area and add a studio to the East part of the house was replaced at a second stage by the introduction of a self-contained flat for the owner's parents. The angles of the corrugated "Eternit" pitched roof are reflected indoors, the underside being lined with larch wood battens.

34

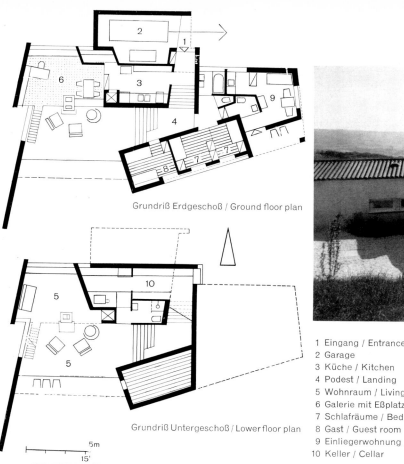

Grundriß Erdgeschoß / Ground floor plan

Grundriß Untergeschoß / Lower floor plan

5m
15'

1 Eingang / Entrance
2 Garage
3 Küche / Kitchen
4 Podest / Landing
5 Wohnraum / Living room
6 Galerie mit Eßplatz / Gallery with dining space
7 Schlafräume / Bedrooms
8 Gast / Guest room
9 Einliegerwohnung / Separate flat
10 Keller / Cellar

4 Wohnraum. Blick auf Kamin und Sitzgruppe; die Treppe führt zum Eßplatz auf der Galerie.
  Living room, looking towards the fireplace and sitting area. The stairs lead to the dining room in the gallery.
5 Blick auf den rückwärtigen Teil des Wohnraumes zur Süd-terrasse.
  View from the back of the living room towards the South terrace.

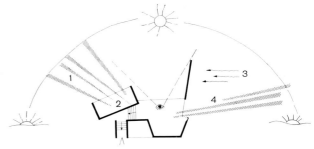

Besonnungsschema / Sun-exposure diagram
1 Morgensonne / Morning sun
2 Schlafzimmer / Bedrooms
3 Westwinde / West winds
4 Abendsonne / Evening sun

Wohnhaus des Architekten in Köln-Müngersdorf – 1958–59
Architekt: Oswald Mathias Ungers, Köln

The architect's house, Cologne-Müngersdorf – 1958–59
Architect: Oswald Mathias Ungers, Cologne

1 Ansicht von Westen.
  View from the West.
2 Dachaufsicht (Modellfoto).
  Roof view (model).

Das stark gegliederte, aus einander durchdringenden Baukörpern zusammengesetzte Haus nimmt bewußt die Beschränkungen auf, die die Bebauung des Eckgrundstückes weitgehend festlegen: vorgeschriebene Bautiefe und Traufhöhe, auf die Himmelsrichtung falsch bezogene Bauflucht und der Giebel des Nachbarhauses. Ein erdgeschossiges Büro, die Wohnung des Architekten im ersten und zweiten Obergeschoß und die beiden Einliegerwohnungen, die bei Bedarf auch Büro oder Wohnung erweitern können, sind so aneinandergefügt, daß eine gegenseitige Störung ausgeschlossen ist. Der unbebaute Teil des Grundstücks ist in verschieden große Gartenhöfe aufgeteilt. Sie können von außen nicht eingesehen werden und ergänzen zusammen mit den Balkonen und Dachterrassen die Wohn- und Arbeitsbereiche in einer differenzierten Folge von Freiräumen. Einheitliches Material bindet die Vielfalt der Bauformen: rote Klinker und Sichtbeton.

A bold design in interrelated volumes, this house skilfully exploits the drastic limitations of a corner site, restrictions on depth of substructure and height to eaves, an arbitrarily imposed building line, and the pitched roof of the house next door. A ground floor office, the architect's home on the first and second floors, and the two self-contained flats which, when required, can serve as extensions to office and living space, are so arranged that no disturbance occurs to the balance of the design. The "unbuilt-upon" part of the plot is split up into garden courts of different sizes. These cannot be overlooked from outside and complement together with balconies and roof-terraces the living and working areas in forming a varied sequence of open spaces. Widely differing architectural forms are compensated by uniform materials: red brick and exposed, untreated, concrete.

39

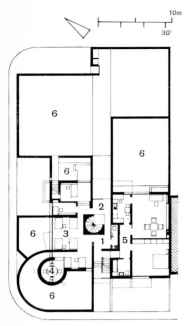

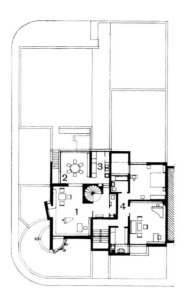

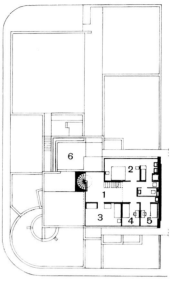

Grundriß Erdgeschoß / Ground floor plan
1 Büroeingang / Office entrance
2 Eingang zur Wohnung / Flat entrance
3 Büroräume / Office space
4 Besprechungsraum / Clients' room
5 Einliegerwohnung / Self-contained flat
6 Gartenhöfe / Garden courts

Grundriß 1. Obergeschoß / First floor plan
1 Wohnraum / Living room
2 Eßplatz / Dining area
3 Küche / Kitchen
4 Einliegerwohnung / Self-contained flat

Grundriß 2. Obergeschoß
Second floor plan
1 Flur / Landing
2 Eltern / Parents
3 Kind / Child
4 Gast / Guest
5 Mädchen / Maid
6 Dachterrassen / Roof terraces

3 Ansicht von Norden.
  North view.
4 Dachterrasse und Treppenhauskopf mit Lichtkuppel.
  Roof terrace and top of stair tower with dome light.
5 Wohnraum mit Blick zum Eßplatz. Die Materialien der Innen-
  räume sind rote Klinker, Holz und weiß gestrichener Verputz.
  Living room, looking towards dining area. The materials used
  in the interior are red brick, wood, and white-painted plaster.
6 Flur im zweiten Obergeschoß. Der Treppenturm in der Haus-
  mitte wird durch eine Lichtkuppel belichtet. Die Tür links
  führt zur Dachterrasse.
  Second floor landing. The stair tower in the middle of the
  house is lit by a dome light. The door on the left leads to the
  roof terrace.

Wohnhaus in Braunschweig – 1956
Architekt: Friedrich Wilhelm Kraemer, Braunschweig

House at Brunswick – 1956
Architect: Friedrich Wilhelm Kraemer, Brunswick

Ein Stahlskelett auf quadratischem Raster bildet das konstruktive Gerüst, in das die Räume ihrer funktionellen Bedeutung entsprechend eingeordnet sind. Die Schlafräume im Obergeschoß füllen mit ihren Balkonen neun Felder des Rasters. Die Erdgeschoßwände, die den Wohnbereich gliedern, greifen nach allen Seiten über diesen strengen Umriß hinaus und verbinden das Innere mit den überdeckten Sitzplätzen und dem Garten. Arbeitsraum, Wohnraum, Eßzimmer und die Küche mit Frühstücksplatz und Wirtschaftsraum sind um die Eingangsdiele gruppiert und bilden eine vielfältige, zusammenhängende Raumfolge. Das Obergeschoß nimmt die Schlafräume der Eltern, ein Mädchenzimmer und ein kleines Appartement für den Sohn auf. Das Äußere wird bestimmt durch die Raumabschlüsse – glasierte Ziegelsteine, Holzschalung, Glaswände, Lamellengitter und Drahtglasbrüstungen am Balkon – mit ihrem Wechsel von Offenheit, Transparenz und Geschlossenheit.

A steel skeleton on a square grid forms the structural framework, into which the rooms are fitted according to their particular function. The bedrooms on the upper floor including their balconies fill nine squares of the grid. The ground floor partition walls, which divide the living area, extend on each side beyond this strict pattern, linking the interior to the covered sitting spaces and garden. Study, living room, dining room and kitchen with breakfast alcove and pantry are grouped about the entrance hall to form a logical sequence of interrelated rooms. The upper floor comprises the parents' bedrooms, a maid's room, and a small flat for the son of the house. The exterior is determined by the variety of ways in which rooms and living spaces are defined – glazed handmade bricks, timber sidings, glass partitions, lattice screens, and wired-glass panels to the balcony parapets – by alternate open, transparent and closed, effects.

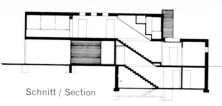

Schnitt / Section

Grundriß Erdgeschoß / Ground floor plan

Grundriß Obergeschoß
Upper floor plan

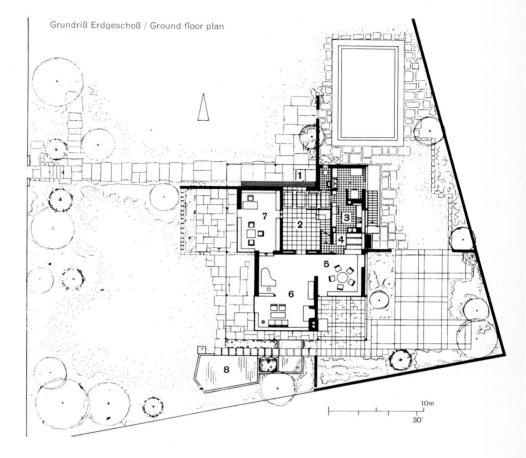

1 Eingang / Entrance
2 Diele / Hall
3 Küche / Kitchen
4 Frühstücksplatz / Breakfast alcove
5 Eßzimmer / Dining room
6 Wohnraum / Living room
7 Arbeitsraum / Study
8 Wasserbassin / Pool
9 Dame / Wife's room
10 Herr / Husband's room
11 Sohn / Son
12 Mädchen / Maid
13 Balkon / Balcony

10m
30'

1 Ansicht von Westen.
  View from the West.
2 Detail der Südwestecke.
  Detail of the South-West corner.
3 Ansicht von Osten.
  View from the East.

Mietshaus am Hansaring in Köln – 1959
Architekt: Oswald Mathias Ungers, Köln

Flats, Hansaring, Cologne – 1959
Architect: Oswald Mathias Ungers, Cologne

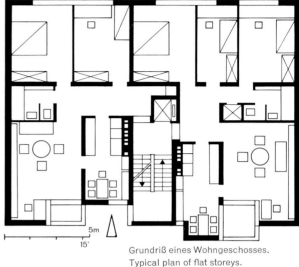

Grundriß eines Wohngeschosses.
Typical plan of flat storeys.

Das Wohnhaus schließt die Baulücke an einer Hauptgeschäftsstraße – eine der häufigsten Aufgaben beim Wiederaufbau der deutschen Städte nach dem Kriege. Das Erdgeschoß enthält außer dem Eingang mit Treppenhaus und Aufzug zwei Läden. In jedem der fünf Obergeschosse liegen zwei Drei- bis Vierzimmer-Wohnungen. Wohnräume und Küchen sind nach Süden orientiert. Vor- und zurückspringende Bauteile und tiefeingezogene Loggien rücken den Wohnbereich von der verkehrsreichen Straße und ihrem Lärm ab, ohne den Blick auf den im Südosten gegenüberliegenden Park zu behindern. Die verwendeten Materialien unterstreichen die kraftvolle, kubische Gliederung der Fassade: 30 cm starkes, unverputztes Gitterziegelmauerwerk, Sichtbeton und Stahlrahmen für Fenster und Türen.

The building fills a gap in a principal commercial street – one of the commonest tasks in German post-war urban reconstruction. Besides the entrance with stairs and lift, the ground floor contains two shops, while each of the five upper storeys holds two three to four-room flats. Sitting rooms and kitchens face South. The projecting and indented formal elements and deeply recessed balconies protect the living areas from the busy street and traffic noises without obstructing the South-East view across the park opposite. The materials used emphasise the powerful, cubic, design of the façade: 12-inch, unrendered, brick masonry; exposed concrete; steel frames for doors and windows.

Wohnhochhäuser ›Romeo‹ (1957) und ›Julia‹ (1959) in Stuttgart-Zuffenhausen
Architekten: Hans Scharoun, Berlin, und Wilhelm Frank, Stuttgart

"Romeo" (1957) and "Julia" (1959), two blocks of flats, Stuttgart-Zuffenhausen
Architects: Hans Scharoun, Berlin, and Wilhelm Frank, Stuttgart

1 Ansicht von Südosten. Links Julia, rechts Romeo.
View from the South-East. Left Julia, right Romeo.

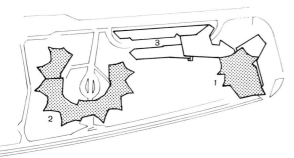

Lageplan / Site plan
1 Romeo
2 Julia
3 Garagen und Restaurant / Garages and restaurant

Die Wohnhochhäuser Romeo und Julia bekrönen, umgeben von den Zeilenbauten der neuen Siedlung, den Hügel östlich des alten Ortes Zuffenhausen. Rund 200 Eigentumswohnungen sind auf ein neunzehngeschossiges Punkthaus mit sechs durch einen Innengang erschlossenen Einheiten je Geschoß (Romeo) und ein hufeisenförmiges, in seiner Höhe von fünf bis zwölf Geschossen gestaffeltes Laubenganghaus (Julia) verteilt. Die aufgefächerte Grundrißform läßt Luft und Sonne zu allen Wohnungen Zugang finden. Gegen Wind und Einblick geschützte Balkone ergänzen den Wohnbereich als Räume unter freiem Himmel. Das zurückgesetzte Dachgeschoß beider Häuser enthält Atelierwohnungen mit windgeschützten Terrassen und überdeckten Freiplätzen. Im Erdgeschoß des Romeo finden Läden des täglichen Bedarfs und ein kleines Café Platz. Über der dort anschließenden Wäscherei und dem Garagentrakt liegt ein auf mehreren Bodenhöhen terrassiertes Restaurant.

Two high blocks of flats, Romeo and Julia, set among the terraces of a new housing estate, crown the hill lying to the East of the old locality of Zuffenhausen. Some 200 privately-owned flats are provided in a nineteen-storey point block, with six dwellings to each floor, entered from a central landing (Romeo) and in a horseshoe-shaped building, varying in height from five to twelve floors with enclosed balcony access (Julia). The irregular, fanlike, plan offers air and sun to every flat. Balconies, protected from wind and intrusion, complete the living area in the form of open-air rooms. The recessed roof storeys of both blocks contain studio flats with terraces shielded from the wind and sheltered open-air spaces. Shops for routine needs and a small café are located on the ground floor of Romeo. Above the adjoining laundry and range of garages there is a restaurant disposed on several levels.

Romeo, Grundriß Dachgeschoß
Romeo, roof (penthouse) floor plan
1 Wohnraum-Atelier / Studio sitting room
2 Schlafraum / Bedroom

Romeo, Grundriß eines Wohngeschosses
Romeo, typical floor plan
1 Innenflur / Central hall
2 Putzbalkon mit Müllschlucker
  Service balcony, with refuse disposal plant
3 Nottreppe / Emergency stairs

2 Ostansicht des Romeo.
   East view of Romeo.
3 Westseite des Romeo. In der Mitte die offene Nottreppe.
   West façade of Romeo. In the centre the open emergency
   stairs.
4 Julia von Süden. Das Haupttreppenhaus ist in jedem Geschoß
   mit einer zentralen Halle verbunden.
   Julia from the South. The main stair tower opens on to a
   central hall at each landing.
5 Blick vom Dach des Romeo zur Julia. Der Wechsel von Sicht-
   betonflächen und farbigem Putz betont die Gliederung der
   Baukörper.
   View of Julia from the roof of Romeo. The alternation of exposed concrete and coloured rendering emphasises the
   physical features of the building.

Julia, Grundriß eines Normalgeschosses
Julia, typical floor plan
1 Treppenhalle / Landing
2 Putzbalkon mit Müllschlucker
   Working balcony, with refuse disposal plant
3 Laubengänge / Enclosed access balconies
4 Nottreppen / Emergency stairs

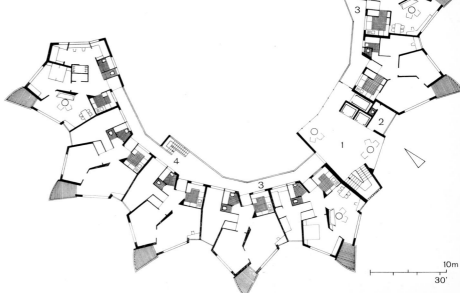

Unité d'Habitation ›Typ Berlin‹ – 1957–58
Architekt: Le Corbusier, Paris; Mitarbeiter: André Wogensky, Paris

Unité d'Habitation, Berlin – 1957–58
Architect: Le Corbusier, Paris; Assistant: André Wogensky, Paris

Die Größe des 17 Wohngeschosse umfassenden Hochhauses schloß seine Errichtung innerhalb des Hansaviertels aus. Die Stadt Berlin stellte deshalb das Heilsberger Dreieck zwischen der Heerstraße und dem Olympiastadion als Baugelände zur Verfügung. Die 527 Wohneinheiten sind an neun Innenflure angeschlossen, die das Gebäude der Länge nach durchziehen und zu den Fahrstühlen und Treppen führen. Die Wohnungen mit zwei und drei Zimmern sind doppelgeschossig. Küchen, Bäder und WC-Räume wurden im Inneren angeordnet. Die Wohnungen öffnen sich mit Loggien nach Osten und Westen und an der Schmalseite nach Süden. Die nördliche Schmalseite des Hochhauses ist geschlossen. Das Gebäude steht auf sieben Meter hohen Stahlbetonpfeilern. Decken und Fahrstuhlturm sind in Ortbeton ausgeführt. Wohnungstrennwände und Loggien bestehen aus Betonfertigteilen, die auf der Baustelle gegossen wurden, die Wände innerhalb der Wohnungen aus Gipsplatten.

The size of the 17-storey block precluded its erection inside the Hansa Quarter, but the City Council offered the Heilsberger Dreieck between the Heerstrasse and the Olympic stadium. The 527 dwellings are served by nine internal corridors, which extend to the full length of the building and lead to the lifts and staircases. The two- and three-room flats are on two floors. In all flats the kitchens, baths and W.C.'s are placed internally. They have balconies facing East and West and, on the narrow side, towards the South. The corresponding North side has no openings. The building stands on reinforced concrete piers, 23 feet high. Floors and lift-towers are concrete, cast in situ. Party walls and balconies are composed of prefabricated concrete units made on the building site; internal partitions are plasterboard.

1 Ansicht von Westen.
  West view.
2 Ansicht von Süden.
  South view.

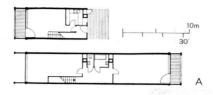

10m
30'

Typengrundrisse der Wohnungen / Typical flat plans
A Dreizimmerwohnung / Three-room flat
B Zweizimmerwohnung / Two-room flat
C Einzimmerwohnung / One-room flat

A

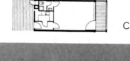

B

C

Schnitt / Section

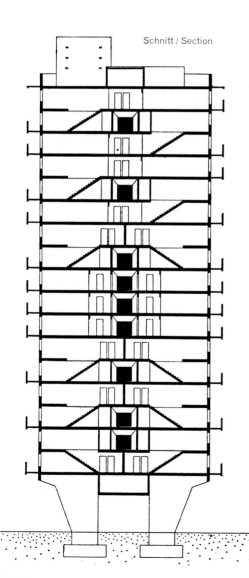

3 Ausschnitt aus der Westfassade. Von den in halber Höhe des Gebäudes geplanten Läden wurde nur die Fassadenaufteilung mit den senkrechten Lamellen übernommen, die den jetzt dahinter angeordneten Appartements die Aussicht verstellen.

West front: details. Of the proposed shops half way up the building, only the section of the façade with vertical sunshields was used, and these now obstruct the daylighting of flats placed behind them.

4 Darstellung des Modulor auf der Betonwand neben dem Haupteingang.

The Modulor exemplified on the concrete wall by the main entrance.

5 Innenflur.
  Internal corridor.
6 Blick aus einem Wohnraum zur Loggia.
  Looking towards the balcony from one of the living rooms.
7 Treppe vom Wohnraum zu den Schlafräumen, links Küche
  und Eßplatz.
  Staircase from the living room to the bedrooms; left, the
  kitchen and dining area.

Hansaviertel, Berlin – 1957
Bauträger: Aktiengesellschaft für den Aufbau des Hansaviertels

Hansa Quarter, Berlin – 1957
Promoters: Hansa Quarter Redevelopment Group

Der Wiederaufbau des im Krieg zerstörten südlichen Hansaviertels sollte als Hauptausstellungs-objekt der Internationalen Bauausstellung in Berlin 1957 den gegenwärtigen Stand der Architektur in ihrer ganzen Vielfalt aufzeigen. Zugleich mußte das neue Wohngebiet auf die besonderen Bedingungen seiner innerstädtischen Lage und die wirtschaftlichen Beschränkungen im Rahmen des sozialen Wohnungsbaues abgestimmt werden. Das alte sternförmig auf den Hansaplatz bezogene Straßennetz wurde auf wenige Erschließungsstraßen reduziert, die mit Ausnahme der Altonaer Straße vom Durchgangsverkehr frei bleiben. In Einfamilienhäusern, Zeilenbauten, scheibenförmigen und Punkthochhäusern sind nach Plänen von 53 in- und ausländischen Architekten die unterschied-lichsten Wohnformen verwirklicht. Zwischen den mit ihren Wohnfronten von den Verkehrsstraßen abgewandten Gebäuden setzen Grünanlagen den im Südosten anschließenden Tiergarten fort.

The reconstruction of the Southern Hansa Quarter, destroyed in the war, was intended as the chief exhibit of the 1957 International Building Exhibition in Berlin to demonstrate the present state of architecture in all its diversity. At the same time the new residential area had to respect the special conditions of its central urban site and the economic limitations of buildings sponsored by government. The old star-shaped network of streets centred upon the Hansaplatz was reduced to a few service roads which, with the exception of the Altonaer Strasse, carry no through traffic. Widely differing forms of dwellings – single-family houses, terrace houses, slab and point blocks – have been built to the designs of 53 architects from Germany and abroad. Between these buildings, the living areas of which are turned away from traffic ways, broad green spaces extend South-East to the adjoining Tiergarten.

1 Blick von der Siegessäule zum nördlichen Teil des neuen
  Hansaviertels mit den fünf Punkthäusern.
  View from the Siegessäule towards the Northern part of the
  new Hansa Quarter with its five point blocks.
2 Lageplan.
  Site plan.
3 Blick von Norden auf die acht- bis zehngeschossigen Schei-
  benhäuser (links) und die viergeschossigen Zeilenbauten
  (rechts). In die Grünanlagen sind zwei Kirchen, Kinderhorte
  und Spielplätze, Einkaufs- und Erholungszentren eingebettet.
  View from the North towards the eight- to ten-storey slabs
  (left) and the four-storey terrace homes (right). Two churches,
  day-nurseries and play grounds, and a shopping and amusement centre are placed in the green spaces.
4 Ansicht der fünf Punkthäuser von Südwesten.
  View of the five point blocks from the South-West.

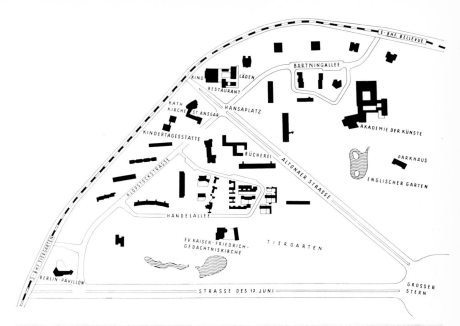

Eingeschossige Einfamilienhäuser im Hansaviertel, Berlin – 1957
Architekt: Arne Jacobsen, Kopenhagen

One-storey houses, Hansa Quarter, Berlin – 1957
Architect: Arne Jacobsen, Copenhagen

Der unterschiedliche Bedarf der einzelnen Räume an Belichtung und Intimität bestimmt die Abfolge der Raumgruppen innerhalb der durch die Haustrennwände begrenzten Grundfläche. Der Straße zugewandt sind zwei Abstellräume – einer davon ist von außen zugänglich – und das Bad. Die Schlafräume sind mit Südfenstern auf einen kleinen Innenhof geöffnet, der zusammen mit Küche und Eßplatz den zentralen Wohnplatz der Familie bildet. Er gestattet den Bewohnern einen Aufenthalt im Freien, der weder von den Nachbargrundstücken noch von der Straße her beobachtet werden kann. Der Wohnraum nimmt die ganze Südfront des Hauses ein. Er ist in seinem vorderen Teil, der die Sitzgruppe enthält, mit drei großen Fenstern zum Garten gerichtet. Der kleinere rückwärtige Teil, den eine Glaswand und ein durchlaufendes Blumenbeet mit dem Innenhof verbinden, kann nach den Wünschen des Besitzers durch einen Vorhang als Arbeitsplatz abgetrennt werden.

The differing needs of particular rooms for light and privacy decided the sequence and grouping of spaces within the area defined by the party walls. Two storage rooms, one accessible from the outside, and the bath are placed at the road end. The bedrooms, with South windows, open on to a small, internal court which together with kitchen and dining space forms the family's central living area. This provides the occupants with open-air relaxation without being overlooked by their neighbours or passers-by. The living room occupies the whole South front of the house. The front part, which comprises the sitting area, has three large windows facing the garden. The smaller back section, linked to the internal court by a glass wall and a long flower bed, can be separated by a curtain to form a study, if the owners wish.

10m
30'

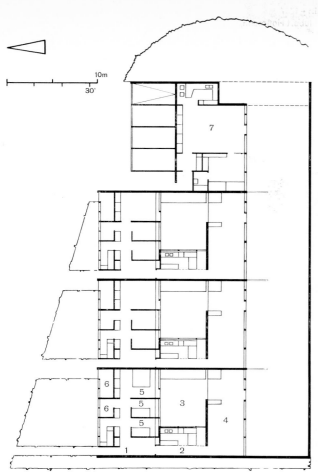

7

6 5 3
6 5 4
5
1 2

Grundriß / Floor plan
1 Eingang / Entrance
2 Küche und Eßplatz / Kitchen and dining room
3 Innenhof / Internal court
4 Wohnraum / Living room
5 Schlafräume / Bedrooms
6 Abstellräume / Storage space
7 Zweizimmerwohnung / Two-roomed house

1 Sitzplatz vor der Südfront des Wohnraumes. Die geschlossenen Wandteile bestehen aus Siropex-Tafeln mit einem Bodex-
Überzug, die Fugen sind mit eloxierten Aluminiumstreifen
abgedeckt.
Sitting space, outside the South front of the living room. The
unglazed wall units consist of Siropex (light concrete) panels
with a Bodex finish; the joints are concealed by anodized
aluminium fillets.
2 Innenhof zwischen Wohn- und Schlafteil.
Internal court between living and sleeping sections.
3 Blick von der Wohnküche zum Innenhof; der Küchenbereich
kann durch einen Vorhang vom Gang getrennt werden.
View from the kitchen-dining room into the internal court.
The kitchen can be separated from the entrance by a curtain.
4 Wohnraum.
Living room.

Wohnhaus im Hansaviertel, Berlin – 1957
Architekten: Wassili Luckhardt und Hubert Hoffmann, Berlin

Flats, Hansa Quarter, Berlin – 1957
Architects: Wassili Luckhardt and Hubert Hoffmann, Berlin

Das Haus gehört zu den fünf in Ost-Westrichtung gebauten, viergeschossigen Zeilenbauten im Westen des Hansaviertels. Drei verglaste Treppenhäuser gliedern den Baukörper in der Länge und lassen seine Konstruktion als Schottenbau deutlich erkennen. Die tragenden Wände bestehen aus Ziegelsplitt-Einkornschüttbeton, die Trennwände innerhalb der Wohnungen sind gipsgebundene Koksschlacken-Anwurfwände. Die unterschiedliche Größe und Aufteilung der 28 Wohnungen ergibt eine Vielfalt von Wohnungstypen. Vier Einheiten haben je 95 bzw. 94 qm, acht je 73 qm, sechs je 68 qm, vier je 50 qm, die sechs Einzimmerwohnungen je 27 qm. Zwei Einheiten sind doppelgeschossig mit einer Innentreppe ausgebildet. Ein Teil der Zwei- und Dreizimmerwohnungen kann durch Einbeziehung einer benachbarten Einzimmerwohnung auch später noch vergrößert werden. Waschküchen und Abstellräume für die Mieter sind im Keller vorgesehen.

The block is one of five four-storey terrace structures, sited in an East-Westerly direction at the West end of the Hansa Quarter. Three glazed staircase towers divide the range of buildings longitudinally, and bring the box-frame construction into sharp relief. The load-bearing walls are no fines concrete and crushed brick aggregate, the internal partitions being plastered breeze. The different sizes and plans of the 28 flats permit a wide variety of dwelling types. Four are each approximately 1,000 sq.ft., eight 750 sq.ft., six 700, four 550, while there are six one-room flats of about 300 sq.ft. Two of the flats are on two floors with inside staircases. Some of the two and three-room dwellings can eventually be made larger by incorporating their one-room neighbours. Laundries and storage space are provided for the tenants in the basement.

1 Ansicht von Süden. Alle Wohn- und Schlafräume liegen hinter einer durchgehenden Loggia auf der Südseite, Küchen und Nebenräume auf der Nordseite.
View from the South. All living rooms and bedrooms are placed behind continuous balconies on the South side. Kitchens and subsidiary rooms face North.
2 Ansicht von Südosten.
View from the South-East.
3 Ansicht von Nordosten.
View from the North-East.

Grundriß Obergeschoß / Typical floor plan

Grundriß Erdgeschoß
Ground floor plan

10m
30'

Wohnhaus im Hansaviertel, Berlin – 1957
Architekt: Kay Fisker, Kopenhagen

Flats, Hansa Quarter, Berlin – 1957
Architect: Kay Fisker, Copenhagen

Durch die Staffelung von drei zu vier Geschossen leitet dieses Gebäude von den zweigeschossigen Flachbauten über zu den Hochhäusern im Nordosten des Hansaviertels. Vier Einheiten im Erdgeschoß sind wie Eigenheime von außen zugänglich, die übrigen zwölf werden über Laubengänge von einem zentralen Treppenhaus erschlossen. Treppe, Laubengänge, Küchen, Bäder und ein Teil der Schlafräume liegen auf der Ostseite; auf der Westseite nehmen Balkone die ganze Breite der Wohnungen ein. Die acht Dreieinhalbzimmerwohnungen sind doppelgeschossig. Innentreppen verbinden Wohn- und Schlafteil. Vier Einzimmerwohnungen haben je eine kleine abgetrennte Küche. Bei den übrigen Einraum-Appartements ist der Kochbereich in den Vorplatz einbezogen. Das Gebäude ist als Schottenbau konstruiert. Tragende Querwände und Außenwände sind aus farbig verputztem Hohlblockmauerwerk, die leichten Trennwände aus Ziegelsplittplatten, die Decken aus Stahlbeton.

The stepped three- to four-storey elevations mark a transition stage between the low, two-floor, buildings and the high blocks at the North-East of the Hansa Quarter. Four of the ground floor units have direct access from the outside, the remainder being reached by access galleries from a central staircase. Stairs, passages, kitchens, baths and some of the bedrooms are on the East side; balconies occupy the entire width of the flats on the West. The eight three-and-a-half-room dwellings have two storeys, with their own stairs linking the living space with the bedrooms. Four of the one-room flats have small separate kitchens, in the others, cooking space is provided in the hall. The building has box-frame construction. The load-bearing cross-walls and external walls consist of colour-rendered hollow blocks, while the light internal partitions are built of crushed brick slabs. The floors are reinforced concrete.

1 Die Ansicht der Westseite zeigt den Wechsel von Wohn- und
  Schlafgeschossen.
  This West view shows the alternation of living and sleeping
  floors.
2 Wohnraum einer Dreieinhalbzimmerwohnung.
  Living room in one of the three-and-a-half-room flats.
3 Ostfassade.
  East façade.

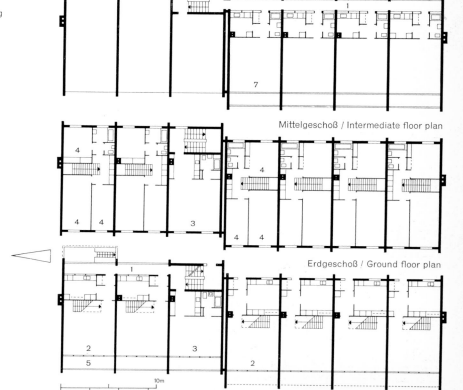

Obergeschoß / Upper floor plan

Mittelgeschoß / Intermediate floor plan

Erdgeschoß / Ground floor plan

1 Laubengang / Access gallery
2 Wohnraum / Living room
3 Einzimmerwohnung mit Kochnische / One-room flat with
  cooking space
4 Schlafräume der größeren Wohnungen / Bedrooms of larger
  flats
5 Loggien / Balconies
6 Überdeckte Terrassen / Covered terraces
7 Einzimmerwohnung mit abgetrennter Küche / One-room flat
  with separate kitchen

10m
30

Viergeschossiges Wohnhaus im Hansaviertel, Berlin – 1957
Architekt: Otto H. Senn, Basel

Four-storey block of flats, Hansa Quarter, Berlin – 1957
Architect: Otto H. Senn, Basel

Das über einem Fünfeck entwickelte Wohnhaus steht im nordöstlichen Teil des Hansaviertels als Bindeglied zwischen den sechzehngeschossigen Punkthäusern und der niedrigen Bebauung. In den drei Normalgeschossen sind je eine Vier-, eine Drei- und zwei Zweizimmerwohnungen um die Treppenhalle gruppiert. Durch die Auffächerung des Grundrisses ist jede Wohnung zwei Himmelsrichtungen zugewandt. Den Wohnräumen ist eine Loggia vorgelagert. Falttüren ermöglichen das Einbeziehen von Eßplatz und Küche in den Wohnraum. Die innengelegenen Bäder und WC-Räume sind, wie auch die Küchen, künstlich belüftet. In den vier Atelierwohnungen des zurückgesetzten Dachgeschosses gehen Wohnraum, Vorplatz und Küche ineinander über. Die Außenwände, Brüstungen und Decken sind in Stahlbeton, die inneren Tragwände in Trümmerstein ausgeführt. Der in Berlin erprobte Wohnhaustyp ist die Vorstufe für zwei Wohnhochhäuser, die im Hechtliacker bei Basel gebaut werden.

The flats, erected upon a pentagonal plan, stand in the North-Easterly section of the Hansa Quarter and form a linking feature between the sixteen-floor tower blocks and the low buildings. Each of the three typical floors has one 4-room dwelling, one with three rooms and two 2-room flats, grouped about a central staircase and landing. The disposition of the ground-plan provides daylighting for each flat from two directions. The living rooms open on to balconies. Folding doors make it possible for dining-room, kitchen and living room to be combined. Bath-rooms and lavatories, all internally placed, are as the kitchens artificially ventilated. In the four studio flats of the recessed roof storey, living-room, entrance-lobby and kitchen are merged into one. The external walls, parapets and floors (ceilings) are reinforced concrete; the internal load-bearing walls are reconstructed stone aggregate. This experimental building in Berlin is the prototype for two multi-storey blocks of flats to be built at Hechtliacker, near Basel.

1 Ansicht von Süden. Von den Sichtbetonmauern der Obergeschosse sind die farbigen Loggienwände, das hell gestrichene Dachgeschoß und das dunkle Sockelgeschoß abgehoben. Fenster und Loggientüren sind als Horizontal-Schiebeflügel ausgebildet.

View from the South. The coloured balcony walls, brightly painted roof storey and dark basement contrast with the exposed concrete finish of the upper storeys. Windows and balcony doors are arranged as horizontal sliding panels.

2 Ansicht von Nordosten mit dem Eingang im Sockelgeschoß.
View from the North-East, showing basement entrance.

3 Blick aus einem Wohnraum durch die geöffnete Falttüre auf den Eßplatz.
Looking from a living room, through the folding doors, towards the dining alcove.

4 Blick vom Eßplatz zum Wohnraum. Rechts die eingebaute Küche.
View from the dining alcove into the living room. Right, the built-in kitchen.

Nordwestansicht / Perspective from the North-West

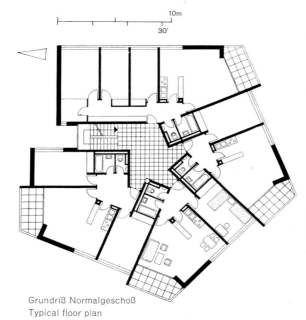

Grundriß Normalgeschoß
Typical floor plan

Achtgeschossiges Wohnhaus im Hansaviertel, Berlin – 1957
Architekt: Alvar Aalto, Helsinki

Eight-storey flats, Hansa Quarter, Berlin – 1957
Architect: Alvar Aalto, Helsinki

Das achtgeschossige Wohnhaus enthält, an zwei Treppenhäuser mit Aufzug und Müllschlucker angeschlossen, 78 Wohnungen, deren Größe von einem bis viereinhalb Zimmern variiert. Eine offene Eingangshalle nimmt den mittleren Teil des Erdgeschosses ein. Sie ist von Osten über eine Treppe, von Westen über eine Rampe zugänglich. Die Dachfläche steht den Mietern als Terrasse zur Verfügung. Die Räume der größeren Wohnungen sind um den zentralen Wohnraum und die tief eingezogene Loggia gruppiert und nach zwei Himmelsrichtungen geöffnet. Der Eßplatz ist mit der Küche zusammengefaßt. Die innenliegenden Kochnischen der Zweizimmerwohnungen sind durch eine Absaugvorrichtung künstlich entlüftet. Die Außenwände bestehen aus 20 cm starkem, bewehrtem Ziegelsplittbeton. Sie sind außen mit Leca-Platten verkleidet. Die betonierten tragenden Innenwände sind mit Schalldämmplatten belegt und verputzt.

This eight-storey block, served by two staircases with lift and refuse disposal system, contains 78 flats, varying in size from one to four-and-a-half rooms. An open entrance hall, occupying the middle of the ground floor, is reached on the East side by a flight of steps and from the West by a ramp. The flat roof provides a terrace for the tenants. The rooms of the larger flats, which are grouped about a central living room and a deeply recessed balcony, face the open on two sides. The bedroom area can be separated by folding partitions; the dining room and kitchen are combined. The kitchens of the two-room flats, placed internally, are artificially ventilated by an air-extraction plant. The external walls consist of 8″ broken brick concrete with "Leca" facings. The concrete load-bearing internal walls have acoustic panels, and are plastered.

1 Ansicht von Südwesten.
  View from South-West.
2 Ostansicht. Die offene Halle im Erdgeschoß ist über eine
  Treppe mit dem Park verbunden.
  East view. The open ground-floor hall is linked by a flight of
  steps to the garden.
3 Wohnraum einer Viereinhalbzimmerwohnung.
  Living room of a four-and-a-half room flat.

Grundriß / Floor plan

10m

30'

Zehngeschossiges Wohnhaus im Hansaviertel, Berlin – 1957
Architekten: Fritz Jaenecke und Sten Samuelson, Malmö

Ten-storey flats, Hansa Quarter, Berlin – 1957
Architects: Fritz Jaenecke and Sten Samuelson, Malmö

Das Erdgeschoß des scheibenförmigen Hochhauses wird durch Läden, Lagerräume und Büros gewerblich genutzt; ein Teil bleibt zwischen den tragenden Stützen als Freiplatz erhalten. Vier Aufzüge erschließen 68 Wohneinheiten in den neun Obergeschossen. Vor die Südfront ist eine flache Balkonzone gelegt, die sich jeweils vor dem Allzweckraum zu einer Loggia vertieft. Dieser Raum bildet in Verbindung mit der Küche den Mittelpunkt jeder Wohnung. Die Decken werden von den betonierten Querwänden getragen. Die Giebelwände sind in Schwerbeton gegossen und mit Kunststeinplatten verblendet. Die nichttragenden Wände im Innern bestehen aus Schlackenbetonplatten, die Ausfachungen der Außenwände aus vorfabrizierten Leichtbau-Fertigteilen. Das Gebäude hat nach schwedischem Muster eine in den Estrich einbetonierte Fußbodenheizung.

The ground floor of the slab-shaped block is used for shops, store rooms and offices; part of the area between the stanchions is left unoccupied. Four lifts serve 68 flats on nine upper floors. Flush with the front of the South façade balconies have been erected; and these are recessed in every case to form a loggia for the "all-purpose" room behind. This room, communicating with the kitchen, is the central feature of each flat. The floors are carried on the concrete, faced with artificial stone panels. For the non-bearing internal walls breeze and concrete blocks are used; those on the outside have a skin of light prefabricated units. The building has floor heating of Swedish design laid in concrete.

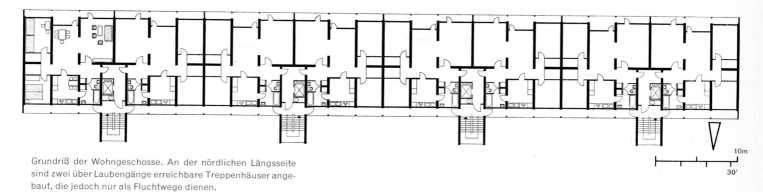

Grundriß der Wohngeschosse. An der nördlichen Längsseite sind zwei über Laubengänge erreichbare Treppenhäuser angebaut, die jedoch nur als Fluchtwege dienen.
Typical floor plan. Along the North side two staircase towers are erected which serve as emergency exits and are reached by access galleries.

10m
30'

1 Ansicht von Südosten.
  View from the South-East.
2 Treppenhaus und Laubengänge an der Nordseite.
  Staircase tower and access balconies on the North side.
3 Nordfassade mit den zwei Treppenhäusern.
  North façade, showing the two staircase towers.
4 Allzweckraum und Küche einer Vierzimmerwohnung.
  All-purpose room and kitchen in a four-room flat.

Sechzehngeschossiges Wohnhaus im Hansaviertel, Berlin – 1957–60
Architekten: J H van den Broek und J. B. Bakema, Rotterdam

Sixteen-storey flats, Hansa Quarter, Berlin – 1957–60
Architects: J. H. van den Broek and J. B. Bakema, Rotterdam

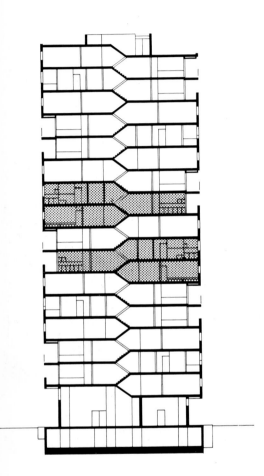

Dieses Wohnhochhaus stellt den Versuch dar, ein Punkthaus wirtschaftlich zu nutzen, die Verkehrsfläche zu verringern und möglichst vielen Wohnungen Querlüftung und zweiseitige Belichtung zu geben. Treppenhaus und Aufzüge nehmen den Kern des Grundrisses ein. Je acht Dreizimmer- und vier Einzimmerwohnungen werden von einem der sechs Korridore erschlossen. Am Nordende der Korridore befindet sich die Nottreppe, an ihrem Südende erweitern sie sich zu doppelgeschossigen Spiel- und Sonnenterrassen. Die Kleinwohnungen liegen mit dem Korridor auf einer Ebene. Zu den um ein halbes Geschoß versetzten größeren Einheiten, die sich über die ganze Tiefe des Hauses erstrecken, gelangt man über eine kurze Differenztreppe. Vom Wohnteil aus ist der Schlafteil über eine weitere Differenztreppe zu erreichen. Im Erdgeschoß sind die Hausmeisterwohnung und Abstellräume für Fahrräder und Kinderwagen, im Dachgeschoß die Waschküche untergebracht.

This building reflects an attempt to exploit the economic possibilities of a point block, to reduce traffic ways and provide as many flats as possible with cross-ventilation and daylighting on two sides. Staircase and lifts are the core of the plan. Each of six corridors serve eight three-room and four one-room dwellings. The emergency stairs are at the North end of the corridors, which widen at the South end to form play- and sun-terraces two storeys high. The small flats and corridors are on one plane. The larger units, which stretch the entire depth of the house, are split-level and reached by a short flight of steps, of half storey height. The living room area is also linked to the bedroom section by a short staircase. The ground floor contains the caretaker's flat and storage space for bicycles and perambulators; the laundry is on the top floor.

Grundriß von je zwei zusammenge-
hörigen Wohngeschossen.
Plan of two interrelated floors.

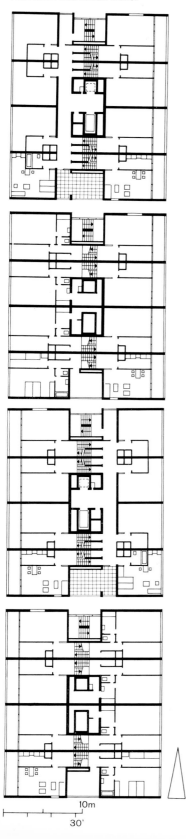

10m

30'

1 Ansicht von Südwesten.
   View from the South-West.
2 Haupteingang auf der Westseite. Vor allen Wohnräumen
   breite Loggien. Die Außenwände des Stahlbetonbaues sind
   mit vorgefertigten Betonplatten verkleidet.
   Main entrance on the West side. All living rooms have wide
   balconies. The external walls of the reinforced concrete building are faced with prefabricated concrete panels.
3 Eingangshalle im Erdgeschoß.
   Entrance hall (ground floor).

Wohnhochhaus im Hansaviertel, Berlin – 1958
Architekt: Gustav Hassenpflug, München

Residential tower block in the Hansa Quarter, Berlin – 1958
Architect: Gustav Hassenpflug, Munich

Das im Rahmen der Interbau errichtete Gebäude ist das mittlere der fünf turmartigen Hochhäuser, die das Hansaviertel im Norden begrenzen. Im Erdgeschoß sind zu beiden Seiten einer sieben Meter breiten, in ganzer Gebäudetiefe durchgehenden Eingangshalle eine Hausmeisterwohnung, Abstellräume und Waschküchen angeordnet. Die vierzehn Obergeschosse enthalten je vier Dreizimmer- und eine Zweizimmerwohnung, die verschieden unterteilt werden können. Die atelierartigen Wohnungen des Dachgeschosses sind zurückgesetzt und mit einer umlaufenden Terrasse verbunden. Der Hauptteil der senkrechten Lasten und die Windkräfte werden von zwei sich rechtwinklig kreuzenden Betonwandscheibenpaaren aufgenommen. Die Außenwände wurden ohne äußeres Gerüst aus vorgefertigten Elementen – Stahlbetonpendelstützen, Ausfachung mit Eternitplatten – trocken montiert. Als Montagebühne konnte jeweils die fertige Geschoßdecke verwendet werden.

The building is the middle one of five tower blocks, which form the Northern boundary of the Hansa Quarter and were erected within the framework of the Interbau exhibition. On the ground floor, on both sides of a 23' wide entrance hall penetrating to the full extent of the building, are placed a caretaker's flat, store rooms and laundries. The fourteen upper storeys each contain four three-room and one two-room flats, which can be variously subdivided. The studio type dwellings on the top floor are set back and surrounded by a terrace. Most of the vertical load and the wind stresses are taken by two pairs of concrete slab walls which intersect at right angles. The exterior walls were dry mounted without external scaffolding from prefabricated elements, reinforced concrete hinged stanchions, cladding with "Eternit" panels. Each completed floor could be used as an assembly stage for the next.

Sechs Varianten der Dreizimmerwohnung mit 71 qm, die zeigen, wie die Wohnungen entsprechend den Bedürfnissen und der Familiengröße unterteilt werden können: 1 vier Betten; 2 vier Betten, mit größerer Loggia; 3 zwei Betten; 4 sechs Betten; 5 vier Betten, Kinderzimmer vom Wohnraum durch einen Schrank und einen Vorhang getrennt; 6 Praxiswohnung mit Warteraum und Sprechzimmer.

Six variations of the 800-square-foot three-room flat, showing how the flats can be divided according to particular needs and the size of families: 1 four beds; 2 four beds, with larger loggia; 3 two beds; 4 six beds; 5 four beds, children's room separated from living room by a storage wall and curtain; 6 professional man's flat with waiting and consulting rooms.

1 Südfassade
  South façade.
2 Ansicht von Westen mit den dahinterliegenden Häusern von Lopez/Beaudouin und Schwippert.
  View from the West with the blocks by Lopez/Beaudouin and Schwippert behind.

Grundriß eines Obergeschosses
Plan of a typical upper storey

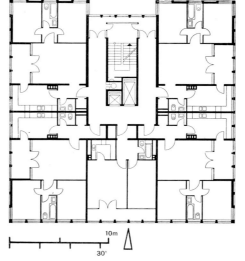

10m
30'

1 Gesamtansicht von Süden. In der Mitte das Bettenhaus, links die Kapelle, rechts vor der gynäkologischen Abteilung der Personalspeisesaal.
General view from the South. In the middle, the ward block; left, the chapel; right, the staff dining room in front of the gynaecological department.

Die Südost-Orientierung des Krankenhauses ergab sich aus der Hanglage und der vorherrschenden Windrichtung im Donautal. Die Raumgruppen sind nach ihrer Funktion auf fünf verschiedene, miteinander verbundene Baukörper verteilt. Zwölf selbständige Stationen mit je 15 Krankenbetten nehmen die sechs Obergeschosse, Ambulanz, Röntgenraum, Unfallaufnahme und Verwaltung das Erdgeschoß, Bäderabteilung, Labor und Apotheke das Untergeschoß des Hauptbaues A ein. Im Erdgeschoß des Bauteils B liegt die Küche, im Obergeschoß Geburtshilfe und gynäkologische Abteilung, im nordwestlichen Bauteil C die OP-Räume und die Personalunterkunft (später Kinderabteilung). Der nach Südosten herausgezogene Bauteil D dient in Höhe des Erdgeschosses von Block A als Speisesaal für das Personal. Die auf Stützen stehende Kapelle schließt die Baugruppe nach Südwesten ab. Vor dem Bettenhaus wurde ein tiefliegender Ziergarten angelegt.

The South-East orientation of the hospital is due to the sloping site and the direction of the prevailing wind in the Danube valley. The accommodation is divided according to function into five separate, but interconnected, blocks. Twelve self-contained stations, each with fifteen beds, occupy the six upper storeys of block "A"; outpatients, X-ray, casualty departments and administration the ground floor; baths, laboratory and pharmacy the basement. The kitchens are on the ground floor of block "B", with the gynaecological department above and, in the North-West "C" block, the operating theatres and staff quarters. Block "D", which extends South-East, contains the staff dining room on the ground floor level of block "A". The group of buildings is terminated on the South-West side by a chapel raised on stilts. A sunken flower garden has been laid out in front of the ward block.

70

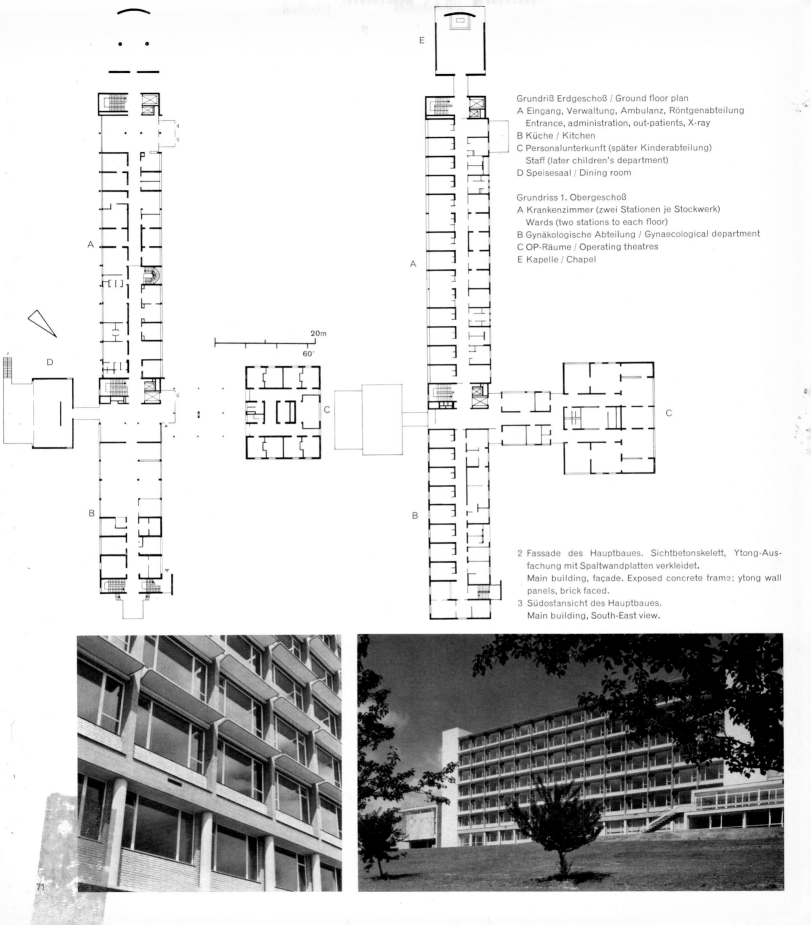

Grundriß Erdgeschoß / Ground floor plan
A Eingang, Verwaltung, Ambulanz, Röntgenabteilung
  Entrance, administration, out-patients, X-ray
B Küche / Kitchen
C Personalunterkunft (später Kinderabteilung)
  Staff (later children's department)
D Speisesaal / Dining room

Grundriss 1. Obergeschoß
A Krankenzimmer (zwei Stationen je Stockwerk)
  Wards (two stations to each floor)
B Gynäkologische Abteilung / Gynaecological department
C OP-Räume / Operating theatres
E Kapelle / Chapel

20m
60'

2 Fassade des Hauptbaues. Sichtbetonskelett, Ytong-Ausfachung mit Spaltwandplatten verkleidet.
  Main building, façade. Exposed concrete frame; ytong wall
  panels, brick faced.
3 Südostansicht des Hauptbaues.
  Main building, South-East view.

4 Ansicht von Südwesten. Vor dem achtgeschossigen Bettenhaus die auf Stützen stehende, verglaste Kapelle. Links Bauteil C.
  View from the South-West. The glass-walled chapel, set on
  stilts, in front of the eight-storey ward block. On the left
  block C.

5 Innenraum der Kapelle.
  Chapel interior.

1 Ansicht von Nordosten. Vor dem Bettenhaus der erdgeschossige Behandlungsbau.
View from the North-East. In front of the ward block is the treatment department.

Die vier Obergeschosse des Bettenhauses enthalten 126 Krankenbetten für Chirurgie, innere Medizin, Geburtshilfe und Gynäkologie. Jedes Geschoß ist in zwei Halbstationen mit getrennten Installationsräumen aufgeteilt. Die Krankenzimmer liegen nach Süden. Der um einen Innenhof angelegte Behandlungsflachbau ist unter das Bettenhaus geschoben, um die das Personal belastenden horizontalen Wege kurz zu halten. Die Untersuchungs- und Behandlungsabteilungen sind so zusammengefaßt, daß sie von einer einzigen Wartezone aus zugänglich sind und eine gute gegenseitige Ergänzung der einzelnen Disziplinen gewährleisten. Die Zufahrt erfolgt von Norden. Aus psychologischen Gründen ist der Eingang für Unfälle und Liegendkranke vom Haupteingang der gehfähigen Kranken, Ambulanten und Besucher getrennt. Durch Anfügung eines weiteren Stationstraktes nach Osten und Vergrößerung des Behandlungsbereiches kann die Bettenzahl später verdoppelt werden.

The four upper floors of the ward block hold 126 beds for surgical cases, general medicine, obstetrics and gynaecology. Each floor is divided into two half ward units with their own clinical and utility suite. The bedrooms face South. The low treatment building, disposed about a courtyard, extends beneath the ward block to keep staff movements short and reduce strain. The examination and treatment departments are so placed that they are accessible from a single waiting area and an effective balance between their individual functions is obtained. Vehicles approach from the North. For psychological reasons the entrance for accident and stretcher cases is separated from the main entrance for walking cases, out-patients and visitors. By the addition of a further ward block on the East side and the enlargement of the treatment department the number of beds can eventually be doubled.

Grundriß Normalgeschoß / Typical floor plan
1 Krankenzimmer / Sick room
2 Arzt / Doctor
3 Schwesternarbeitsraum / Sisters' room
4 Stationsküche / Ward kitchen
5 Tagesraum / Day room
6 Bereitschaftsraum / Duty room

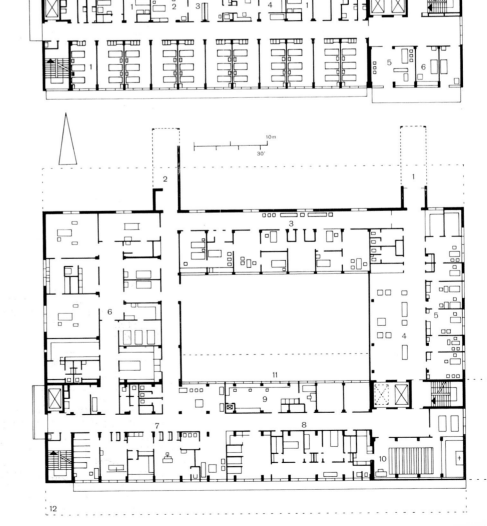

Grundriß Erdgeschoß / Ground floor plan
1 Haupteingang / Main entrance
2 Eingang für Unfälle / Entrance (accident)
3 Ambulanz / Out-patients
4 Halle / Hall
5 Verwaltung / Administration
6 Operationsräume / Operating theatre suite
7 Röntgenabteilung / X-ray department
8 Physikalische Therapie / Physiotherapy
9 Labor / Laboratory
10 Kapelle / Chapel
11 Innenhof / Courtyard
12 Erweiterung / Extension

2 Ansicht des Bettenhauses von Süden. Im Untergeschoß Wirtschafts- und Versorgungsräume, im Erdgeschoß die Behandlung, darüber die vier Stationen und ein Dachgarten. Links das Personalwohnhaus.

South view of the ward block. The basement contains rooms for mechanical and domestic services; the ground floor, treatment rooms; above, four ward units and a roof garden. Left, staff accommodation.

3 Dreibettzimmer.

Three-bed room.

4 Stationsdienstzimmer mit anschließendem Schwestern-arbeitsraum.

Ward utility room connected to sisters' work room.

5 Operationsraum.

Operating theatre.

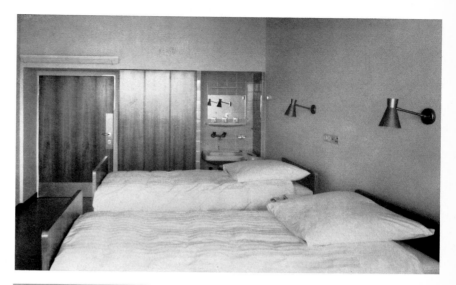

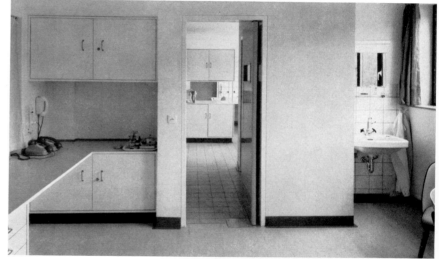

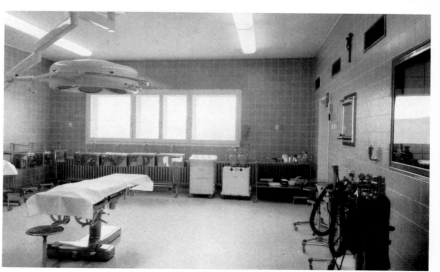

Sozialgebäude der Firma Linde's Eismaschinen AG, Mainz-Kostheim – 1957
Architekt: Hans-Joachim Lenz, Mainz; Mitarbeiter: Eugen Müller

Welfare building for Linde's Ice Machine Co., Mainz-Kostheim – 1957
Architect: Hans-Joachim Lenz, Mainz; in collaboration with Eugen Müller

Das Sozialgebäude enthält im Erdgeschoß Küche und Speisesaal für die Betriebsangehörigen, im Untergeschoß Umkleide-, Wasch- und Brauseräume, getrennt für Frauen und Männer. Die WC-Räume sind über eine Treppe auch vom Windfang im Hauptgeschoß aus zugänglich. Der Speisesaal umgreift U-förmig die Küche mit ihren Nebenräumen. Hier können täglich 1200 Essen gekocht und in drei Schichten von je einer halben Stunde ausgegeben werden. Die Stahlbinderkonstruktion des Daches wird von zwei Reihen aus U-Profilen zusammengeschweißter Stahlstützen an den beiden Längsseiten getragen. Abstand der Stützen vier Meter, Stützweite 20,30 Meter. Das ganze Erdgeschoß bleibt im Innern stützenfrei, die umlaufend verglasten Außenwände sind mit Jalousetten versehen. Die Umfassungen des Untergeschosses – Glasbaustein- und Sichtbetonwände – sind hinter die Flucht des Erdgeschosses zurückgesetzt.

The welfare building contains, on the ground floor, the kitchens and canteen for the firm's employees, and in the basement, changing rooms, washrooms and showers, for women and men. The lavatories are also accessible from the entrance lobby of the main floor. The canteen forms a "U" round the kitchens. 1,200 meals can be cooked and served daily in three half-hour shifts. The steel roof truss construction is carried on two rows of steel stanchions composed of welded channel sections. The interval between stanchions is 13 feet; the span about 66 feet. The entire ground floor is free of internal supports. The glazed external walls are provided with blinds. The walls of the basement – glass brick and exposed concrete – are set back behind the line of the floor above.

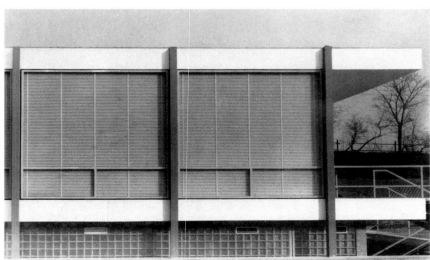

1 Gesamtansicht mit Aufgang zum Erdgeschoß.
  General view, showing way up to ground floor.
2 Treppe zum Erd- und Untergeschoß.
  Steps to ground floor and basement.
3 Detail der Längsfront.
  Detail of long elevation.
4 Speisesaal. In der Mitte hinten der Küchenblock.
  Canteen. Middle background, the kitchens.

1 Gang zu den Kühlräumen im alten Bürogebäude
  Way to cold storage rooms in the old office building
2 Vorräte / Stores
3 Lüftung / Ventilation
4 Warmwasserspeicher / Boiler House
5 Wannenbäder und Brausen / Baths and showers
6 Zur besonderen Verwendung / Special purposes
7 Umkleide- und Waschraum für Männer
  Changing and washroom (men)
8 WC für Männer / W.C. (men)
9 Umkleide- und Waschraum für Frauen
  Changing and washroom (women)
10 WC für Frauen / W.C. (women)
11 Windfang / Entrance lobby
12 Speisesaal / Canteen
13 Küche / Kitchen
14 Ausgabe / Service hatch
15 Anrichte / Counter
16 Küchenchef / Chef
17 Verkauf / Cash
18 Spülküche / Scullery

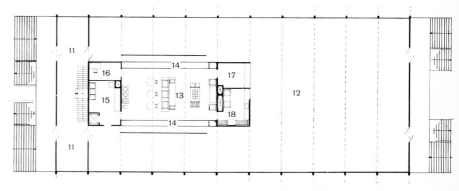

Grundriß Erdgeschoß / Ground floor plan

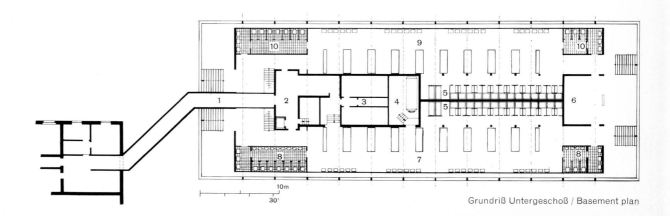

10m
30'

Grundriß Untergeschoß / Basement plan

Restaurant Buschmühle in Dortmund – 1959
Architekten: Otto-Heinz Groth und Werner Lehmann, Dortmund

Buschmühle Restaurant, Dortmund – 1959
Architects: Otto-Heinz Groth and Werner Lehmann, Dortmund

Das Restaurant Buschmühle wurde nach einem prämiierten Wettbewerbsentwurf am Nordufer des gleichnamigen Teiches errichtet und in das Gelände der Dortmunder Bundesgartenschau 1959 einbezogen. Das zweigeschossige Hauptgebäude ist mit der Breitseite zum See gerichtet. Die Küche liegt mit dem Hauptrestaurant auf gleicher Höhe. Frei eingestellte Wandelemente und Ganzglastüren schneiden aus dem Gastraum einen kleinen Bereich für geschlossene Gesellschaften heraus. Das erdgeschossige Bierrestaurant wird durch einen Speiseaufzug versorgt. Der in den Hang einschneidende Teil des Erdgeschosses enthält Vorratsräume, Heizungs- und Lüftungsanlage und Toiletten. Neben der rechtwinklig zum Hauptbau gestellten Pächterwohnung sind die Heizungs- und Lüftungskamine in einem Sammelschornstein zusammengefaßt. Terrassen, offene Überdachungen, Pergolen, Zugangsbrücken und eine geschwungene Fußgängerrampe verbinden das Restaurant mit dem Park.

The Buschmühle Restaurant, a prize-winning competition design, has been built on the North bank of a lake of the same name and was incorporated in the grounds of the 1959 National Garden Show at Dortmund. The broad front of the two-storey main block faces the lake. The kitchen is on the same level as the principal restaurant, a small section of which can be enclosed for private parties by freestanding partitions and glass doors. The beer restaurant on the ground floor is served by a food lift. Part of the ground floor, which has been hewn out of the sloping site, contains store-rooms, heating and ventilating plant, and lavatories. Adjoining the proprietor's house, which stands at right angles to the main block, the heating-plant flue and air-extraction shaft are combined as a single stack. Terraces, roofed open spaces, pergolas, foot-bridges and a curved ramp for walkers link the restaurant with the park.

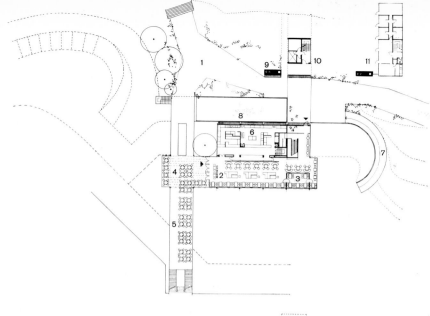

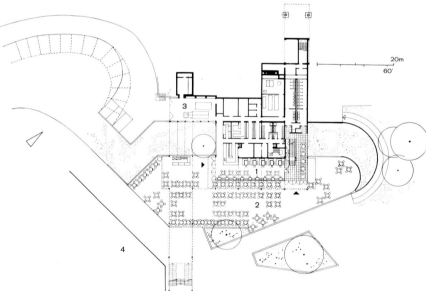

1 Gesamtansicht von Osten. Links das Hauptgebäude mit dem Restaurant im Obergeschoß und dem Bierlokal im Erdgeschoß, rechts das Pächterhaus. Dazwischen der aus gelben Klinkern gemauerte Sammelkamin.
General view from the East. Left, the main building with restaurant on the upper floor and beer hall below; right, the proprietor's home and, in between, the yellow brick composite stack.

2 Durchblick unter der Verbindungsbrücke zur Seeterrasse auf die Südostfront des Restaurants.
View under the bridge leading to the lakeside terrace towards the South-East front of the restaurant.

3 Hauptrestaurant. Das Afzeliaholz der Fenster und Wandelemente kontrastiert zur sichtbaren Stahlskelettkonstruktion.
Principal restaurant. The Afzelia wood of the window frames and wall units contrasts with the exposed steel skeleton frame.

4 Ostecke des Hauptgebäudes.
East corner of the main block.

Grundriß Obergeschoß / Upper floor plan
1 Hauptzugang / Main entrance drive
2 Hauptrestaurant / Principal restaurant
3 Raum für geschlossene Gesellschaften
  Room for private parties
4 Terrasse / Terrace
5 Verbindungsbrücke zur Seeterrasse
  Bridge to the lakeside terrace
6 Küche / Kitchen
7 Rampe / Ramp
8 Wasserbecken / Pools
9 Sammelkamin / Composite stack
10 Erdgeschoß der Pächterwohnung
  Proprietor's home – ground floor
11 Obergeschoß der Pächterwohnung
  Proprietor's home – upper floor

Grundriß Erdgeschoß / Ground floor plan
1 Bierrestaurant / Beer restaurant (hall)
2 Terrasse / Terrace
3 Garage
4 See / Lake

Stadtparkrestaurant in Nürnberg – 1957
Architekt: Friedrich Seegy, Nürnberg

Municipal park restaurant, Nürnberg – 1957
Architect: Friedrich Seegy, Nürnberg

Mit drei Flügeln greift die Baugruppe in die Parklandschaft hinaus. An der Ostseite zur Straße liegt der Gästeeingang. Das Restaurant mit einem Nebenzimmer und der höhere Saalbau stehen rechtwinklig zueinander und öffnen sich mit großen Glasflächen auf eine Terrasse mit 800 Sitzplätzen, die im Süden und Westen in den Stadtpark übergeht und vom Wirtschaftshof durch eine gestaffelte Mauer getrennt ist. Um jede Kreuzung von Kellner- und Gastwegen zu verhindern, wurden Küche und Wirtschaftsräume in das Untergeschoß verlegt. Die Bedienung der Gasträume und der Terrasse erfolgt von einer Anrichte in der Mitte der Anlage. Garderobe und Toiletten sind in einem eigenen Flügel neben dem Eingang untergebracht. Die außen und innen unverputzten Wände sind aus Hartbrandsteinen gemauert. Für die Decken von Restaurant und Café wurden gehobelte, sonst aber unbehandelte Fichtenbretter verwendet.

The group of buildings spreads into the park in three directions. The public entrance from the road being on the East side. The restaurant with its extension and the higher assembly room are sited at right angles to one another, with big windows opening on to a terrace with seating for 800, which stretches to the South and West into the park and is separated from the service yard by a stepped wall. To avoid obstructing the movements of waiters and customers, the kitchen and pantries are placed in the basement, the restaurants and terrace being served from a central distribution counter. Cloakrooms and lavatories are located in a separate wing close to the entrance. External and internal walls are exposed hard stock brick. For the restaurant and café ceilings planed, but otherwise untreated, fir battens are used.

1 Ostfassade mit dem Haupteingang.
  East façade, with main entrance.
2 Ansicht des Restaurants von Südosten.
  View of the restaurant from the South-East.
3 Innenansicht des Saales.
  Interior of the assembly room.
4 Terrasse mit Blick auf die verglaste Südfront des Saales.
  Rechts das Restaurant.
  Terrace, looking towards the glazed South front of the
  assembly room. Right, the restaurant.

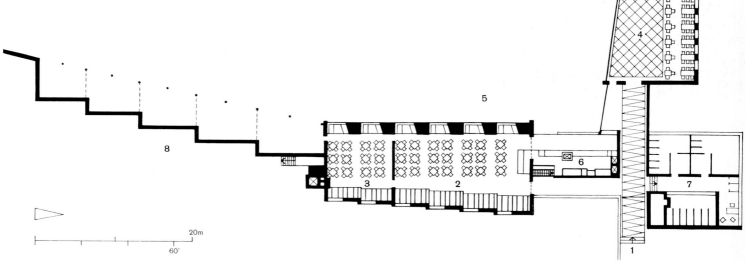

20m
60'

Grundriß / Plan
1 Haupteingang / Main entrance
2 Restaurant
3 Nebenzimmer / Extension of restaurant
4 Saal / Assembly room
5 Terrasse / Terrace
6 Anrichte / Serving counter
7 Garderobe und WC / Cloakroom and lavatories
8 Wirtschaftshof / Service yard

Klubhaus am Hundekehlensee in Berlin-Grunewald – 1958
Architekt: Paul G. R. Baumgarten, Berlin

Club-house on the Hundekehlen Lake, Berlin-Grunewald – 1958
Architect: Paul G. R. Baumgarten, Berlin

Das Klubhaus steht quer zum Hang in einem Parkgrundstück, das nach Südwesten zum Hundekehlensee stark abfällt. Das Hauptgeschoß nehmen die Klubräume ein. Untereinander können sie durch halbhohe Vorhänge getrennt werden. Durch ihre Staffelung in drei verschiedenen Ebenen folgen sie dem abfallenden Gelände. Großflächige Glaswände verbinden sie mit den Terrassen und geben den Blick in den Park und auf den See im Südwesten frei. Die Dachform paßt sich der Staffelung der Räume an und gibt ihnen den gewünschten intimen Charakter. In das Dach ist ein Sattelteil eingearbeitet, der bei niedriger Terrassenüberdachung die für die Klubräume erforderliche Raumhöhe schafft. Von der Küche können die Klubräume und eine Ausgabe im Freien bedient werden. Das Dach wird von einer Stahlpfettenkonstruktion mit Welleternitdeckung gebildet und von Stahlstützen getragen. Das massive Untergeschoß enthält Garderoben, WC, Heizung, Nebenräume und eine Wohnung.

The club-house lies in park surroundings across a slope, which drops sharply in a South-Westerly direction towards the Hundekehlen Lake. The main floor contains the clubrooms, which can be partially divided by curtains and are stepped on three levels down the slant of the site. Wide glass partitions open on to the terraces and offer unobstructed views of the park and towards the lake in the South-West. The design of the roof conforms to the stepped pattern of the rooms and contributes to the intimate character which the clients wanted. A saddle roof over part of the building ensures a low canopy for the terraces and the necessary height for the clubrooms. Composed of "Eternit" corrugated decking, the roof is carried on steel purlins and stanchions. The solid masonry lower floor comprises cloakrooms, lavatories, heating and service rooms, and a flat.

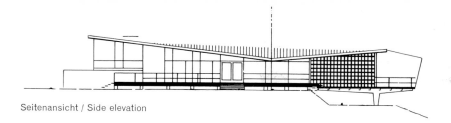

Seitenansicht / Side elevation

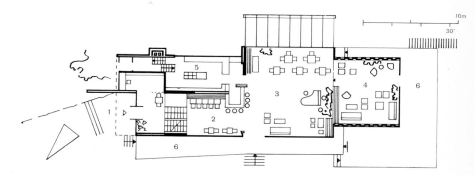

Grundriß Hauptgeschoß / Plan of principal floor
1 Eingang / Entrance
2 Bar
3 Großer Klubraum / Large clubroom
4 Kleiner Klubraum / Small clubroom
5 Küche / Kitchen
6 Terrassen / Terrace

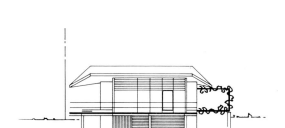

Südwestansicht / South-West elevation

1 Südwestansicht vom Hundekehlensee aus. Die auskragende
  Terrasse ist aus vorfabrizierten Stahlbetonbalken konstruiert,
  die einen Holzbohlenbelag tragen.
  South-West view from the lake. The cantilevered terrace is
  constructed of prefabricated reinforced concrete beams,
  which carry a covering of timber battens.
2 Nordwestfront. Rechts die auskragende Terrasse vor dem
  kleinen Klubraum.
  North-West front. Right, the cantilevered terrace in front of
  the small clubroom.
3 Blick vom großen in den zwei Stufen tiefer liegenden kleinen
  Klubraum. Die geknickte Decke mit Holz verschalt; Riemen-
  fußboden; Holzfenster mit doppelter Verglasung.
  View from the large clubroom into the smaller one, two steps
  below. The ridge roof is timber-lined; simple plank flooring;
  wood-framed windows with double glazing.

Hotel ›Berlin‹ in Berlin – 1958
Architekten: Paul Schwebes und Hans Schoszberger, Berlin

Hotel "Berlin", Berlin – 1958
Architects: Paul Schwebes and Hans Schoszberger, Berlin

Das Erdgeschoß des von weiten Grünflächen umgebenen Hotels ist nur zum Teil ausgebaut. Es nimmt den Empfangsraum, die Hotelhalle, ein Frühstücksrestaurant, eine Bar und die Direktion auf. In einem eigenen Flügel auf der Nordseite liegt das Restaurant, daran anschließend zwei Konferenzräume. Die vier Obergeschosse des 104 Meter langen Gebäudes enthalten insgesamt 257 Zimmer mit 287 Betten, die meisten sind mit einer Loggia verbunden. Sämtliche Installationsleitungen sind in einem niedrigen Zwischengeschoß zusammengefaßt, das sich als dunkler Streifen in der Fassade abzeichnet. Das Gebäude ist in Schottenbauweise errichtet. Auf jede konstruktive Achse kommen zwei Gastzimmer, die durch schwere Betonwände und die Installationsräume akustisch isoliert sind. Im Erdgeschoß sind die tragenden Wände zu kurzen Mauerscheiben zusammengezogen. Im zweiten Bauabschnitt soll ein sechzehnstöckiges Hochhaus mit etwa 300 Betten errichtet werden.

The ground floor of the hotel, sited in open green surroundings, which is only partly built up, houses the reception area and hall, a breakfast room, a bar and offices for the management. The restaurant is located in a separate wing on the North side, and is connected to two conference rooms. The four upper storeys of the building, which is nearly 350 feet long, contain 257 bedrooms with 287 beds, most of which open on to balconies. All service mains are located in a low intermediate floor, which appears as a dark ribbon on the façade. The building has box-frame construction, with two guest rooms to each structural axis, insulated against noise by the heavy concrete partition walls and toilet space. On the ground floor the load-bearing walls are contracted into short vertical slabs. As a second stage, a sixteen-storey tower block with about 300 beds is to be built.

1 Hauptansicht von der Kurfürstenstraße.
  General view from the Kurfürstenstrasse.
2 Das Modell zeigt den fertiggestellten fünfgeschossigen Trakt
  und das geplante Hochhaus.
  The model shows the completed five-storey building and the
  projected tower block.
3 Hotelhalle im Erdgeschoß.
  Ground floor hall.

Grundriß Obergeschoß / Typical upper floor plan
1 Aufzüge / Lifts
2 Büro / Office
3 Einbettzimmer mit Balkon / Single room with balcony
4 Einbettzimmer ohne Balkon / Single room without balcony
5 Zweibettzimmer mit Balkon / Twin-bed room with balcony

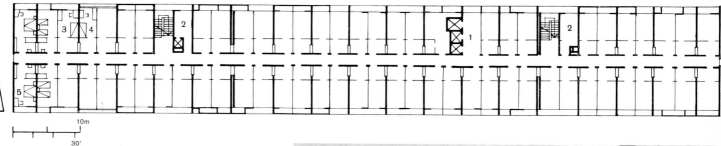

10m
30'

Geschwister-Scholl-Gymnasium, Lünen – 1960
Architekt: Hans Scharoun, Berlin

Scholl High School for girls, Lünen – 1960
Architect: Hans Scharoun, Berlin

Durch ihre Anordnung im Pavillonsystem fügt sich die Schule in den Grünzug ein, der die Altstadt umgibt. Die achtzehn Klassen sind in drei Typen aufgegliedert. Die achtklassige Unterstufe und die sechsklassige Mittelstufe sind erdgeschossig angelegt und zu ihren Pausenhöfen geöffnet. Die vier Klassen der Oberstufe liegen, um ein Geschoß gehoben, auf der Betonplatte über der gemeinsamen Pausenhalle. Jeder Klassenraum ist mit Garderobe, Gruppenraum und Freisitz zu einer Klassenwohnung zusammengefaßt, in der die Schülerinnen, je nach Altersstufe, zwei bis vier Jahre verbringen. An die große Pausenhalle im Erdgeschoß sind Schülerselbstverwaltung, Schülerbibliothek, die Gruppe der naturwissenschaftlichen Hörsäle und Übungsräume und die für unterschiedliche Nutzung geplante Aula angeschlossen. Zeichensaal und Handarbeitsräume im Obergeschoß gehen ineinander über. Im Schulgarten ist ein freistehender Musikpavillon vorgesehen.

Exemplifying the pavilion system, the school fits sympathetically into the green belt surrounding the old town. The eighteen classes are divided into three types. The eight-class junior grade and the six-class middle grade are on the ground floor and open on to their own play areas. The four classrooms of the upper school are placed, one storey higher, on the concrete slab roof of the general recreation hall. Each classroom has cloakroom, common room and open-air teaching space, and forms a class "house", in which the girls spend two to four years according to their age group. The large recreation area on the ground floor gives access to the students' council, the library, the series of natural science rooms for lectures and practical work, and a multi-purpose hall. Art and handicraft departments open into one another on the upper storey. A free-standing music pavilion is provided in the garden.

1 Luftbild von Süden.
Air view from South.
2 Blick von Osten auf die Klassen der Unterstufe.
Looking West towards the junior school classrooms.
3 Atriumklasse gegen Osten.
Classroom facing East across courtyard.
4 Atriumklasse der Mittelstufe gegen Westen.
Middle school classroom facing West on to courtyard.

86

Grundriß Erdgeschoß / Ground floor plan

1 Haupteingang / Main entrance
2 Nebeneingang / Side entrance
3 Halle / Hall
4 Aula / Assembly hall
5 Turm / Tower
6 Schülerselbstverwaltung / Students' council
7 Milchbar / Milk bar
8 Schülerbibliothek / Library
9 Aquarien / Aquarium
10 Direktion / Principal's room
11 Lehrerzimmer / Staff room
12 Unterstufe / Junior school
13 Mittelstufe / Middle school
14 Physik / Physics
15 Biologie / Biology
16 Chemie / Chemistry
17 Musikraum / Music room

Grundriß Obergeschoß (Seite 89 links)
Upper storey plan (page 89, on the left)

1 Oberstufe / Senior school
2 Reserveklasse / Additional (spare) classroom
3 Zeichensaal / Art
4 Handarbeit / Handicraft

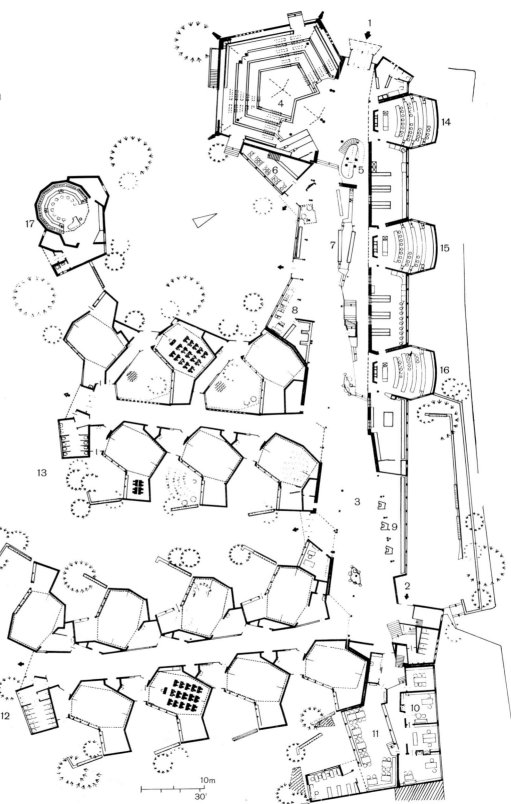

10m

30'

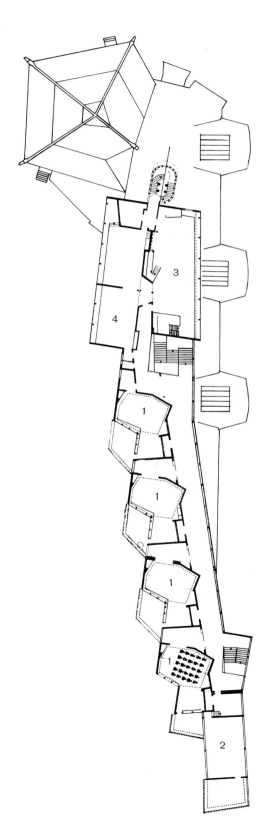

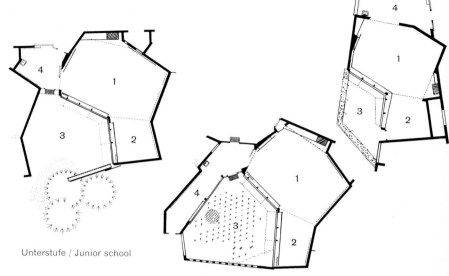

Typengrundrisse / Typical floor plans
1 Klassenraum / Classroom
2 Gruppenraum / Common room
3 Freiraum-Unterricht / Open-air classes
4 Garderobe / Cloakroom

Oberstufe / Senior school

Unterstufe / Junior school

Mittelstufe / Middle school

5 Eine Klassenwohnung der Unterstufe, darüber eine Ober-
stufenklasse.
A junior school class "house", with senior classroom above.

Aufbau- und Abendgymnasium in Dortmund – 1956–59
Architekt: Friedrich Wilhelm Kraemer, Braunschweig

High School and Evening Secondary School, Dortmund – 1956–59
Architect: Friedrich Wilhelm Kraemer, Brunswick

1 Pausenhof im Winkel zwischen Atriumbau (links) und Sonderklassentrakt. Rechts die Mensa.
  Recreation area between the quadrangle group (left) and
  special-classroom wing. Canteen on right.
2 Modell von Nordosten.
  Model, from the North-East.

Um die stark gestiegenen Aufwendungen für den Bau einer höheren Schule – Ausbau der naturwis-senschaftlichen Sonderklassen, Räume für die musische und handwerkliche Erziehung – wirtschaft-lich tragbarer zu machen, wird der Dortmunder Schulneubau täglich zweimal benützt: vormittags als Gymnasium, nachmittags und abends als Abendschule für den zweiten Bildungsweg. Der Bauplan – das Projekt erhielt 1954 in einem Wettbewerb den zweiten Preis – gliedert das umfangreiche Pro-gramm in mehrere Baukörper: Zwölf Stammklassen, Bibliothek und zwei Pausenhallen nehmen einen zweigeschossigen Atriumbau ein, die Sonderklassen und die Verwaltung einen dreigeschossigen Flügel. Von ihnen führen verglaste Gänge zum Gemeinschaftshaus mit Mensa und Küche und zur Aula, deren Untergeschoß einen Musiksaal, Garderoben und den Zugang für Besucher enthält. Sportplatz, Turnhalle und Hausmeisterwohnung liegen am Nordende des Grundstücks, eine Freilicht-bühne mit in einem Viertelkreis amphitheatralisch angeordneten Zuschauerreihen neben dem Pausenhof.

In order to place upon an economically practicable footing the greatly increased cost of building a High School (e. g., provision of special facilities for natural science studies, and rooms for education in the arts and crafts) this new Dortmund school building is used twice daily; in the morning as a High School and in the afternoon and evening for its second educational purpose, the evening classes. The scheme – it won second prize in a competition in 1954 – translates the comprehensive programme into a group of several buildings: twelve ordinary classrooms, a library and two recreation areas occupy a two-storey building ranged about a quadrangle, while the special classrooms and administrative offices are housed in a three-storey wing. Glazed covered ways lead to the common room block with canteen and kitchen, and to the assembly hall, the lower floor of which contains a music room, cloak-rooms and the visitors' entrance. The sportsground, gymnasium and caretaker's house are located at the North end of the site, while an open-air stage with spectators' seats is arranged in a quadrant and approached from the play area.

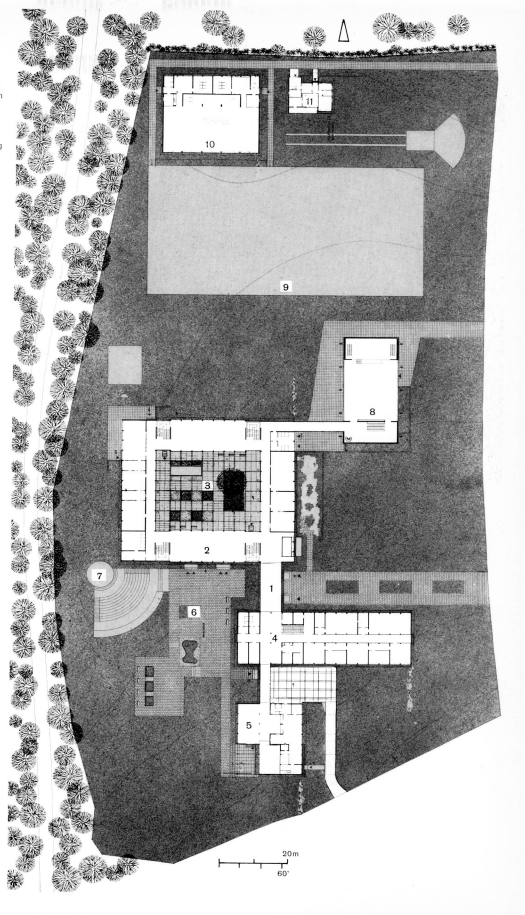

Grundriß Erdgeschoß / Site and ground floor plan
1 Haupteingang / Main entrance
2 Normalklassenbau / Ordinary classrooms
3 Innenhof / Quadrangle
4 Sonderklassentrakt / Special-classroom wing
5 Gemeinschaftshaus / Common room block
6 Pausenhof / Recreation area
7 Freilichtbühne / Open-air stage
8 Aula / Assembly hall
9 Sportplatz / Sports ground
10 Turnhalle / Gymnasium
11 Hausmeister / Caretaker

20m
60'

3 Westansicht des Gemeinschaftshauses.
West view of common room block.

4 Innenansicht der Aula.
Interior of assembly hall.

5 Zwischen dem Sonderklassenflügel (links) und dem Atriumbau liegt der Haupteingang. Rechts, durch eine Brücke mit dem Hauptbau verbunden, die Aula.
The main entrance lies between the special-classroom wing (left) and the quadrangle group. Right, the assembly hall, linked by a bridge to the main building.

6 Blick vom Innenhof des Atriumbaues durch eine Pausenhalle zur Turnhalle. Das Sichtbetonskelett ist mit gelben Klinkern ausgefacht.
View from the quadrangle, through one of the recreation areas, towards the gymnasium. The exposed concrete frame has yellow brick in-filling.

7 Südfassade des Atriumbaues. Im Erdgeschoß eine der Pausenhallen.
South front of the quadrangle block. One of the recreation halls on the ground floor.

8 Blick von der Freilichtbühne zum Haupteingang, der die Normalklassen und die Sonderklassen verbindet.
View from the open-air stage towards the main entrance, which links the ordinary classrooms to the special classrooms.

1 Ansicht von Nordosten. Links die Turnhalle, rechts der
Hauptbau, davor die Hausmeisterwohnung.
View from North-East. Left, the gymnasium; right, the main
building with caretaker's flat in front.

Die Planung ging von einem prämiierten Wettbewerbsentwurf der Architektengemeinschaft Fritz
Novotny und Paulfriedrich Posenenske aus. Die Anlage auf einem Gelände von circa 7800 qm gliedert
sich in mehrere Baukörper, die durch überdeckte Wege miteinander verbunden sind. Der dreigeschossige Hauptbau enthält in jedem Geschoß sechs beidseitig belichtete Normalklassen, von
denen je zwei an ein Treppenhaus angeschlossen sind. Das Erdgeschoß des zweigeschossigen
Paralleltraktes steht auf Stützen und dient als Pausenhalle. Ein Teil ist als WC-Anlage ausgebaut.
Darüber liegen die Sonderklassen, Lehrerzimmer und Rektorat. Drei Klassenräume mit Freiluftklassen für die unteren Jahrgänge sind zu einem Pavillonbau zusammengefaßt. Die Turnhalle hat
einen eigenen Zugang von der Straße. Die Ytong-Ausfachung des schalungsrauhen Stahlbeton-
skeletts ist teils verputzt, teils mit Sichtmauerwerk verblendet. Die Decken sind als Stahlbeton-
rippen-Decken ausgebildet.

The scheme is based on a prize-winning design by the Fritz Novotny and Paulfriedrich Posenenske
architectural group. Erected on a 2-acre site, it incorporates several blocks linked to one another by
covered ways. Each of the three storeys of the main building contains six ordinary classrooms, lit from
both sides and served by three staircases, one for every two classrooms. The ground floor of the parallel
two-storey building is carried on stilts and serves as a recreation hall. Part is occupied by lavatories.
Above are special classrooms, staff room and principal's office. Three classrooms with open air
spaces are arranged for the younger pupils in the form of a pavilion. The gymnasium has direct access
from the road. The ytong infill of the reinforced concrete frame which shows the pattern of the shuttering is partly rendered and partly masked by exposed brick. The ceilings (floors) are reinforced concrete. 94

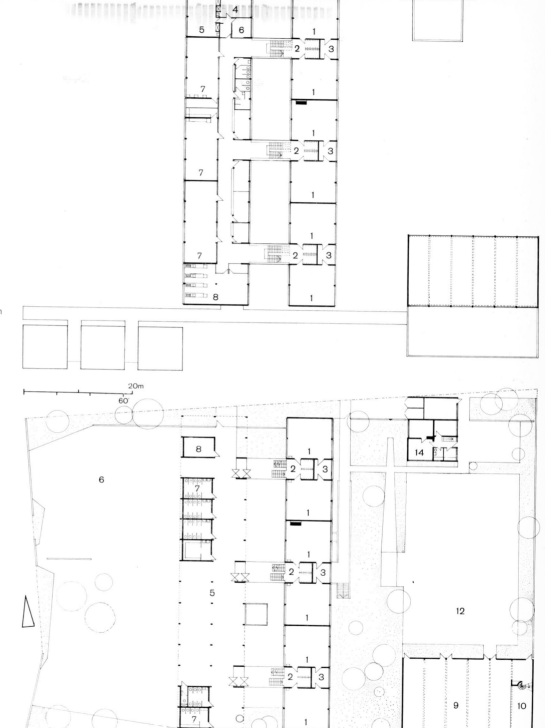

Grundriß 1. Obergeschoß / First floor plan
1 Klasse / Classroom
2 Garderobe / Cloakroom
3 Gruppenraum / Assembly area
4 Direktor / Principal
5 Lehrer / Staff
6 Sprechzimmer / Consulting room
7 Sonderklassen / Special classes
8 Lehrküche / Cooking classes

20m
60'

Erdgeschoßgrundriß / Ground floor plan
 1 Klasse / Classroom
 2 Garderobe / Cloakroom
 3 Gruppenraum / Assembly area
 4 Freiluftklasse / Open-air class
 5 Pausenhalle / Recreation hall
 6 Pausenhof / Recreation yard
 7 WC
 8 Hausmeister / Caretaker
 9 Turnhalle / Gymnasium
10 Bühne / Stage
11 Umkleideräume / Changing rooms
12 Turn- und Spielplatz
    Gym and play area
13 Gedeckter Gang / Covered way
14 Hausmeisterwohnung
    Caretaker's flat

95

2 Südansicht. Links über der offenen Pausenhalle die Sonderklassen, rechts der Hauptbau mit den Normalklassen, davor
der gedeckte Gang zur Turnhalle.
South aspect. Left, above the open recreation hall, the special
classrooms; right, the main block with ordinary classrooms;
in front, the covered way to the gymnasium.

3 Das verglaste Treppenhaus führt zu den Normalklassen.
Glazed stair tower leading to the ordinary classrooms.

4 Westansicht des erdgeschossigen Hausmeisterhauses.
West view of the single-storey caretaker's home.

5 Ansicht von Südwesten. Hinter dem erdgeschossigen Pavillonbau mit den Freiluftklassen die Sonderklassen, der
Hauptbau mit den Normalklassen und die Turnhalle.
South-West view. Behind the single-storey pavilion for open-
air classes lie the special classrooms, the main building containing the ordinary classrooms and the gymnasium.

Rudolf-Koch-Gymnasium, Offenbach am Main – 1957
Architekt: Adolf Bayer, Offenbach am Main

Rudolf Koch Secondary School, Offenbach-on-Main – 1957
Architect: Adolf Bayer, Offenbach-on-Main

Die Normalklassen im gestaffelten, von der Straße 40 m entfernten Ostflügel dieses Gymnasiums haben teilweise doppelseitige Belichtung und Querlüftung, mindestens jedoch Überecklüftung. Verwaltung und Spezialklassen bilden den gewinkelten Westflügel. In der naturwissenschaftlichen Abteilung (Biologie, Physik, Chemie) sind in jedem der drei Obergeschosse ein Lehrsaal, ein Vorbereitungszimmer, ein Sammel- und ein Übungsraum angeordnet. Der Verkehrsraum zwischen Klassen- und Verwaltungsflügel ist zu einer dreigeschossigen, von Galerien umgebenen Gemeinschaftshalle erweitert. Im Erdgeschoß sind außer den Räumen für die unterste Klasse die Groß- und Sonderräume eingeplant, da sie gelegentlich auch außerhalb des Schulbetriebes zur Verfügung stehen sollen (Musik-, Film- und Zeichensaal). Zur Vergrößerung des Hofes und zur Schaffung einer überdeckten Pausenhalle ist der nördliche Teil des Klassenflügels im Erdgeschoß auf Stützen gestellt.

The classrooms in the East wing of this Secondary School, which are stepped on plan and set back 130 feet from the road, have partial daylighting from two sides and cross, or diagonal, ventilation. Administration and special classes occupy the East wing. In the natural sciences department (biology, physics, chemistry) there are on each of the three upper floors a teaching room, a preparation room, a general room and a room for practical work. The circulation area between the classrooms and administrative wing has been elaborated into an assembly hall, three storeys high and enclosed by galleries. The ground floor, besides the junior-class rooms, also provides accommodation for large gatherings and special purposes, since it has sometimes to be used for activities outside the normal curriculum (music, films, drawing). The North part of the classroom wing is carried on stilts in order to extend the recreation area under cover.

1 Gemeinschaftshalle.
   Assembly hall.
2 Anschluß des Klassenflügels an die große Halle.
   Link between the classroom wing and the great hall.
3 Klassenflügel mit offener Pausenhalle.
   Classroom wing with its covered open-air play area.
4 Ansicht von Südosten.
   View from South-East.

Grundriß Erdgeschoß
Ground floor plan

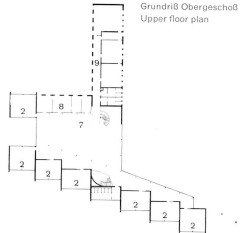

Grundriß Obergeschoß
Upper floor plan

1 Eingangshalle / Entrance hall
2 Klassenräume / Classrooms
3 Filmsaal / Film theatre
4 Musiksaal / Music room
5 Zeichensaal / Drawing studio
6 Überdeckte Pausenhalle
   Covered play area
7 Gemeinschaftshalle/Assembly hall
8 Verwaltung / Administration
9 Naturwissenschaftliche Abteilung
   Natural sciences department

Wilhelm-Busch-Schule, Hannover-Ricklingen – 1956–58
Architekt: Dieter Oesterlen, Hannover

Wilhelm Busch School, Hanover-Ricklingen – 1956–58
Architect: Dieter Oesterlen, Hanover

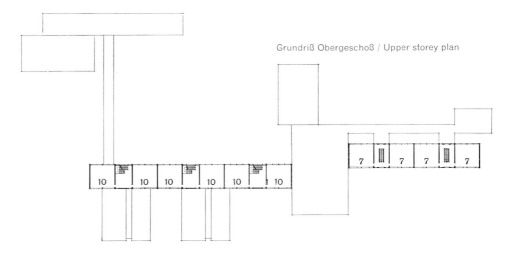

Grundriß Obergeschoß / Upper storey plan

Die Klassentrakte sind möglichst weit von der Hauptverkehrsstraße im Westen abgerückt. Der Eingang liegt im Zentrum der Anlage. In seiner Nähe sind Verwaltung, Bücherei und Hausmeisterwohnung mit einem Dienstraum angeordnet. Die große Eingangshalle dient auch als Vorhalle zur Aula, die nach Westen anschließt. Die Klassen der Unterstufe liegen im zweigeschossigen nördlichen Haupttrakt, die der Oberstufe in den zwei Obergeschossen des Südtraktes. Große Ostfenster und ein Fensterband auf der Westseite geben ihnen Licht. Die Pausenhalle der Unterstufe ist dem Klassentrakt vorgelagert und bildet kleine bepflanzte Höfe. Die Pausenhalle der Oberstufe liegt im Erdgeschoß unter den Klassenräumen. Von ihr sind auch die zwei erdgeschossigen Flügel mit den Sonderklassen zugänglich. Auch sie werden durch Fensterbänder über den niedrigen Fluren zweiseitig belichtet. Im Westteil des Grundstücks zwei Pausenhöfe und die Turnhalle.

The classroom blocks are set back as far as possible from the main road which passes on the West side. The entrance lies in the centre of the scheme, and close to it are the administrative offices, and the library and caretaker's flat. The large entrance hall also serves as an anteroom to the assembly hall on its West flank. The junior classrooms are in the two-storey North block; those for seniors occupy the two upper storeys of the building to the South. Daylighting comes from the big East windows, and from ribbon windows along the West wall. The junior recreation area is arranged in front of the series of classrooms. The recreation space for seniors is on the ground floor beneath the classrooms. It provides access as well to the two single-storey wings housing the special classrooms, which are also lit by ribbon windows placed above the low passages. Two separate playgrounds and the gymnasium are located on the Western half of the site.

1 Ostansicht des zweigeschossigen Unterstufentraktes.
  East elevation of the two-storey junior school block.
2 Modell von Südosten.
  Model, from the South-East.
3 Haupteingang. Dahinter links die Oberstufe, rechts die
  Unterstufe.
  Main entrance. Behind (left) the senior school, (right) the
  junior school.

Legende / Legend
 1 Eingangshalle / Entrance hall
 2 Rektor / Headmaster
 3 Lehrerzimmer / Staff room
 4 Bücherei / Library
 5 Hausmeisterdienstraum / Caretaker's office
 6 Hausmeisterwohnung / Caretaker's flat
 7 Klassenräume Unterstufe / Junior classrooms
 8 Pausenhalle Unterstufe / Junior recreation area
 9 Pausenhof Unterstufe mit Freiunterricht
   Junior playground, and space for open-air teaching
10 Klassenräume Oberstufe / Senior classrooms
11 Pausenhalle Oberstufe / Senior recreation area
12 Pausenhof Oberstufe / Senior playground
13 Sonderklassen / Special classrooms
14 Aula mit Bühne / Assembly hall and stage
15 Turnhalle / Gymnasium

Grundriß Erdgeschoß / Ground floor plan

Die Konstruktion der Klassentrakte besteht aus einem Stahlbetonskelett mit Betonschotten und Massivdecken. Der Sichtbeton an den Stirnseiten und an der östlichen Erdgeschoßwand des Oberstufentraktes ist schalungsrauh gelassen. Die Lüftungsflügel der Holzfenster ermöglichen die Querlüftung, die Fensterbrüstungen sind mit Teakholz verkleidet. Der erdgeschossige Verwaltungsbau und die Stirnwände der Sonderklassenflügel wurden wie die Brüstungen unter den Fensterbändern der Westseite mit gelben Klinkern verblendet. Aula, Turnhalle, der offene Verbindungsgang zur Turnhalle und die Pausenhalle der Unterstufe sind Stahlkonstruktionen.

The construction of the classroom blocks is reinforced concrete frame with concrete partitions and solid slab ceilings. The concrete on the front façades and on the East ground floor wall of the senior school building has been left rough. Sections of the wood-framed windows open to provide cross-ventilation; the panels beneath the windows have teak cladding. The single-storey administration building and the front façades of the special classroom wings have yellow brick in-filling, as do the panels below the ribbon windows on the West walls. The assembly hall, the gymnasium, the open-sided covered way to the gymnasium and the recreation area of the junior school are steel structures.

◁ 4 Oberstufentrakt von Südwesten mit dem Verbindungsgang
zur Turnhalle. Im Erdgeschoß die Pausenhalle.
Senior school block from the South-West, with the covered
way to the gymnasium. The recreation area can be seen on
the ground floor.

5 Ein Klassenraum mit zweiseitiger Belichtung und Homaton-
Akustikdecke.
Classroom with acoustic ceiling, lit from two sides.
6 Turnhalle.
Gymnasium.
7 Treppe in der Pausenhalle des Oberstufentraktes. An der
Südwand Mosaik ›Stelzengänger‹ von Claus Arnold.
Staircase in the recreation area of the senior school block.
Mosaic by Claus Arnold on the South wall, ''the Stiltwalkers''.

Musische Bildungsstätte, Remscheid – 1959
Architekten: Werner und Grete Wirsing, München

Arts Training Centre, Remscheid – 1959
Architects: Werner and Grete Wirsing, Munich

In der sechs Kilometer vom Remscheider Stadtkern entfernt gelegenen Musischen Bildungsstätte werden Jugendpfleger, Lehrer und Seelsorger für die musische Erziehung der Jugend in vierwöchigen Kursen ausgebildet. Schulungsräume, Wohnungen und Wirtschaftsteil sind auf drei durch verglaste Gänge verbundene Baukörper verteilt. Ihre Staffelung ermöglicht unter Ausnutzung des nach Süden fallenden Geländes eine gute Besonnung aller Aufenthaltsräume und freien Ausblick in die Wupperberge. Im Schulungsbau sind dem doppelgeschossigen Hauptarbeitsraum von zwei Seiten Ausbildungsräume für Musik, Tanz, Spiel, Fotografie und Film und Werkräume angegliedert. Die Räume des Wohntraktes sind zu kleinen Raumgruppen zusammengefaßt. Mensa und Wirtschaftsräume sind bereits auf die später durch einen zweiten Bauabschnitt zu erweiternde Gesamtkapazität bemessen. Zwischen den Baukörpern aufgeschüttete Terrassen gestatten Tanz und Laienspiel im Freien.

1 Ansicht des Schulungsbaues von der Talseite.
  View of the teaching block from the valley side.
2 Gesamtansicht.
  General view.

At the Arts Training Centre four miles from the centre of Remscheid, youth leaders, teachers and clergy are trained in four-week courses for educating young people in arts and crafts. Teaching, residential and domestic sections are divided into three blocks linked by glazed covered ways. The stepped design, exploiting a South-sloping site, ensures good natural lighting for all rooms and an unobstructed view of the Wupper range. In the teaching block, instruction rooms for music, dancing, acting, photography, films and various crafts are linked on two sides to the principal study room, which is two storeys high. Rooms in the residential building are arranged in small groups. The refectory and domestic accommodation take into account the future larger general capacity of the centre, when an extension is built. Raised terraces between the blocks provide space for open-air dancing and theatricals.

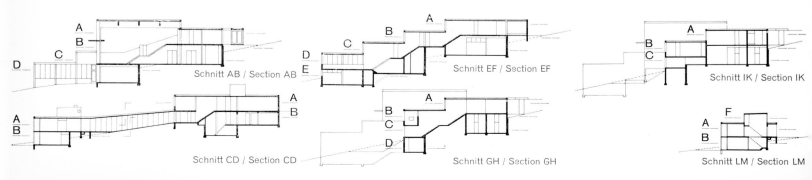

Schnitt AB / Section AB

Schnitt CD / Section CD

Schnitt EF / Section EF

Schnitt GH / Section GH

Schnitt IK / Section IK

Schnitt LM / Section LM

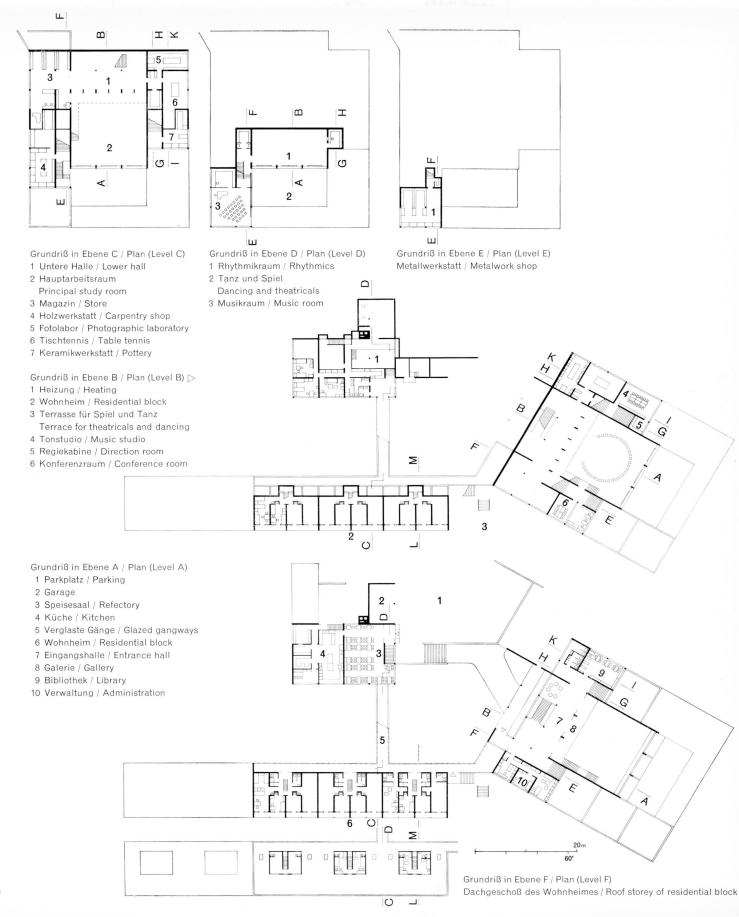

Grundriß in Ebene C / Plan (Level C)
1 Untere Halle / Lower hall
2 Hauptarbeitsraum
  Principal study room
3 Magazin / Store
4 Holzwerkstatt / Carpentry shop
5 Fotolabor / Photographic laboratory
6 Tischtennis / Table tennis
7 Keramikwerkstatt / Pottery

Grundriß in Ebene B / Plan (Level B) ▷
1 Heizung / Heating
2 Wohnheim / Residential block
3 Terrasse für Spiel und Tanz
  Terrace for theatricals and dancing
4 Tonstudio / Music studio
5 Regiekabine / Direction room
6 Konferenzraum / Conference room

Grundriß in Ebene D / Plan (Level D)
1 Rhythmikraum / Rhythmics
2 Tanz und Spiel
  Dancing and theatricals
3 Musikraum / Music room

Grundriß in Ebene E / Plan (Level E)
Metallwerkstatt / Metalwork shop

Grundriß in Ebene A / Plan (Level A)
1 Parkplatz / Parking
2 Garage
3 Speisesaal / Refectory
4 Küche / Kitchen
5 Verglaste Gänge / Glazed gangways
6 Wohnheim / Residential block
7 Eingangshalle / Entrance hall
8 Galerie / Gallery
9 Bibliothek / Library
10 Verwaltung / Administration

20 m
60'

Grundriß in Ebene F / Plan (Level F)
Dachgeschoß des Wohnheimes / Roof storey of residential block

3 Schulungsbau von Südwesten. Die Fertigbetonstützen und die am Ort betonierten Brüstungen bleiben unverputzt.
  Teaching block from the South-West. The prefabricated concrete piers and the spandrels cast in-situ are left exposed.
4 Wirtschaftsbau von Südwesten. Rechts die Verbindungs-rampe zum Wohntrakt.
  Domestic block from the South-West. Right, the covered ramp giving access to the residential building.
5 Wohntrakt.
  Residential building.

6 Hauptarbeitsraum. Zwischen die Sichtbetonbalken der Dachkonstruktion ist eine Unterdecke aus Herakustikplatten eingehängt.
Principal study room. An acoustic panel ceiling is suspended
between the exposed concrete beams of the roof.
7 Eingangshalle im Schulungsbau. Links Durchblick zur Galerie des Hauptsaales.
Teaching block entrance hall. Left, a glimpse into the gallery
of the main hall.
8 Blick vom Parkplatz zur Eingangshalle des Schulungsbaues.
Looking from the parking space towards the entrance hall of
the teaching block.

Hochhaus der Fakultät für Bauwesen, Technische Hochschule Stuttgart – 1956–60
Architekten: Rolf Gutbier, Günter Wilhelm, Curt Siegel, Stuttgart

Faculty of Building, Technical High School, Stuttgart – 1956–60
Architects: Rolf Gutbier, Günter Wilhelm, Curt Siegel, Stuttgart

In dem rund 55 Meter hohen Gebäude sind die Abteilungen für Architektur und Bauingenieurwesen vereinigt. Übungs- und Vorlesungssäle nehmen die nördliche, Lehrstuhl- und Institutsräume die südliche Längsseite der Obergeschosse ein. Ihr unterschiedlicher Raumhöhenbedarf erfordert einen Wechsel der Geschoßhöhen. Je zwei hohe Geschosse an der Nordseite sind mit drei Geschossen an der Südseite zusammengefaßt. Aufzugsturm, Treppenhäuser und Toiletten sind in einer mittleren Zone angeordnet. Die Erschließungsgänge erweitern sich zu kleinen Hallen, die die Einheit jeder Geschoßgruppe anschaulich machen. Differenztreppen vermitteln zwischen den versetzten Stockwerksebenen. Das Erdgeschoß ist als große Eingangshalle ausgebildet, in deren südlicher Hälfte eine Milchbar eingerichtet wurde. Tragendes Sichtbetonskelett, später eingefügte Klinkermauern, Türen, Schränke und Zwischenwände aus Eschenholz sind deutlich gegeneinander abgesetzt.

The departments of architecture and structural engineering are housed together in this building, which is about 170 feet high. Rooms for lectures and practical work occupy the long North flank; the tutorial and study rooms being located on the upper floors of the South side. The different height requirements of the rooms entail a variation in the heights of stories. Every two floors on the North side correspond to three on the South façade. Lift and stair towers, and lavatories, are placed in the middle. Access passages widen into small halls and emphasize the unity of each group of floors. Shallow flights of steps compensate for the changes in floor levels. The ground floor is arranged as a large entrance hall; it contains a milk bar in the South half. The exposed concrete load-bearing frame, the later added brick walls, the doors, built-in storage fitments and partitions, all of ash, are sharply differentiated.

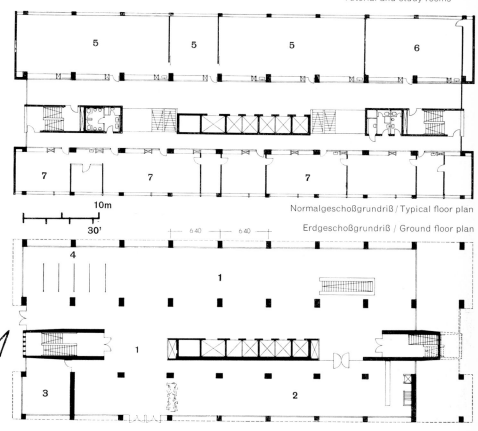

Schnitt / Section
1 Eingangshalle im Erdgeschoß
  Entrance hall (ground floor)
2 Übungsräume und Hörsaal
  Studios and lecture room
3 Lehrstuhl- und Institutsräume
  Tutorial and study rooms
4 Dachterrasse / Roof terrace

Grundrisse / Plans
1 Eingangshalle / Entrance hall
2 Milchbar / Milk bar
3 Hausmeister / Caretaker
4 Anschlagtafeln / Notice boards
5 Übungsräume / Studios
6 Hörsaal / Lecture room
7 Lehrstuhl- und Institutsräume
  Tutorial and study rooms

Normalgeschoßgrundriß / Typical floor plan

Erdgeschoßgrundriß / Ground floor plan

1 Südfassade. Die Fensterbänder der Lehrstuhl- und Institutsräume wechseln mit kunststeinverkleideten Brüstungen.
  South façade. Ribbon windows of tutorial and study rooms
  alternate with reconstructed stone spandrels.
2 Ansicht von Westen. An der Schmalseite links die Wandscheiben der breiteren und höheren Übungs- und Hörsäle,
  rechts die schmäleren und niedrigeren Lehrstuhl- und Institutsräume. In der Mitte das Treppenhaus, das zwischen den
  Geschoßdifferenzen vermittelt.
  View from the West. Narrow side left, the wall panels of
  the broader and higher studios and lecture rooms; right, the
  narrower and lower tutorial and study rooms. In the centre,
  the staircase compensating for the changes in floor levels.

3 Nordfassade. Hohe Glaswände vor den Übungsräumen und Hörsälen.
North façade. High glass walls front the lecture rooms and studios.

4 An den Schmalseiten treten zwischen den verglasten Gängen die Treppenhäuser hervor.
The staircases stand out from the narrow sides between the glazed end-panels of the passages.

5 Eingangshalle im Erdgeschoß. Links hinten die Aufzugs-
türen.
Ground-floor entrance hall. Left background, the lift doors.
6 Differenztreppen innerhalb einer Geschoßgruppe mit Blick
in die Übungssäle.
Compensating stairways in a floor group, and a glimpse
inside one of the studios.

Akademie der Künste, Berlin – 1959–60
Architekt: Werner Düttmann, Berlin

Academy of Arts, Berlin – 1959–60
Architect: Werner Düttmann, Berlin

1 Gesamtansicht von Norden. Hinter dem Ausstellungsbau links der fünfgeschossige Trakt, rechts der Studiobau.
General view from the North. To the left, behind the exhibition building, the five-storey block; to the right, the studio building.

Der Neubau der Akademie der Künste wurde durch eine großzügige Stiftung des Deutsch-Amerikaners Henry H. Reichhold an seine Vaterstadt ermöglicht. Die Lage des Grundstückes im Tiergarten, am Rande des neuerbauten Hansaviertels, veranlaßte den Architekten, das vielfältige Raumprogramm in einer Gruppe von drei Gebäuden anzuordnen, deren Gestalt ihrer funktionellen Bestimmung Ausdruck gibt. Im Obergeschoß des der Straße zugewandten Ausstellungsflügels sind drei Ausstellungshallen um einen Skulpturenhof gruppiert. Im Erdgeschoß liegen Haupteingang, Archiv- und Arbeitsräume. Ein fünfgeschossiger Bau für die interne Arbeit der Akademie enthält Ateliers, Konferenz- und Clubräume, Bibliothek, Arbeitsräume für wissenschaftliche Mitarbeiter und Verwaltung. Der Studiobau mit seinem gefalteten Dach dient als Saal für Vorträge, Filme und experimentelles Theater. Foyers, verglaste Gänge und Gartenhöfe verbinden die drei Bauteile.

The new building of the Academy of Arts was made possible by a munificent endowment by a German American, Henry H. Reichhold, to the city of his birth. The nature of the site in the Tiergarten, on the perimeter of the newly constructed Hansa Quarter, induced the architect to organize the complex programme in a group of three buildings, the design of which expresses their functional purpose. The upper floor of the exhibition range, which faces the street, contains three exhibition halls disposed about a court for sculpture. The main entrance, records and work-rooms are on the ground floor. A five-storey block for the internal activities of the Academy incorporates studios, conference and club rooms, library, workrooms and administration. The studio building, with its folded roof, serves as a hall for lectures, films and an experimental theatre. Foyers, glazed corridors and garden courts link the three parts of the scheme.

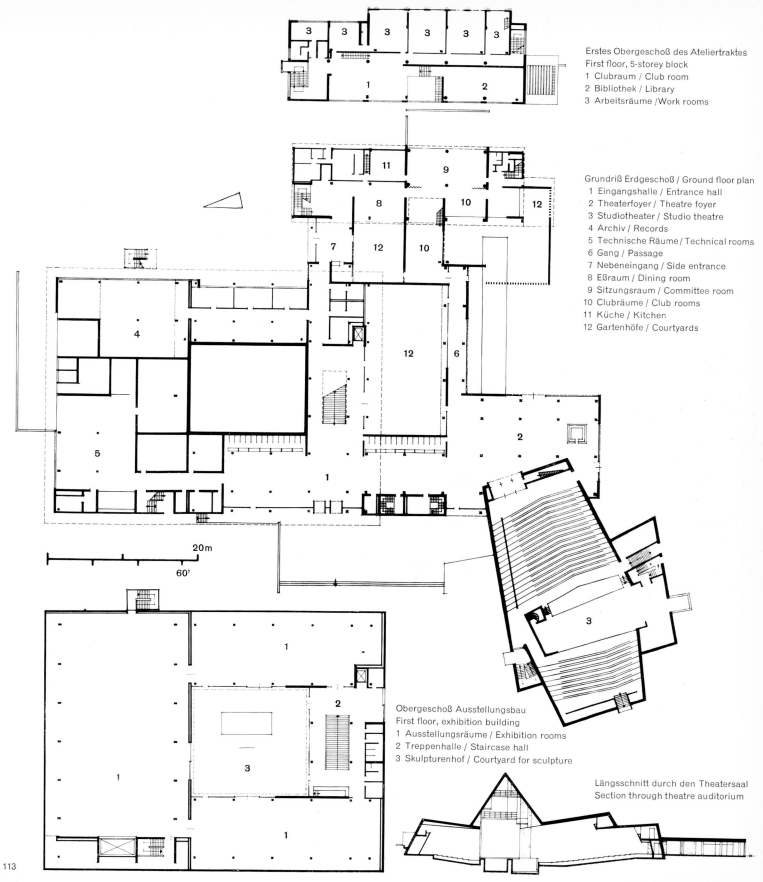

Erstes Obergeschoß des Ateliertraktes
First floor, 5-storey block
1 Clubraum / Club room
2 Bibliothek / Library
3 Arbeitsräume /Work rooms

Grundriß Erdgeschoß / Ground floor plan
1 Eingangshalle / Entrance hall
2 Theaterfoyer / Theatre foyer
3 Studiotheater / Studio theatre
4 Archiv / Records
5 Technische Räume / Technical rooms
6 Gang / Passage
7 Nebeneingang / Side entrance
8 Eßraum / Dining room
9 Sitzungsraum / Committee room
10 Clubräume / Club rooms
11 Küche / Kitchen
12 Gartenhöfe / Courtyards

20m
60'

Obergeschoß Ausstellungsbau
First floor, exhibition building
1 Ausstellungsräume / Exhibition rooms
2 Treppenhalle / Staircase hall
3 Skulpturenhof / Courtyard for sculpture

Längsschnitt durch den Theatersaal
Section through theatre auditorium

2 Gesamtansicht von Westen. Im Erdgeschoß des Ausstellungsflügels der Haupteingang.
General view from the West. The main entrance on the ground floor of the exhibition building.

3 Freitreppe an der Ostseite des Ausstellungsflügels. Holländische handgestrichene Ziegel und Waschbeton unter Zusatz von Marmorflußkieseln sind die dominierenden Materialien.
Open staircase on the East side of the exhibition building. Dutch hand-painted bricks and pebble-dash rendered concrete are the principal materials.

4 Treppenhalle des Ausstellungsflügels.
Staircase hall of the exhibition building.

5 Die Ausstellungshallen sind zum Skulpturenhof hin weitgehend verglast.
Continuous windows separate the exhibition rooms from the
sculpture courtyard.
6 Der große Ausstellungssaal wird durch ein Sheddach belichtet.
The large exhibition hall has saw-tooth roof lighting.
7 Sitzungsraum und Clubräume im Erdgeschoß des Ateliertraktes können durch Schiebewände getrennt werden.
Committee and club rooms on the ground floor of the
5-storey block can be separated by sliding partitions.

8 Studiotheater. Die Zuschauer sitzen auf beiden Seiten der
  Bühne. Deckenschalung aus brasilianischem Kiefernholz.
  Studio theatre. The audience sit on both sides of the stage.
  Ceiling lined with Brazilian pine.
9 Wasserbecken vor dem Foyer des Theatersaals.
  Pool in front of the theatre foyer.

Nationaltheater Mannheim – 1954–57
Architekt: Gerhard Weber, München und Frankfurt

National Theatre, Mannheim – 1954–57
Architect: Gerhard Weber, Munich and Frankfurt

1 Giebelseite mit dem Foyer des Großen Hauses.
  Gable end from the Luisenplatz, showing the foyer of the large theatre.
2 Ansicht der Längsseite mit der vorgelagerten Eingangshalle.
  View from the Goetheplatz, with the projecting entrance hall.

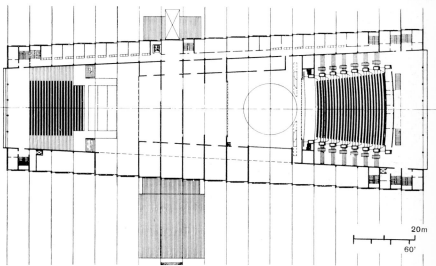

20m
60'

Grundriß Bühnengeschoß / Stage floor plan

Großes Haus – 1200 Plätze – und Kleines Haus – rund 800 Plätze – sind so angeordnet, daß die beiden Bühnenbezirke in der Mitte des Gebäudes über der gemeinsamen Wandelhalle im Erdgeschoß liegen. Im Großen Haus, das vorwiegend der Aufführung von Opern und großen Schauspielen dient, sind der Zuschauerraum und die mit allen technischen Einrichtungen ausgestattete Bühne wie im konventionellen Theaterbau räumlich getrennt und einander gegenübergestellt. Dagegen ist es im Kleinen Haus möglich, die Verteilung von Szene und Zuschauergruppen für jede Inszenierung abzuwandeln. Der Regisseur kann nicht nur zwischen Guckkasten- und Arenabühne wählen, das Spiel kann auch auf den seitlichen Galerien, die mit der rückwärtig schwebenden Regiezone verbunden sind, um die Zuschauer herumgeführt werden. Da die Lage der Bühne nicht fixiert ist, wurde auf einen Bühnenturm und den eisernen Vorhang für das Kleine Haus verzichtet.

The large "house" (1,200 seats) and the small "house" (about 800 seats) are so arranged that both stage areas lie in the middle of the building above the general concourse on the ground floor. In the big theatre, which is principally used for opera and spectacular pieces, the auditorium and the stage (which is equipped with every technical device) are separated and placed opposite one another in the conventional theatre tradition. In the small theatre, on the other hand, the shape and area of the stage and the grouping of the audience can be altered for each production. The producer can not only choose between a picture-frame or an arena stage, but the action of the play can also be extended round the audience in the side galleries, which are linked to the stage direction "bridge" suspended over the back of the hall. Since the position of the stage is not fixed no scenery tower or safety curtain is provided for the small theatre.

3 Garderoben- und Wandelhalle im Erdgeschoß.
  Cloakrooms and concourse on the ground floor.
4 Großes Haus. Blick zur Bühne.
  Large theatre, looking towards the stage.
5 Kleines Haus. Blick von der Hinterbühne. Zuschauer auf beiden Seiten der Bühne. Auftritt von den seitlichen Galerien.
  Die Regiezone im Hintergrund ist an der Decke aufgehängt.
  Small theatre. Back stage view. Audience on both sides of
  stage. Entrance from side galleries. The stage direction room
  in the background is suspended from the roof.

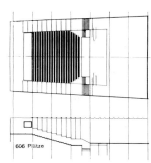

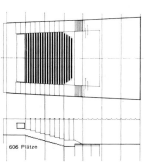

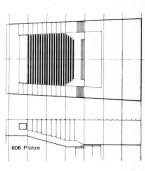

606 Plätze 606 Plätze 606 Plätze

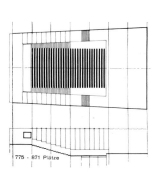

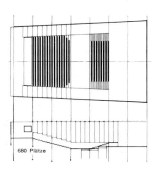

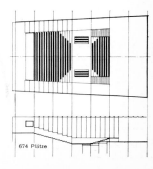

775 - 871 Plätze 680 Plätze 674 Plätze

Variationsmöglichkeiten des Kleinen Hauses
A Schauspiel mit Orchester
B Schauspiel mit erweiterter Vorbühne
C Schauspiel aus dem Parkett ansteigend
D Vortragsraum
E Arenabühne zweiseitig
F Arenabühne allseitig

Small theatre: possible variations
A Play with orchestra
B Stage with apron widened
C Stage rising from stalls
D Lecture hall
E Two-sided arena stage
F Arena stage with audience on four sides

Stadttheater Gelsenkirchen – 1958–59
Architekten: Werner Ruhnau, Gelsenkirchen, Ortwin Rave, Max von Hausen, Münster

Municipal Theatre, Gelsenkirchen – 1958–59
Architects: Werner Ruhnau, Gelsenkirchen, Ortwin Rave, Max von Hausen, Münster

Der Theaterneubau, nach dem wenig veränderten Wettbewerbsentwurf des Jahres 1954 errichtet, bildet den Kern eines Platzgefüges, das später zum kulturellen Forum werden soll. Eingang, Kasse und Garderoben liegen im Erdgeschoß auf der Südseite. Das Zuschauerhaus enthält 1050 Sitzplätze. Es ragt mit seinen Umgängen und Zugangstreppen halbrund in das hohe, zum Forum hin geöffnete Foyer. An den Bühnenbereich schließen auf der Nordseite die Magazinräume an. Darüber sind Werkstätten, Montagesaal, Probebühne und Ballettsaal angeordnet. Die Künstlergarderoben sind in sechs Geschossen an der westlichen Außenwand untergebracht und durch Treppen mit der Szene verbunden. An der Ostseite liegen die Räume für Intendanz und Verwaltung. Im Kleinen Haus, einem Studiotheater für 400 Zuschauer, ist die Bestuhlung im Parkett so variabel, daß die Zuordnung von Bühne und Zuschauern auch während eines Stückes verwandelt werden kann.

The new theatre, a slightly modified version of a competition design in 1954, forms the centre-piece of a scheme which will eventually become a "cultural forum". The entrance, box-office and cloakrooms are on the South side and at ground level. The auditorium contains 1,050 seats and, with its access corridors and staircases, makes a semicircular projection into the high foyer opening on to the square. On the North side storerooms connect with the stage area, while above there are workshops, a scenery construction room, a rehearsal stage and a ballet studio. The actors' dressing rooms are disposed in six tiers along the West wall and linked by stairs to the stage. On the East side are the administrative offices. In the smaller theatre, which accommodates 400, provision is made for varying the seating plan of the stalls, and for changing the relationship of stage and audience, even during the course of a performance.

120

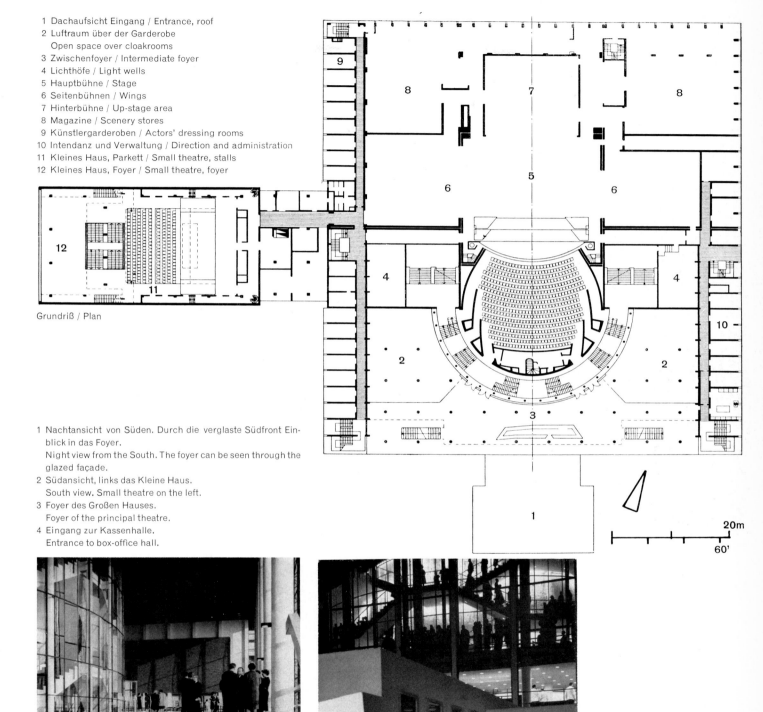

1 Dachaufsicht Eingang / Entrance, roof
2 Luftraum über der Garderobe
  Open space over cloakrooms
3 Zwischenfoyer / Intermediate foyer
4 Lichthöfe / Light wells
5 Hauptbühne / Stage
6 Seitenbühnen / Wings
7 Hinterbühne / Up-stage area
8 Magazine / Scenery stores
9 Künstlergarderoben / Actors' dressing rooms
10 Intendanz und Verwaltung / Direction and administration
11 Kleines Haus, Parkett / Small theatre, stalls
12 Kleines Haus, Foyer / Small theatre, foyer

Grundriß / Plan

1 Nachtansicht von Süden. Durch die verglaste Südfront Einblick in das Foyer.
  Night view from the South. The foyer can be seen through the
  glazed façade.
2 Südansicht, links das Kleine Haus.
  South view. Small theatre on the left.
3 Foyer des Großen Hauses.
  Foyer of the principal theatre.
4 Eingang zur Kassenhalle.
  Entrance to box-office hall.

20m
60'

5+6 Foyer des Großen Hauses mit den blauen Wänden von
Ives Klein. Schon während der Planung wurden die Künstler
zur Mitarbeit herangezogen.
Foyer of the principal theatre, with Ives Klein's blue murals.
Artists were invited to collaborate during the planning stage.
7 Treppe des Kleinen Hauses. Im Foyer bewegliches Relief von
Jean Tinguely.
Staircase in the small theatre. In the foyer, mobile by Jean
Tinguely.

8 Zuschauerraum des Großen Hauses. Die knappe Grundfläche des steil ansteigenden Parketts und die zwei bis zur Bühnenöffnung vorgezogenen Ränge ermöglichen einen engen Kontakt der Zuschauer zur Bühne. Die Bühnenöffnung kann durch einfahrbare Portale variiert werden, die die Rundung der Raumwände fortsetzen.

Auditorium of large theatre. The unobstructed plan of the steeply raked stalls, and the two higher "circles" of seats thrust forward towards the proscenium opening, allow close contact between the audience and the stage. The position of the opening can be varied and the stage extended at the sides.

Liederhalle, Stuttgart – 1955–56
Architekten: Adolf Abel, München, und Rolf Gutbrod, Stuttgart

Liederhalle, Stuttgart – 1955–56
Architects: Adolf Abel, Munich, and Rolf Gutbrod, Stuttgart

1 Außenansicht. Links der kleine, rechts der mittlere Saal. In der Mitte hinten der große Saal, davor der Haupteingang mit dem großen Vordach.
External view. Left the small, right the medium-sized hall. In the middle background the big hall; in front of it the main entrance with its large canopy.

Die Liederhalle am Rand der Innenstadt grenzt an den geplanten Hochschulpark. Die drei Säle sind nach Größe, Raumform und Material deutlich unterschieden. Der große Saal mit den gekurvten Außenwänden und weit geschwungener Empore bietet Platz für 2000 Personen und dient für musikalische Veranstaltungen, Kongresse, Bankette und größere Feiern. Die 750 Plätze des Kammermusiksaals sind auf ansteigenden, gegeneinander versetzten Estraden zum Podium ausgerichtet, das eine der fünf Raumecken einnimmt. Während die beiden größeren Säle nach außen völlig abgeschlossen sind, wird der kleine Saal durch eine Glasbausteinwand direkt belichtet. Er faßt 350 Zuschauer und ist vor allem für Schülerkonzerte, Proben und Vorträge gedacht. Das doppelgeschossige Foyer, das die Säle verbindet, wird bei festlichen Veranstaltungen selbst als Hauptsaal benützt. Von der zentral gelegenen Küche aus können das Restaurant, das Foyer und die Säle bedient werden.

The concert hall, on the perimeter of the city centre, borders the proposed High School Park. The three auditoria differ sharply in size, shape and treatment. The big hall, with curved external walls and wide, flowing, "circle" seats 2,000 people and is intended for musical festivals, congresses, banquets and larger celebrations. The 750 seats of the pentagonal chamber music room are asymmetrically disposed in raked tiers to face the platform, which occupies one of the five angles. While the two larger halls are completely enclosed, the small one is lit by a stepped glass-brick wall. It holds an audience of 350 and is designed chiefly for students' concerts, rehearsals and lectures. The two-storey foyer, linking the halls, is itself used as a focal centre for festival occasions. The restaurant, foyer and auditoria are served from a common kitchen.

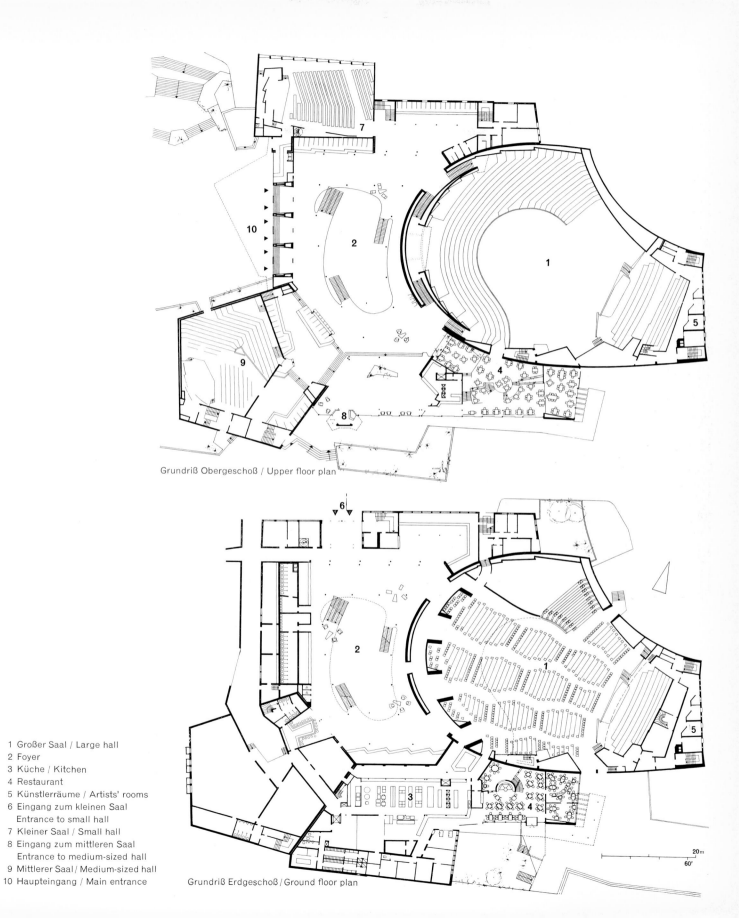

Grundriß Obergeschoß / Upper floor plan

1 Großer Saal / Large hall
2 Foyer
3 Küche / Kitchen
4 Restaurant
5 Künstlerräume / Artists' rooms
6 Eingang zum kleinen Saal
  Entrance to small hall
7 Kleiner Saal / Small hall
8 Eingang zum mittleren Saal
  Entrance to medium-sized hall
9 Mittlerer Saal / Medium-sized hall
10 Haupteingang / Main entrance

Grundriß Erdgeschoß / Ground floor plan

2 Doppelgeschossiges Foyer. Rechts die Eingänge zum mittleren Saal.
  Two-storey foyer. To the right, the entrances to the medium-
  sized hall.

3 Mittlerer Saal für Kammermusikaufführungen. Die Wände
  sind mit Eichenholz verkleidet, die Eschenholzdecke ist frei
  eingehängt.
  The middle-sized hall for chamber music. The walls are faced
  with oak; the ash-wood ceiling is suspended.

4 Kleiner Saal, Blick gegen die Bühne.
  Small hall, looking towards the platform.

5 Großer Saal. Blick von der Galerie zur Bühne. Die linke Wand ist aus veredeltem Beton, die übrigen Wände sind mit Teakholz verkleidet. Die Bühne kann durch Schiebewände in ihrer Größe verwandelt werden.
Large hall. View from the circle towards the platform, the size of which can be changed by means of sliding partitions. The left wall is fair-faced concrete; the other walls have teak cladding.
6 Galerie des großen Saales.
Circle of large hall.

Beethovenhalle, Bonn – 1959
Architekt: Siegfried Wolske, Hamburg

Beethoven Hall, Bonn – 1959
Architect: Siegfried Wolske, Hamburg

1 Luftaufnahme von Südwesten.
Air view from South-West.

Die Beethovenhalle dient als kulturelles Zentrum für Veranstaltungen verschiedenster Art, in erster Linie der Pflege der Musik. Sie liegt am Westufer des Rheins am Rande des mittelalterlichen Stadtmauerringes. Die Foyers und das zur Rheinseite gerichtete Restaurant umschließen ringförmig die in der Mitte des Gebäudes zusammengefaßten Säle und vermitteln zwischen den geschlossenen Festräumen und dem Freiraum der Umgebung. Die Podien werden von einem gemeinsamen Zugang erschlossen. Der Hauptteil der Garderoben und der Eingang sind in einem gesonderten Baukörper dem großen Foyer vorgelagert. Zugang und Garderoben für die Künstler und die Nebenräume sind im Untergeschoß untergebracht. Der Hauptsaal ist vor allem für Konzerte bestimmt, das Studio für Kammermusik und Theater. Vortragssaal, Kammermusiksaal und Ausstellungsraum erhalten von einem Innenhof her Tageslicht. Sie können für große Ausstellungen zusammengefaßt werden.

The Beethoven Hall serves as a cultural centre for performances of various kinds, and of music in particular. It lies on the West bank of the Rhine on the perimeter of the mediaeval city wall. The foyers, and the restaurant overlooking the Rhine, are ringed about the several auditoria grouped in the middle of the building, and break the contrast between these rigidly enclosed spaces and their open surroundings. The stages share a common access corridor. Most of the cloakrooms and the main entrance are located in a special block sited in front of the large foyer. The artists' entrance, dressing rooms and adjoining rooms are at a lower level. The principal hall is primarily intended for concerts; the "studio" for chamber music and plays. Daylight enters the lecture room, chamber music studio and exhibition room from an internal court. They can be combined for large exhibitions.

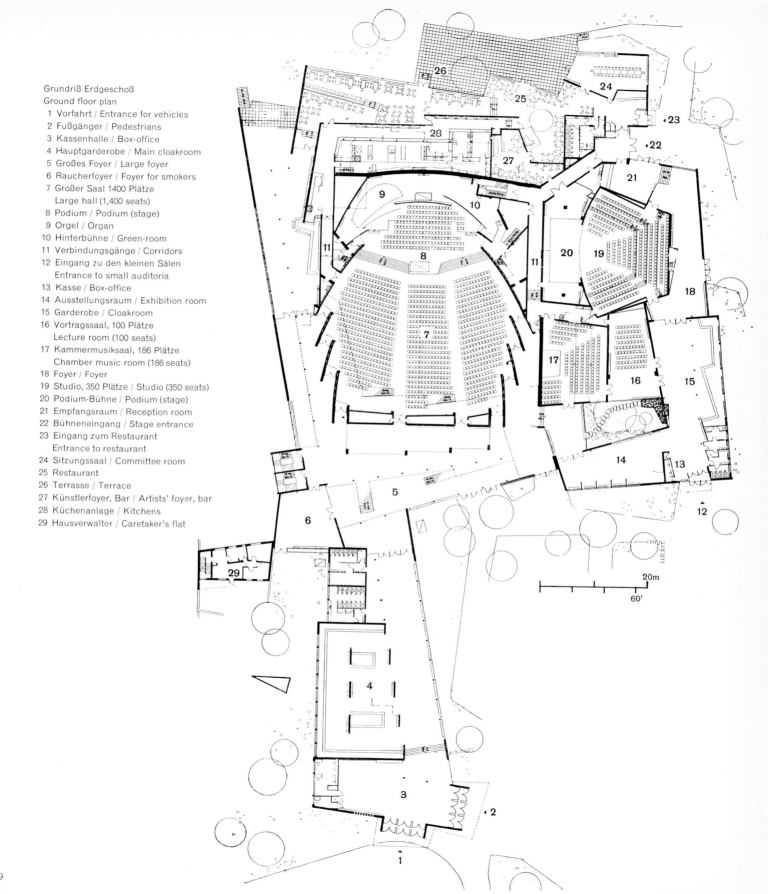

Grundriß Erdgeschoß
Ground floor plan

1 Vorfahrt / Entrance for vehicles
2 Fußgänger / Pedestrians
3 Kassenhalle / Box-office
4 Hauptgarderobe / Main cloakroom
5 Großes Foyer / Large foyer
6 Raucherfoyer / Foyer for smokers
7 Großer Saal 1400 Plätze
  Large hall (1,400 seats)
8 Podium / Podium (stage)
9 Orgel / Organ
10 Hinterbühne / Green-room
11 Verbindungsgänge / Corridors
12 Eingang zu den kleinen Sälen
   Entrance to small auditoria
13 Kasse / Box-office
14 Ausstellungsraum / Exhibition room
15 Garderobe / Cloakroom
16 Vortragssaal, 100 Plätze
   Lecture room (100 seats)
17 Kammermusiksaal, 186 Plätze
   Chamber music room (186 seats)
18 Foyer / Foyer
19 Studio, 350 Plätze / Studio (350 seats)
20 Podium-Bühne / Podium (stage)
21 Empfangsraum / Reception room
22 Bühneneingang / Stage entrance
23 Eingang zum Restaurant
   Entrance to restaurant
24 Sitzungssaal / Committee room
25 Restaurant
26 Terrasse / Terrace
27 Künstlerfoyer, Bar / Artists' foyer, bar
28 Küchenanlage / Kitchens
29 Hausverwalter / Caretaker's flat

2 Ansicht vom Rheinufer aus. Im Vordergrund das Restaurant.
  View from the bank of the Rhine. Restaurant in the foreground.
3 Großes Foyer mit Aufgang zu den Galeriegeschossen. Wand-
  malerei von Joseph Fassbender.
  Large foyer, with way up to circle. Mural by Joseph Fassbender.
4 Restaurant.

5 Großer Saal. Lose Bestuhlung im Parkett. Die gestaffelten Rangplätze können durch ein herabklappbares Deckenelement abgetrennt werden.
Large hall. Movable seats in the stalls. The raked circle seating at the back can be partitioned off by a folding device descending from the roof.

6 Die Decke des großen Saales besteht aus Trockenstuck-Hohlkörpern.
The ceiling of the large hall is composed of dry-anchored hollow concrete blocks.

7 Vortragssaal.
Lecture hall.

Kongreßhalle in Berlin – 1957
Architekt: Hugh A. Stubbins, Cambridge, Mass.; Mitarbeiter: W. Düttmann und F. Möcken, Berlin

Congress Hall, Berlin – 1957
Architect: Hugh A. Stubbins, Cambridge, Mass.; Assistants: W. Düttmann and F. Möcken, Berlin

Die Kongreßhalle ist der Beitrag der Vereinigten Staaten zur Interbau Berlin 1957. Sie steht unweit der Ruine des Reichstagsgebäudes am Nordostrand des Tiergartens. Die überbaute Grundfläche von 92 × 94 Metern ist annähernd quadratisch. In dem zweigeschossigen Unterbau sind Eingangshalle und Garderobe, die in mehreren Ebenen angeordneten Foyers, eine Ausstellungshalle, ein Studiotheater, Konferenz- und Büroräume und ein Restaurant zusammengefaßt. Er wird von einer als Dachgarten ausgebildeten Plattform überdeckt. Eine breite Freitreppe verbindet sie mit dem Tiergarten. Das geschwungene Dach des Kongreßsaales berührt die Plattform nur an zwei Punkten. Das fensterlose Auditorium faßt 1250 Sitzplätze. Seine gewölbte Decke folgt der Form der Dachschale. Die Neigung des Fußbodens ergibt von allen Seiten eine gute Sicht auf das Podium. Vier Ausgänge führen vom Saal auf den Dachgarten.

The congress hall was the contribution of the United States to "Interbau", Berlin, 1957. It stands not far from the ruins of the Reichstag building on the Northern perimeter of the Tiergarten. The "built-up" area of approximately 302 × 309 feet is almost square. The two-storey substructure contains entrance hall and cloakroom, the foyers arranged on several levels, an exhibition hall, a studio-theatre, conference rooms, offices and a restaurant. Above this is a terrace laid out in the form of a roof garden and linked to the Tiergarten by a wide, open, stairway. The hanging roof of the congress hall touches this terrace at only two points. The windowless auditorium holds 1,250 people, its vaulted ceiling conforming to the shape of the roof shell. The sloping floor provides a good view of the platform from every side. Four exits lead from the hall to the roof garden.

1 Nachtaufnahme von Süden.
  Night view from the South.
2 Ansicht vom Tiergarten aus. Auf der Südseite ist vor dem
  Haupteingang ein Teich angelegt. Die Freitreppe führt zur
  Plattform hinauf.
  View from the Tiergarten. On the South side a pool is placed
  in front of the main entrance. The open stairway leads to the
  platform.
3 Ansicht von Westen.
  View from the West.

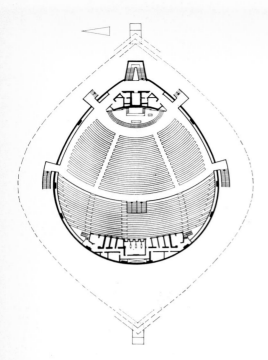

Grundriß des Auditoriums / Plan of the auditorium

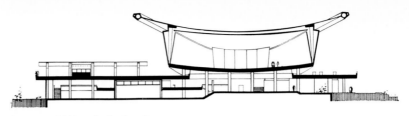

Längsschnitt / Longitudinal section

Querschnitt / Cross-section

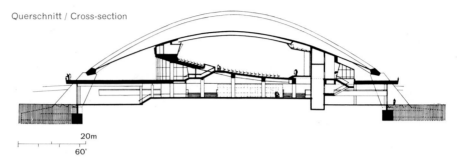

20m
60'

Die Trennwände im Erd- und Zwischengeschoß des in Stahlbeton konstruierten Baues sind vom tragenden Stützensystem unabhängig. Das sattelförmige Hängedach ist zwischen zwei ebene, schrägliegende Bögen gespannt, die in einer Höhe von zwei Metern über der Plattform auf zwei Widerlagern aus Stahlbeton ruhen. Die Länge der Bögen beträgt 110 Meter, ihre Scheitelhöhe über der Plattform 18 Meter, die größte Spannweite von Scheitel zu Scheitel 60 Meter. Sie können nur Kräfte aufnehmen, dle in ihrer Ebene liegen. Deshalb ist über den Umfassungswänden des Saales ein 40 cm starker Ring in die Dachfläche eingefügt, der durch Stützen in der Auditoriumswand und durch Verstärkungsstrelfen in der Dachhaut gegen die Bogenwiderlager hin ausgesteift wird. Die 7 cm starke tragende Stahlbetondachhaut ist quer zur Längsachse vorgespannt. Die Spannglieder sind an den Bögen und am inneren Versteifungsring befestigt.

Pile foundations were required for this reinforced concrete structure. The walls of the ground floor and mezzanine are unconnected with the load-bearing structural system, the saddle-shaped hanging roof being stretched between two oblique-angled arches, which rest on two reinforced concrete abutments 6' 6" above the platform. The length of the arches, which are almost 60' above the platform at their highest point, is 360'. Their widest span is approximately 195'. Since they can only withstand stresses in their own plane, a ring 15 inches thick is inserted over the circumference walls of the hall into the roof and this is braced against the abutments by supports in the auditorium wall and reinforcement ribs in the roof skin. The $2^3/_4$ inch thick, load-bearing reinforced concrete, roof is crossbraced to the long axis of the building. The suspension members are secured to the arches and to the inner reinforcement ring.

4 Auditorium.
5 Blick in die Eingangshalle von Osten. Stahlbetonpfeiler tragen
  die gekrümmte Fußbodenplatte des Auditoriums.
  The entrance hall from the East. Reinforced concrete piers
  support the curved floor of the auditorium.

Zeltbauten
Architekt: Frei Otto, Berlin, in Zusammenarbeit mit Peter Stromeyer, Konstanz

Tent buildings
Architect: Frei Otto, Berlin; in collaboration with Peter Stromeyer, Constance

1 Zeltcafé auf der Interbau Berlin 1957. Die Haut des Buckelzeltes wird durch Masten mit Holzfeder-Ausrundung nach oben und durch Zugseile nach unten verformt.
Tent café, Interbau, Berlin, 1957. The skin of the humped-back tent is pressed upwards by masts with wooden umbrella heads, and stretched downwards by guy ropes.

2 Eingangsdach zur Bundesgartenschau in Köln 1957. Eine Haut aus kunststoffbeschichtetem Glasgewebe ist zwischen vier kleine Masten über einen 34 Meter überbrückenden Stahlrohrbogen gespannt.
Entrance canopy at the National Garden Show, Cologne, 1957. A skin composed of a fibre glass and plastic sandwich is stretched from four small masts across a, 110-foot span, steel tube arch.

Die Zeltbauten auf der Bundesgartenschau 1955 in Kassel und 1957 in Köln sind Ergebnisse einer langjährigen Entwicklungsarbeit, die im Zusammenwirken der Zeltfabrik L. Stromeyer & Co. in Konstanz und des Arbeitskreises Frei Otto an der Entwicklungsstätte für Leichtbau in Berlin geleistet wurde. Erst die in den letzten Jahren geschaffenen wissenschaftlichen Grundlagen ermöglichten es, beliebig große Weiten unter sparsamster Ausnutzung des Materials zu überspannen. Durch ihr geringes Eigengewicht, ihre Beweglichkeit und Anpassungsfähigkeit eignen sich die Zeltkonstruktionen vor allem für zeitlich begrenzte Bauaufgaben, die raschen Auf- und Abbau, leichte Transportierbarkeit und die Möglichkeit einer Wiederverwendung an anderer Stelle erfordern: Ausstellungsbauten, Sonnenschutzdächer, bei Verwendung dauerhaften Materials und entsprechender Wärme- und Schallisolierung auch Versammlungs- und Industriehallen.

The tent structures at the National Garden Shows at Kassel (1955) and Cologne (1957) were the products of many years of research carried out in collaboration between the tent factory L. Stromeyer & Co. at Constance and the Frei Otto group at the Light Building Development Station in Berlin. Thanks to scientific studies in recent years, it is now possible to span areas of any width with the most economical expenditure of materials. Because of their extreme lightness, mobility and adaptability, tent structures are particularly suitable for temporary purposes, entailing rapid erection and dismantling, easy transport and the possibility of further use on other sites; e. g., exhibition buildings, sun canopies and even assembly and industrial halls, if durable materials and appropriate insulation are specified.

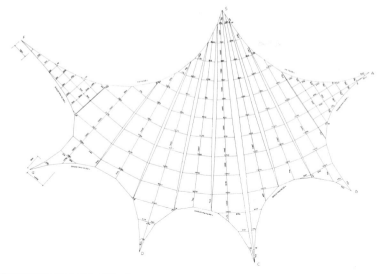

3 Zuschnitt der Bahnstreifen für ein Spitzzelt auf der Bundesgartenschau in Köln 1957.
Plan of a pointed tent at the National Garden Show, Cologne,
1957.

4 +5 Tanzbrunnen auf der Bundesgartenschau in Köln 1957.
Die Sternwellenmembrane wird von sechs leichten Fachwerk-
stützen gehalten.
Fountain pool with dance floor at the National Garden Show,
Cologne, 1957. The star-shaped, wave-like, skin is held by
six light, laced, supports.

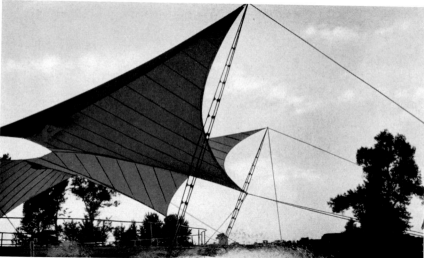

6+7 Wellenförmiges Schattendach an einem Hang auf der Bundesgartenschau in Kassel.
Wave-shaped sun-shading device on a slope at the National Garden Show, Kassel.

8–11 Musikpavillon auf der Bundesgartenschau in Kassel. Erste Ausführung einer sattelförmig gekrümmten, vorgespannten Membrane zwischen vier Punkten, die mit Fangseilen verbunden sind. Spannweite 18 Meter.
Music pavilion at the National Garden Show, Kassel. First example of a saddle-shaped four-pointed and prestressed, tent membrane secured with guys. Width of span 59 feet.

Als Material für die Zeltmembranen werden homogene Stoffe – vor allem Kunststoffolien –, Vliese aus geklebten Fasern und Gewebe aus Leinen, Hanf, Baumwolle oder aus synthetischen Fasern, die mit plastischen Massen beschichtet oder mit Aluminiumfolien beklebt sind, verwendet. Gewebe, die in der Fabrik oder nachträglich mit wärmedämmenden Schaumstoffen versehen sind, eignen sich für winterfeste Bauten auch in den kältesten Regionen. Bei größeren Spannweiten nehmen vorgefertigte Netze aus Fäden, Seilen oder Drähten, deren Maschen durch Aufkleben von Kunststoffbahnen geschlossen werden, die Zugkräfte auf. Zugseile und Druckstäbe mit weich ausgerundetem Kopfteil verformen die dehnfähige, ursprünglich ebene Zelthaut zur sattelförmigen Membrane und leiten die auf die Konstruktion einwirkenden Kräfte ab. Durch diese Vorspannung erhält die Haut ihre Steifigkeit gegen wechselnden Winddruck und Sog.

As tent cloth, homogeneous materials – especially artificial yarns, sheets of glued fibres, and fabrics of linen, hemp and cotton or synthetic threads with plastic linings or sandwiched to aluminium foil, are used. Fabrics subjected during manufacture, or subsequently, to foam spray insulating processes are suitable for winter conditions, even in the coldest climates. For spanning wider areas prefabricated nets of wire, rope or thread, the meshes of which are fitted with strips of plastic, absorb tensile stresses. Guy ropes, and struts with gently rounded heads, stretch and compress the tent cloth, which is initially level, into saddle-shaped skins and counteract strains on the construction. By this prestressing the skin obtains its rigidity in face of changes in wind pressure and suction.

Ausstellungshalle ›Die Stadt von morgen‹ auf der Interbau, Berlin – 1957
Architekt: Karl Otto, Berlin; Mitarbeiter: Günter Günschel und Frei Otto

"The Town of To-morrow" Exhibition Hall, Interbau, Berlin – 1957
Architect: Karl Otto, Berlin; Assistants: Günter Günschel and Frei Otto

Für die Dauer der Ausstellung wurde ein Regendach errichtet, unter dem die Ausstellungsobjekte frei angeordnet werden konnten. Für die Dachkonstruktion wurde ein räumliches Tragwerk aus MERO-Stahlrohren entwickelt. Zwei quadratische Raster aus Stäben von zwei Metern Länge, im Grundriß gegeneinander um die halbe Stablänge verschoben, bilden die obere und untere Begrenzung des Tragwerkes. Ihr Abstand ist so gewählt, daß für die diagonalen Verstrebungen gleichlange Stäbe Verwendung finden. Die Dachkonstruktion wird von Stahlbetonschleuderstützen getragen. Vier MERO-Stäbe verbinden jeden Stützenkopf mit je vier Netzknotenpunkten. Die Dachhaut besteht aus kunstharzbeschichtetem Baumwolltuch. Um starke Windkräfte aufnehmen zu können, ist das Tuch durch Aufspreizen räumlich gekrümmt und vorgespannt. Die Konstruktion ermöglicht einen schnellen Auf- und Abbau, jede Veränderung der Hallengröße und die Wiederverwendung aller Teile.

For the duration of the exhibition a rainproof covering was erected, under which exhibits could be arranged at will. For this purpose a "transpatial" supporting structure was developed out of MERO-steel tubes. Two superimposed square frames composed of rods, 6 ft..6 in. long, reciprocally displaced by half a rod's length on plan, formed the upper and lower limits of the supporting structure; the interval between them was so adjusted that rods of the same length could be used for the diagonal braces. This construction was carried on reinforced concrete piers, their heads each linked by four MERO-rods to four intersection points in the roof frame. The "roof" skin consisted of a resin-impregnated cotton fabric, spatially curved and prestressed to withstand strong wind pressure. The system of construction permitted rapid erection and dismantling, any variation in the size of the hall and the re-utilization of all component parts.

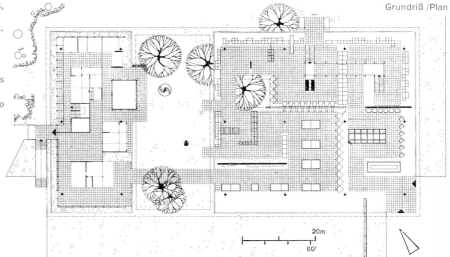

1 Innenansicht. Die Öffnungen in der Decke ermöglichten es,
den Baumbestand zu schonen.
Interior view. Openings in the roof made it possible to pre-
serve the trees.

2 Ansicht von Süden mit dem Eingang.
South view, and entrance.

3 Im Garten des offenen Mittelteils ist der Tiergartenpark als
Freiraum in die Ausstellung einbezogen.
The Tiergarten park was introduced as an open space into
the garden of the middle section.

Grundriß /Plan

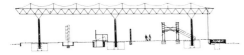

Schnitt / Section

Deutscher Pavillon auf der Weltausstellung in Brüssel – 1958
Architekten: Egon Eiermann, Karlsruhe, und Sep Ruf, München; Gartenarchitekt: W. Rossow, Berlin

German Pavilion at the 1958 Brussels International Exhibition
Architects: Egon Eiermann, Karlsruhe; Sep Ruf, Munich; Landscape architect: Walter Rossow, Berlin

Die alten Baumbestände des 18 000 Quadratmeter großen, hügeligen Geländes und das unter den Leitgedanken ›Leben und Arbeiten in Deutschland‹ gestellte Programm, das eine monumentale Gestaltung ausschloß, legten es nahe, das in neun Abteilungen gegliederte Ausstellungsgut in einer lockeren Baugruppe unterzubringen. Acht Pavillons von verschiedener Größe, alle über quadratischem Grundriß teils zwei-, teils dreigeschossig errichtet, sind durch Stege zu einer Kette verbunden und umschließen einen Innenhof. Das konstruktive Gerüst der Bauten ist aus Stahl, die Außenwände bestehen aus Glas. Alle Konstruktionsteile sind schwarz, die Wandflächen weiß gestrichen. Zur Durchlüftung der Räume wurde unterhalb der Decke ein Streifen unverglast gelassen. Erschlossen wird die Anlage von der höher gelegenen Straße her über einen 57 Meter langen Brückensteg, der an einem 50 Meter hohen Stahlpylon einseitig auskragend aufgehängt ist.

The 4¹/₂-acre hilly tree-clad site, and the theme of the programme "Life and Work in Germany", ruled out any monumental conception, and suggested an informal group of buildings in which the nine sections of the exhibition are evenly dispersed, but interrelated. Eight pavilions of different sizes, all erected upon a square ground plan of two or three storeys, are linked by footbridges into a chain arranged about an internal court. The skeleton frame in each case is steel and the external walls are glass. All structural elements are painted black and wall surfaces white. The rooms are cross-ventilated by leaving a 20-inch band below the ceiling unglazed. Access to the roadway, which lies at a higher level, is provided by a footbridge, 185 feet long, supported on one side by a 160-foot steel pylon, from which it projects.

1 Pavillon 1 mit dem Verbindungssteg zum Pavillon 8, von Norden gesehen.
Pavilion 1 with its communicating bridge to Pavilion 8, seen from the North.
2 Pavillon 1 und 2 von Westen.
Pavilions 1 and 2, from the West.
3 Der an einem Stahlpylon aufgehängte Brückensteg bildet den Zugang von der Straße her.
The footbridge, suspended from a steel pylon, provides access from the road.

Grundriß / Site and floor plan
1 Landwirtschaft, Handwerk, Restaurant / Agriculture, handicrafts, restaurant
2 Industrielle Arbeit / Industry
3 Stadt und Wohnung / Community and home
4 Persönlicher Bedarf / The needs of man as an individual
5 Soziale Aufgaben / Social tasks
6 Freie Zeit / Leisure
7 Heilen und Helfen / Welfare
8 Erziehung und Bildung / Education
9 Zugangsbrücke / Access bridge

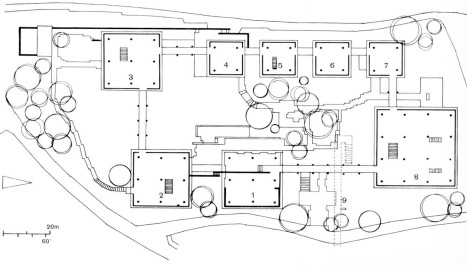

20m
60'

Studio des Kunstkreises Hameln – 1956–57
Architekt: Dieter Oesterlen, Hannover

Studio for Hameln Art Society – 1956–57
Architect: Dieter Oesterlen, Hanover

Die Mauer, die die fast quadratische Anlage umschließt, wird auf der Eingangsseite durch eine Glaswand unterbrochen, die den Blick bis in den Plastikhof im Inneren freigibt. Um die Eingangshalle sind Kasse, Garderobe und WC angeordnet. Der Hauptausstellungsraum erhält durch die große Fensterwand zum Innenhof und durch das Sheddach natürliches Licht, das durch weiß gestrichene Holzlamellen gestreut wird. Die künstliche Beleuchtung entspricht in Richtung, Intensität und Farbe dem Tageslicht, da die Lichtquellen (Leuchtstoffröhren) über der Lamellendecke montiert sind. In den Fußboden sind Hülsen zur variablen Aufstellung von Ausstellungswänden eingelassen. Die Wände sind am Außenbau, in der Eingangshalle und im Gartenhof aus rotem, gesandeltem Backstein. im Ausstellungsraum weiß geschlämmt, die Fußböden von Vorplatz, Eingangshalle und Hof aus dunkelgrünem Dolomit, im Ausstellungsraum aus dunkelgrauen Marley-Fußbodenplatten.

The walls, embracing an almost square plan, are broken on the entrance side by a glass partition, through which can be seen the enclosed court. The pay-office, cloakroom and lavatories are grouped about the entrance hall. Natural light enters the principal exhibition room through the large glass partition facing the courtyard and the roof, and is spread by a system of white-painted, wooden slats. The artificial lighting corresponds in direction, intensity and colour tone to daylight, its source being in the form of fluorescent tubes set in the roof above the slatted ceiling. Sockets have been inserted in the floor to hold display screens. The walls, on the outside, in the entrance hall and in the courtyard are red sand-faced brick, those inside the exhibition room are finished with white emulsion paint; the forecourt, entrance hall and courtyard are paved with dark green Dolomite stone slabs; the exhibition room has Marley patent flooring.

144

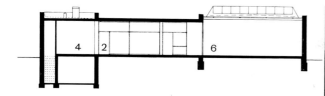

1 Vorplatz / Forecourt
2 Eingangshalle / Entrance hall
3 Packraum / Packing room
4 Garderobe / Cloakroom
5 Kasse / Pay-office
6 Ausstellungsraum / Exhibition room
7 Wasserbecken / Pool
8 Innenhof / Courtyard for exhibitions

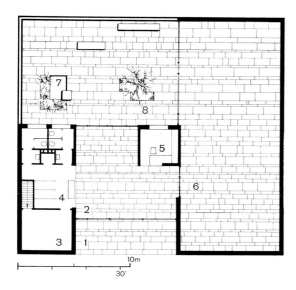

1 Blick vom Vorplatz in die Eingangshalle.
  View from the forecourt into the entrance hall.
2 Modellansicht.
  Model.
3 Sitzgruppe in der Eingangshalle. Dahinter der Innenhof.
  A place to sit in the entrance hall.
4 Innenhof zur Ausstellung von Skulpturen.
  Enclosed courtyard for displaying sculpture.
5 Hauptausstellungsraum mit Blick in den Innenhof.
  Main exhibition room, through which the courtyard can be seen.

Büro- und Wohnhaus an der Berliner Straße in Frankfurt am Main – 1954–55
Architekt: Otto Apel, Frankfurt am Main; Mitarbeiter: Eberhard Brandl

Office block with flats in the Berliner Strasse, Frankfurt-on-Main – 1954–55
Architect: Otto Apel, Frankfurt-on-Main, in collaboration with Eberhard Brandl

1 Straßenfassade.
  Street façade.
2 Ansicht der Südfassade.
  South elevation.

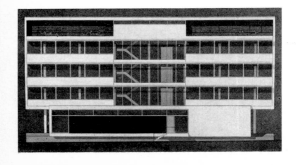

Das an einer neuen Hauptgeschäftsstraße errichtete Gebäude enthält im Erdgeschoß zwei Läden, in den drei Obergeschossen zweibündig angelegte Mietbüroräume und im Dachgeschoß vier Zweizimmerappartements. Seine geringe Länge ermöglicht die Erschließung von nur einem zentralen Treppenhaus auf der Südseite aus, das in den Bürogeschossen mit Aufzug und WC-Räumen zu einem Festpunkt zusammengefaßt ist. Im Erdgeschoß wird die große Eingangshalle durch einen von niedrigen Flügeln dreiseitig umschlossenen Gartenhof erweitert. Die Räume der Dachgeschoßwohnungen sind jeweils um einen kleinen Innenhof gruppiert und mit tiefen Loggien nach Süden geöffnet. Ihre Nordwand ist zum Schutz gegen den Straßenlärm vollkommen geschlossen. Die von Stahlbetonstützen getragenen Obergeschosse kragen auf drei Seiten aus. Fensteraufteilung und Zwischenwände sind vom konstruktiven Gerüst unabhängig.

Erected in an important new business thoroughfare, the building contains two shops at ground level, two parallel rows of rented offices on each of the three storeys above, and four two-room flats on the top floor. Its modest length makes possible a single central staircase on the South side, which on the office floors is provided with a lift and toilets to form a service core. On the ground floor the large entrance hall is extended to incorporate a small garden enclosed on three sides by low ranges of buildings. The rooms of the top-floor flats are each disposed around small internal courts and open on to spacious balconies on the South side. Their North wall is completely closed to exclude street noise. The staircase provides direct access to two of the flats. The others are reached by a covered way. The upper storeys, carried on reinforced concrete piers, project on three sides. The placing of windows and partitions does not reflect the pattern of the structural frame.

146

3 Eingangshalle im Erdgeschoß mit Durchblick in den Hof.
  Ground floor entrance hall with view of garden court beyond.
4 Dachgeschoßappartement. Blick aus dem Wohnraum in den
  Schlafraum und zum Innenhof.
  Top flat. View from living room into bedroom and internal
  court.

Grundrisse / Floor plans
1 Eingangshalle / Entrance hall
2 Aufzug / Lift
3 Laden- und Geschäftsräume / Shops and business premises
4 Innenhof / Garden court
5 Nebeneingang / Alternative entrance
6 Büroraum / Offices
7 Wohnung, um einen Innenhof angeordnet
  Flat (with internal court)
8 Innenhof / Internal court
9 Zugang zu den beiden äußeren Wohnungen / Access to
  two outside flats

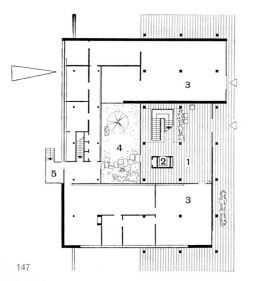

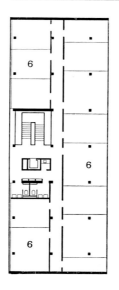

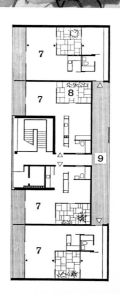

147

10m

30'

Das siebengeschossige Gebäude ist mit seiner Hauptfront der verkehrsreichen Bundesallee zugewandt. Die beiden unteren Geschosse stehen der Verwaltung des ADAC als Büroflächen zur Verfügung. Zu ebener Erde liegen die dem unmittelbaren Publikumsverkehr dienenden Abteilungen. Das Zurückgehen von der Bauflucht an der Straßenecke war wegen des hier geplanten U-Bahn-Ausganges erforderlich. Die Aufteilung der Büroflächen durch Glastrennwände ist von dem tragenden Sichtbetonskelett unabhängig. Von den werbend in das Straßenbild eingreifenden Verwaltungsgeschossen sind die vier oberen Stockwerke und das im Anschluß an die Altbebauung zurücktretende Dachgeschoß abgesetzt. Sie enthalten 35 Wohneinheiten unterschiedlicher Größe. Siebzehn Einraumappartements stehen als Gasträume der Verwaltung des ADAC zur Verfügung. Holzfenster und mit Aluminium-Tafeln verkleidete Brüstungen bestimmen die äußere Erscheinung.

The main front of this seven-storey building faces the busy Bundesallee. The two lower floors are allocated as office space for the administrative needs of the ADAC. Those departments providing direct personal service for the public are located at ground level. A proposed exit from the Underground railway made it necessary to place the building well back from the street corner. The glass partitions, dividing the office areas, are independent of the exposed concrete load-bearing frame. The four upper floors, and the roof storey which is recessed and linked to the old building, are detached from the bold street architecture of the office floors. They contain 35 dwellings of various sizes. Seventeen one-room flats are allotted as guest rooms for the administrative staff of the ADAC. Wood-frame windows, and spandrels faced with aluminium panels, characterize the external appearance.

Grundriß Obergeschoß
First floor plan

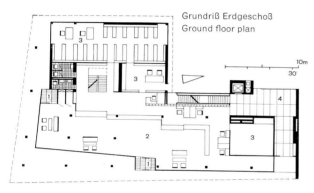

Grundriß Erdgeschoß
Ground floor plan

10m
30'

1 Windfänge / Lobbies
2 Halle / Hall
3 Büros / Offices
4 Eingang und Treppe zu den Wohngeschossen / Entrance and stairs to flats
5 Geschäftsführer / Secretary
6 Erster Vorsitzender / Chairman
7 Büroräume / Offices
8 Sitzungszimmer / Board room
9 Kantine / Canteen

1 Ansicht von dem an der Güntzelstraße liegenden Parkplatz her.
   View from the car park on the Güntzelstrasse.
2 Ansicht von der Bundesallèe. Spiegelglasscheiben in Stahlrahmen trennen die Kundenräume des Erdgeschosses vom Gehsteig.
   View from the Bundesallee. Plate glass windows set in steel frames separate the information offices on the ground floor from the sidewalks (pavement).
3 Ansicht von der Güntzelstraße. Die Staffelung der Wohngeschosse sichert die Besonnung aller Wohnungen.
   View from the Güntzelstrasse. The stepped pattern of the domestic storeys ensures sunshine for every flat.

Bürogebäude für die Ruhrkohlen-Beratung GmbH, Berlin – 1959–60
Architekt: Paul G. R. Baumgarten, Berlin

Office Building for the Ruhr Coal Advisory Board, Berlin – 1959–60
Architect: Paul G. R. Baumgarten, Berlin

1 Nordansicht. Die Stahlbetonbrüstungen sind mit farbig emaillierten Stahlblechelementen verkleidet.
North view. The reinforced concrete units below the windows are faced with enamelled sheet-steel panels.

Das an der Bismarckstraße in Charlottenburg erbaute siebengeschossige Bürogebäude ist auf die besonderen Erfordernisse der Werbung und Schulung abgestimmt. Das Erdgeschoß ist durch große Schaufensterflächen und weitgehende Verwendung von Glastrennwänden von der Straße her voll übersehbar. Um die Eingangshalle sind die Beratungsstelle, ein variabler Ausstellungsraum und die Lehrküche mit Eßraum gruppiert. In einem nach Süden angebauten niedrigen Flügel liegen der Vortragssaal mit 110 Sitzplätzen und zwei Wohnungen. Eine Treppe führt zur Musterheizung im Kellergeschoß. Ein Einblickfenster ermöglicht auch hier die Besichtigung von der Straße aus. Die tragenden Elemente des Stahlbetonbaues bestehen aus den Giebelwandscheiben und einem Kern, der Fahrstühle, Treppe und sanitäre Anlagen enthält. Die dadurch entstehenden stützenfreien Großräume gestatten eine freie Unterteilung der Bürogeschosse.

The seven-storey office building, erected on the Bismarckstrasse in Charlottenburg, is designed to meet the particular needs of publicity and instruction. The ground floor is in full view of the street, thanks to large show windows and extensive use of glass partitions. The advice bureau, an exhibition room with movable partitions and the demonstration kitchen with dining room are grouped about the entrance hall. In a low extension on the South side there are a lecture room with 110 seats and two flats. A staircase leads to the model heating plant in the basement, which can also be inspected from the street through a special window. The load-bearing elements of the reinforced concrete construction consist of solid slab end walls and a core containing the lifts, staircase and service installations. This results in large areas of unobstructed space and flexible planning for the office floors.

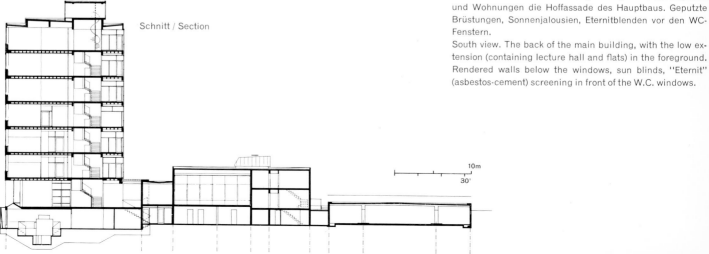

Schnitt / Section

2 Südansicht. Hinter dem niedrigen Flügel mit Vortragssaal und Wohnungen die Hoffassade des Hauptbaus. Geputzte Brüstungen, Sonnenjalousien, Eternitblenden vor den WC-Fenstern.
South view. The back of the main building, with the low extension (containing lecture hall and flats) in the foreground. Rendered walls below the windows, sun blinds, "Eternit" (asbestos-cement) screening in front of the W.C. windows.

10m
30'

3 Eingangshalle im Erdgeschoß mit Blick zum Eßraum.
Entrance hall in the ground floor, through which the dining room can be seen.
4 Treppe in der Eingangshalle.
Stairs in the entrance hall.
5 Vortragssaal. Die Ausbildung von Decke und Wänden entspricht den akustischen Erfordernissen.
Lecture hall. Acoustic requirements dictated the treatment of walls and ceiling.

1 Eingangshalle / Entrance hall
2 Empfang / Reception
3 Ausstellung / Exhibition
4 Beratung / Advice bureau
5 Eßraum / Dining room
6 Lehrküche / Demonstration kitchen
7 Vortragssaal / Lecture hall
8 Wohnungen / Flats
9 Durchfahrt / Vehicle entrance
10 Garagenrampe / Garage ramp
11 Parkplatz / Parking

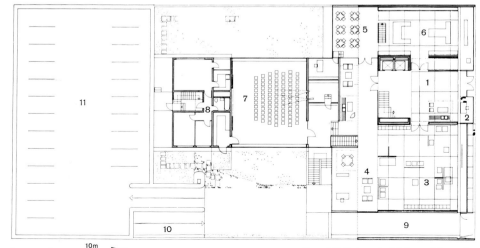

Grundriß Bürogeschoß / Typical office floor

10m
30'

Grundriß Erdgeschoß / Ground floor plan

Technisches Betriebsgebäude der August-Thyssen-Hütte AG, Duisburg-Hamborn – 1957
Architekt: Gerhard Weber, München und Frankfurt am Main

Technical building for the August Thyssen Foundry Co., Duisburg-Hamborn – 1957
Architect: Gerhard Weber, Munich and Frankfort-on-Main

1 Ausschnitt aus der Südwestfassade. Im Erdgeschoß die Eingangshalle.
  Detail of South-West façade. Entrance hall (on ground floor).

Die August-Thyssen-Hütte AG baute auf ihrem Werksgelände inmitten einer Parkanlage ein Betriebsverwaltungsgebäude für die technischen Abteilungen. Unter Beachtung der in Bergschadengebieten notwendigen konstruktiven Forderungen wurde über einem als Betonkasten ausgebildeten Kellergeschoß ein Stahlskelett errichtet. Die zweibündigen Obergeschosse sind durch einen Verkehrs- und Installationskern in der Mitte des Gebäudes erschlossen. Die Stützweite von 7,20 Metern wurde aus dem Mehrfachen eines Zeichentischplatzes entwickelt. Die an der Außenseite und im Erdgeschoß unverkleideten Stahlstützen sind in den Innenräumen ummantelt. Die Fassadenkonstruktion besteht aus Stahlrahmenprofilen mit Wendeflügelfenstern. Die starke Staubentwicklung der nahen Industrie zwang zur Ausbildung einer glatten Außenhaut. In den Brüstungsteil sind schwarze hinterlüftete Glasscheiben eingesetzt.

The August-Thyssen Company has erected an office building to house the firm's technical sections on adjacent parkland belonging to the works. In deference to the special structural needs of an area liable to mining subsidence, a steel skeleton has been constructed over a basement designed as a concrete caisson. The upper storeys are served by a traffic and service core in the middle of the building. The interval of 23′ 6″ between stanchions was developed from the multiple tasks of a drawing office. Exposed on the ground floor and on the outside walls, the steel stanchions covered in the interior of the building. The elevations consist of steel-framed sections with vertically centre-hung windows. Pollution from industrial dust demanded a smooth external skin. Black glass infill panels are inserted below the windows.

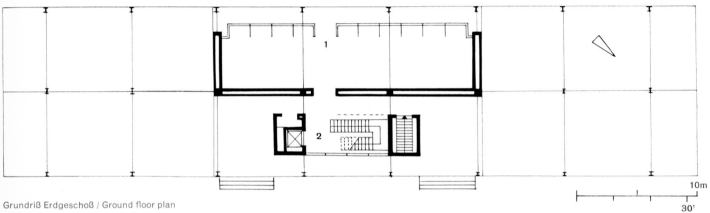

Grundriß der drei Obergeschosse / Floor plan of the three upper storeys

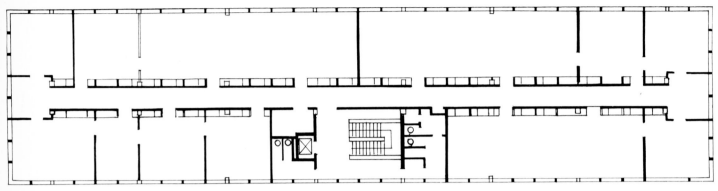

Grundriß Erdgeschoß / Ground floor plan
1 Eingangshalle / Entrance hall
2 Treppe und Aufzug / Stairs and lift

10m
30'

2 Südwestansicht von der Straße her.
  South-West view from road.

3 Nordostfassade.
  North-East façade.
4 Eingangshalle im Erdgeschoß.
  Entrance hall on the ground floor.
5 Schmalseite von Nordwesten. Das freie Erdgeschoß dient zur
  gelegentlichen Ausstellung von Hüttenerzeugnissen.
  Narrow side from the North-West. The open ground floor is
  used for occasional exhibitions of the foundry's products.

Landeshaus in Köln – 1956–59
Architekten: Eckhardt Schulze-Fielitz und Ernst von Rudloff, Essen, mit Ulrich S. von Altenstadt

Provincial Government Building, Cologne – 1956–59
Architects: Eckhardt Schulze-Fielitz and Ernst von Rudloff, Essen; Assistant: Ulrich S. von Altenstadt

1 Südlicher Teil der Ostfassade. Im Erdgeschoß links der Kern mit den Sitzungssälen, rechts die offene Passage um den Innenhof.
Southern part of the East façade. Left, ground floor, the core with comittee rooms; right, the open passage round the internal court.
2 Blick über den Rhein auf die Ostfassade.
View across the river Rhine towards the East façade.

Das Verwaltungsgebäude des Landschaftsverbandes Rheinland wurde nach dem mit einem zweiten Preis ausgezeichneten Wettbewerbsentwurf am Deutzer Rheinufer gegenüber der Kölner Innenstadt errichtet. Seine vier Trakte schließen einen geräumigen Innenhof ein. Die Büroräume der vier Obergeschosse sind durch vier in den Ecken angeordnete Treppenhäuser erschlossen. Die unbelichteten Mittelzonen der tiefen Nord- und Südtrakte werden als Aktenräume und Magazine genutzt. Im ebenerdigen Stützengeschoß ist nur der Nordflügel mit dem Haupteingang und der Südflügel mit Sitzungssälen ausgebaut. Grünstreifen ziehen sich vom Rheinufer zwischen den Stützpfeilern hindurch bis zum Innenhof. Die tragende Konstruktion ist ein Stahlbetonskelett über einem Stützenraster von 7 × 7 Metern. Die massiven Wände der Aufzüge und Treppen versteifen die Konstruktion. Die Außenhaut ist aus grauen Aluminium-Fensterelementen mit dunkelblauen Opakglasbrüstungen montiert.

The administration building of the Rheinland provincial union, a second prize competition design, was erected on the Deutz side of the Rhein, facing the city centre of Cologne. Its four blocks enclose a spacious quadrangle, the offices of the four upper storeys being served by four stair towers placed at each corner. The windowless middle sections of the deeper North and South blocks are used for filing cabinets and storerooms. Of the pillared ground floor, only the North wing with the main entrance and the South wing containing committee rooms have been built for occupation. Ribands of green stretch from the Rhein bank and between the piers to the inner court. The load-bearing elements consist of a reinforced concrete frame erected on a 23 × 23-foot grid. The solid walls of the lift and stair towers provide reinforcement. The external skin comprises grey aluminum window units and dark blue opaque glass spandrels.

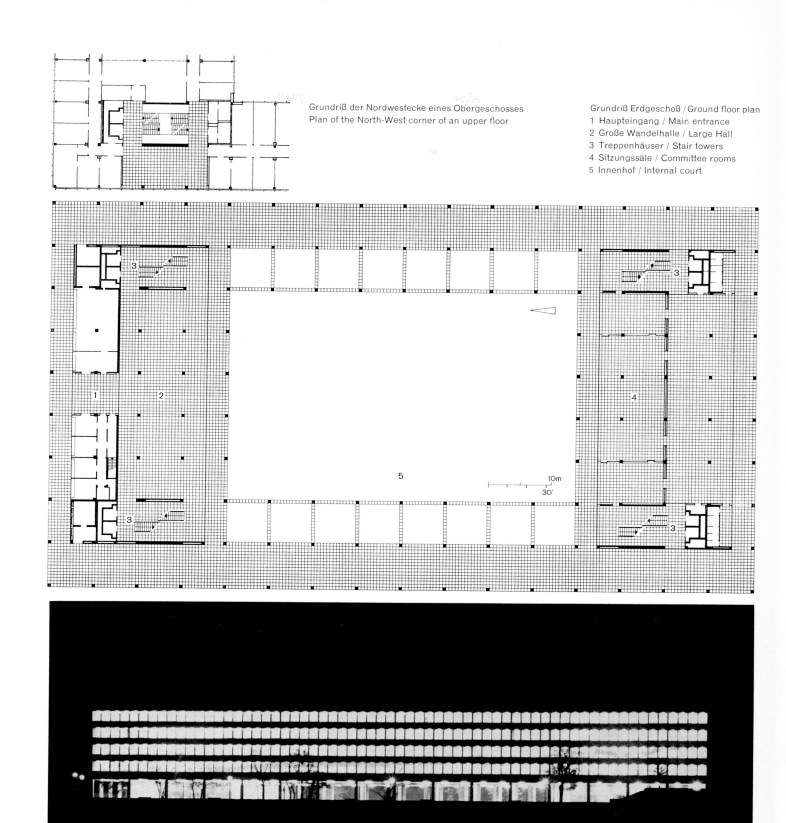

Grundriß der Nordwestecke eines Obergeschosses
Plan of the North-West corner of an upper floor

Grundriß Erdgeschoß / Ground floor plan
1 Haupteingang / Main entrance
2 Große Wandelhalle / Large Hall
3 Treppenhäuser / Stair towers
4 Sitzungssäle / Committee rooms
5 Innenhof / Internal court

10m
30'

3 Nordfassade mit dem Haupteingang und Blick zur Kölner Altstadt.
North façade with main entrance, and view towards the old city of Cologne.

4 Fassadenausschnitt mit nach außen geklappten Ausstellfenstern.
Detail of the façade with top-hung windows opening outwards.

5 Die Treppen und Podeste der vier Haupttreppenhäuser sind mit Nirosta-Stählen an den Unterzügen der Dachdecke aufgehängt.
Stairs and landings of the four main staircases are suspended from the roof joists on slim stainless steel struts.

Landtagsgebäude in Stuttgart – 1959–61
Architekten: Horst Linde, Erwin Heinle, Achim Kießling, Hans Schmidberger, Bernhard Winkler

Provincial Parliament Building, Stuttgart – 1959–61
Architects: Horst Linde, Erwin Heinle, Achim Kießling, Hans Schmidberger, Bernhard Winkler

Der auf quadratischem Grundriß (54 × 54 m) errichtete Baukörper steht zwischen Schloß und Staatstheater frei in einer Grünzone, in die er sich mit seiner kupferbraunen Fassade gut einfügt. Den größten Teil des Erdgeschosses nimmt die Eingangshalle ein, an die sich auf der einen Seite das Restaurant, auf der anderen Sprechzimmer und Büroräume anschließen. Im Zentrum der beiden Obergeschosse liegt der Plenarsaal, dessen Form, Größe und Ausstattung durch die Forderung bestimmt war, daß bei Debatten jeder Abgeordnete von seinem Platz aus im ganzen Saal zu verstehen sein mußte. Als Wandverkleidung sind hohlliegende Holzplatten verwendet. Die Galerie im zweiten Obergeschoß ist Pressevertretern und Zuschauern vorbehalten. Um den Plenarsaal sind an den Außenseiten des Gebäudes die Sitzungs-, Besprechungs- und Arbeitszimmer der Abgeordneten angeordnet. Die Tragkonstruktion besteht aus Stahlbeton mit einem Stützenabstand von 9 m.

Erected on a square ground plan (177′ × 177′), this free-standing block lies between the castle and municipal theatre in a green zone, where its copper-coloured façade fits sympathetically. Most of the ground floor is occupied by the entrance hall, which is connected on one side to the restaurant and, on the other, to members' rooms and offices. In the centre of the two upper stories lies the general assembly hall, its shape, size and equipment designed to ensure that in debates every member can be heard from his particular place in the chamber. For the internal walls hollow-backed wood panels are used. The gallery accommodates the press and public. Members' committee and consulting rooms and offices are ranged about the assembly hall and along the sides of the building. The load-bearing construction is reinforced concrete supported at 30′ intervals.

Schnitt / Section

1 Eingangshalle / Entrance hall
2 Restaurant
3 Garderobe / Cloakroom
4 Presse / Press
5 Abgeordneten-Sprechzimmer / Members' consulting
  rooms
6 Verwaltung / Administration
7 Plenarsaal / Assembly Hall
8 Radio und Fernsehen / Radio and TV
9 Wandelhalle / Lobby
10 Ministerrat / Council of Ministers
11 Sitzungssaal / Comittee Room
12 Verwaltung, Archiv und Bibliothek
   Administration, records, library
13 Landtagspräsident / President of Parliament
14 Abgeordneten-Arbeitszimmer, Fraktions- und Besprechungszimmer / Members' offices, and rooms for party
   groups, conference and interview
15 Zuschauer- und Pressegalerie / Public and Press gallery
16 Obere Wandelhalle / Upper lobby
17 Regierungsvertreter / Government representatives

Grundriß Erdgeschoß
Ground floor plan

Grundriß 1. Obergeschoß
1st floor plan

Grundriß 2. Obergeschoß
2nd floor plan

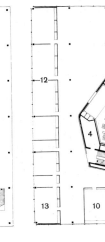

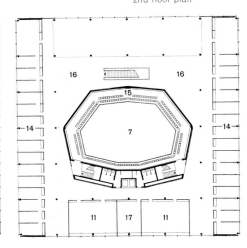

160

2 Blick in die durch zwei Geschosse gehende Wandelhalle im ersten Obergeschoß. Plastik von Marino Marini.
Glimpse into the two-storey-high lobby on the first floor. Sculpture by Marino Marini.

3 Eingangshalle mit Abgeordnetentreppe zur Wandelhalle im ersten Obergeschoß. Boden aus graugelben Travertinplatten, Rückwand aus Schiefer mit eingelassenen Versteinerungen.
Entrance hall, showing members' stairs to the first-floor lobby. The floor is composed of yellow-grey travertine slabs; the wall behind is slate with stone insets.

4 Nordansicht vom Staatstheater aus, rechts das Neue Schloß. Vorgehängte Fassade aus Bronze mit festverglasten Fenstern und wärmeabsorbierendem, graubraunem Glas. Außenstützen als Pendelstützen ausgebildet.
North view from the municipal theatre; right, the New Castle. Bronze curtain-walled façade with sealed windows of greyish brown heat-absorbent glass.

5 Nachtansicht der Eingangsseite. In den Obergeschossen sind die durch Zwischenwände abgeteilten Abgeordneten- und Besprechungszimmer zu erkennen. Im Mittelteil des Erdgeschosses die in ganzer Gebäudetiefe durchgehende Eingangshalle, rechts das Restaurant.
Night view of the entrance front. The members' offices and consulting rooms, separated by partitions, can be seen on the upper floors. In the middle of the ground floor, the entrance hall extending to the full depth of the building; on the right, the restaurant.

Allgemeine Ortskrankenkasse, Groß-Gerau – 1956–57
Architekten: Fritz Novotny und Otto Hoschak, Offenbach

Local health insurance building, Gross-Gerau – 1956–57
Architects: Fritz Novotny and Otto Hoschak, Offenbach

Die Büros der zweigeschossigen Krankenkasse sind um einen Gartenhof von 14,0 × 5,5 m angeordnet. Im Kellergeschoß, über eine Rampe zu erreichen, sind außer den Räumen für Registratur und Archiv ein Baubüro, ein Pfandgutraum, die Wohnung des Hausmeisters und Garagen untergebracht. Hier liegt auch der Eingang für die Angestellten mit Garderoben und Waschräumen. Erd- und Obergeschoß kragen im Süden und Norden über die Kellermauern aus. Eine Freitreppe führt zum Haupteingang, der an der Ostseite dem Gebäude vorgesetzt ist. Das Erdgeschoß enthält die Schalterhalle und Büros, das Obergeschoß Arzträume, Direktion und Sitzungssaal. Die Außenwände an der Nord- und Südseite und die Hoffassaden sind vollständig verglast. Zur Reinigung der Fenster sind balkonartige Laufgänge angebracht, die auf der Südseite zugleich einen Sonnenschutz bieten. Die geschlossenen Ost- und Westfassaden sind nur von schmalen Fensterbändern durchbrochen.

The offices of the two-storey building are arranged about a garden quadrangle 46′ × 18′ in size. The basement, reached by a ramp, contains the caretaker's flat and garages, as well as registration and record offices, etc. The employees' entrance, with cloakrooms and lavatories, is also located here. The ground floor and upper storey project South and North beyond the external walls of the basement. An open staircase leads to the main entrance, which is on the East side of the building. The ground floor accommodates the counter hall and offices, while the storey above houses doctors' consulting rooms, and administration and committee rooms. The external walls on the North and South sides and those facing the internal court are completely glazed. For window cleaning, balcony-like galleries are used, and these also provide sun-protection on the South side. The East and West fronts have no openings apart from narrow ribbon windows.

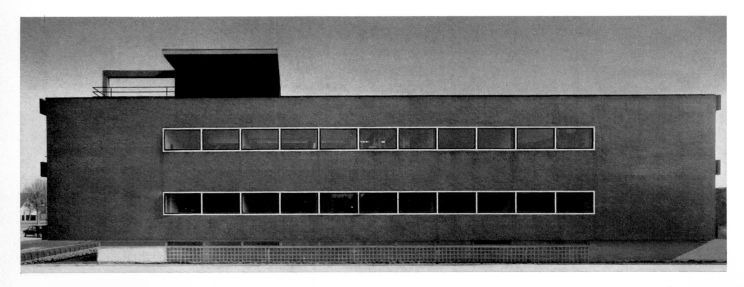

1 Ansicht vom Markt (Nordfassade), links der Anbau mit Eingang.
View from the market (North façade). Left, annexe and
entrance.
2 Westfassade.
West façade.

3 Modell (1 Haupteingang, 2 Schalterhalle, 3 Büros, 4 Innenhof,
5 Treppen).
Model (1 Main entrance, 2 Counter hall, 3 Offices, 4 Internal
court, 5 Stairs).
4 Blick vom ersten Stock in den Gartenhof.
View from the upper floor into the garden quadrangle (internal court).
5 Obergeschoßflur mit Treppe.
Upper floor passage and staircase.
6 Schalterhalle.
Counter Hall.

1 Fassadenausschnitt mit Haupteingang. Die Fenster sind mit Ausnahme der schmalen Schwingflügel fest verglast.
Detail of façade, showing main entrance. Apart from the small, horizontally centre-hung, lights, the windows are sealed.

Das fünfgeschossige Gebäude ist für die Geschäftsleitung und die Konstruktionsbüros des Stahlbauwerks bestimmt. Die Geschosse weisen nur die unbedingt notwendigen Abtrennungen auf und werden im übrigen durch bewegliche Schallschluckwände in Augenhöhe gegliedert. Der Festpunkt aus Stahlbeton, der die Windkräfte aufnimmt, enthält alle Verkehrselemente. Die frei vor der Außenwand stehenden Stützen wurden als Pendelstützen ausgebildet und sind, der Produktion des Werkes entsprechend, aus Stahl. Zu der lebhaften Fassadengliederung tragen vor allem die durchgehend umlaufenden Balkons bei. Sie erlauben eine leichte Reinigung der Fenster von außen und ermöglichten es, die elektrisch bedienten Sonnenstores 1 m vor der Fensterwand anzubringen. Der Sonnenschutz, ein bei dem verhältnismäßig heißen Klima der Oberrhein-Ebene wichtiges Problem, ist daher besonders wirksam, zugleich entsteht blendungsfreies Licht. Die Farbgebung des Gebäudes ist in Schwarz, Grau und Weiß gehalten.

The 5-storey building is intended for the construction offices and management of the steel works. Division of floor space is confined to an absolute minimum, movable sound-proof partitions of eye height being used. The reinforced concrete structural core, which absorbs wind loads, contains all traffic ways. The hinged stanchions, which rise unhampered in front of the external face, are steel, as befits the firm's products. The continuous balconies contribute greatly to the lively pattern of the façade, while making window-cleaning from the outside simple and enabling the electrically operated sun blinds to be placed a full yard in front of the windows. Sun-protection, an important matter in the comparatively hot climate of the Upper Rhine plain, is thus particularly effective and, at the same time, light is provided without dazzle. The colour scheme of the building is black, grey and white.

2 Fassadendetail mit halb herabgelassenen Sonnenschutzlamellen.
   Detail of façade, with sun blinds half lowered.
3 Gesamtansicht der Eingangsseite.
   General view of entrance front.

Grundriß Normalgeschoß mit flexiblen Stellwänden
Typical floor plan with movable partitions

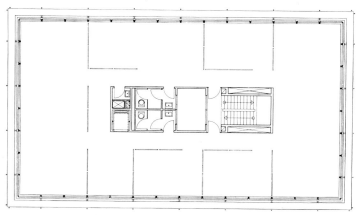

5m
15'

Verwaltungsgebäude der Essener Steinkohlenbergwerke, Essen – 1960
Architekt: Egon Eiermann, Karlsruhe

Headquarters for Essen Coal Mines, Essen – 1960
Architect: Egon Eiermann, Karlsruhe

1 Ansicht des achtgeschossigen Flügels mit Haupteingang.
View of the 8-storey block, with main entrance.

Der Neubau der Steinkohlenbergwerke, in der Essener Innenstadt an der Kreuzung einer Hauptstraße mit dem Ruhrschnellweg gelegen, nimmt Verwaltung und technische Abteilungen der verschiedenen Werkszechen auf. Aufgabe war ein erweiterungsfähiger Bau, der repräsentativen Aufwand vermeidet und eine äußerst ökonomische Lösung darstellt. Das achtgeschossige Hauptgebäude, eine zweibündige Anlage mit Einzelbüros, wird durch zwei Festpunkte erschlossen, die zugleich die Gelenke zu den Seitenflügeln bilden. Der Anbau, der die Verkaufsgesellschaften mit getrennter Organisation beherbergt, besitzt einen weiteren Festpunkt mit Verkehrselementen. Ein geplanter zweiter Seitenflügel soll im Untergeschoß Küche und Kantine enthalten und vom Treppenhaus des Hauptgebäudes aus bedient werden. Der Bau wurde als Stahlbetonskelett errichtet, die Fassadenverkleidung besteht aus schwarzen Keramikplatten.

The new Coal Mines building, erected in the central district of Essen at the crossing of a main road and the Ruhr motorway, accommodates the administrative offices and technical departments of various pits. The requirement was a building capable of extension, which avoided prestige features and offered an extremely economical solution. The 8-storey main building, laid out as two rows of individual offices, is served by two structural (solid) cores, which also provide links with the side wings. One such annexe, which houses the sales associations with their separate organization, has a structural core of its own with traffic ways. A proposed second wing will contain a kitchen and canteen on the ground floor, and be served by the stair tower of the main building. The construction is reinforced concrete frame. The external cladding consists of black ceramic tiles.

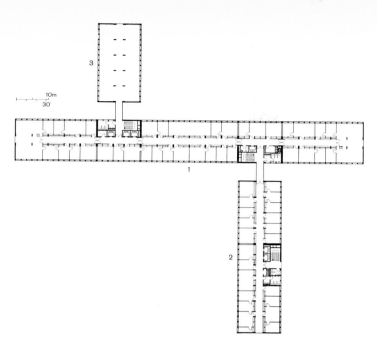

Grundriß 1. Obergeschoß / First floor plan

1 Hauptgebäude für Zechenverwaltungen und technische Abteilungen / Main building for pit administration and technical departments
2 Seitenflügel für die Verkaufsgesellschaften / Annexe for sales associates
3 Geplanter Erweiterungsbau mit Küche und Kantine im Untergeschoß / Proposed extension with kitchen and canteen on ground floor

2 Detail der Fassade mit Dehnungsfuge und Öffnungen für die Belüftung von Transformatorenaggregaten, die sich für jedes Geschoß in den Festpunkten befinden. Der Hauptbau erhielt vier Dehnungsfugen, der Seitenflügel eine, da wegen der benachbarten Bergbaugebiete die Gefahr von Erschütterungen besteht.
Detail of façade, with expansion joint, and ventilator openings for transformer units, which are located on each floor in the structural core. The main building has four expansion joints, and the annexe one, since there is a risk of subsidence owing to the proximity of mining areas.

3 Blick entlang des Hauptgebäudes auf den Seitenflügel. Eine verglaste Spange stellt die Verbindung zwischen beiden Bauten her.
Looking along the main building towards the annexe. A glazed bridge links the two blocks.

4 Konferenzsaal mit Blick auf den Dachgarten im 7. Obergeschoß des Hauptbaus.
Conference room, with a view of the roof garden on the 7th floor of the main building.

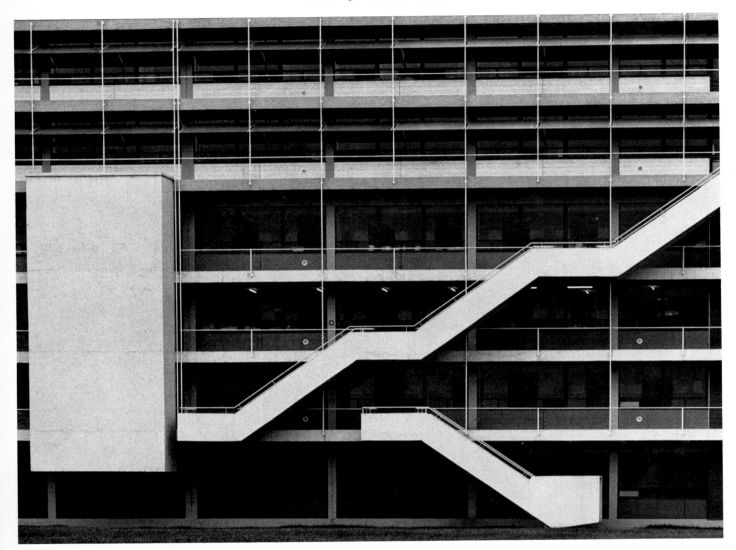

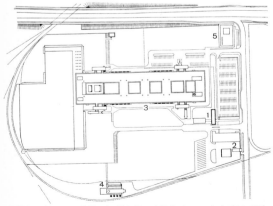

1 Pförtnerhaus und Kontrollstation / Gate-keeper's lodge and check point. 2 Garagen und Tankstelle / Garages and filling station. 3 Versandhaus und Verwaltungsgebäude / Mail-order and administration building. 4 Kesselhaus / Boiler house. 5 Kaufhaus / Store.

Die umfangreiche Anlage im Osten der Stadt umfaßt außer einem im Bau befindlichen Kaufhaus, dem Kesselhaus und einer Reihe kleiner Gebäude ein 257 m langes und 65 m breites Hauptgebäude für Versand und Verwaltung. Dem Stahlbetonskelettbau liegt ein 6×6 m-Raster zugrunde, das größte Freizügigkeit erlaubt. Alle Elemente, die nicht auf diesem Raster aufgebaut sind, wurden als selbständige Bauglieder nach außen gelegt: Treppentürme, Trafostationen, Wasserbehälter, Luftstationen für die Versorgung der Versandgeschosse mit Frischluft, sanitäre Anlagen. Die um das Gebäude geführten Umgänge dienen zusammen mit den frei vorgehängten Nottreppen im Falle eines Brandes als Fluchtweg für die 3000 Angestellten. Die beiden obersten Stockwerke sind für die Verwaltung bestimmt und werden durch vier Innenhöfe aufgelockert.

Besides a department store in course of construction, the boiler house and a number of small buildings, this extensive scheme on the East side of the city comprises a main block for mail-order business and administration approximately 840′ long and 210′ wide. The reinforced concrete frame is based on a 20′ square grid, which allows the greatest flexibility. All elements, not erected on this grid, form external free-standing features: stair towers, transformer sub-stations, water tanks, ventilation units for circulating fresh air to the mail-order floors, and sanitary installations. The balconies extending round the building are connected to the emergency stairs suspended in the open, and provide escape ways for the 3,000 employees in case of fire. Four internal courts open up the two top storeys allotted to administration.

168

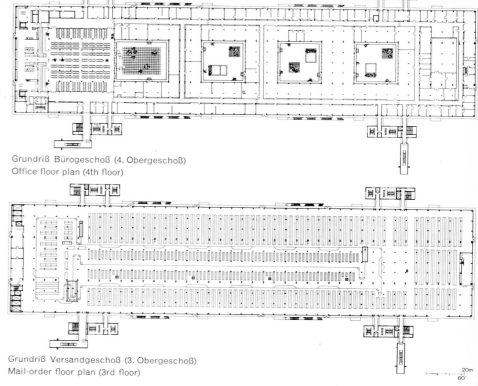

◁ 1 Fassadenausschnitt mit einer der zwölf Luftstationen und Nottreppe.
Detail of façade with one of the 12 ventilating
units and emergency stairs.

Grundriß Bürogeschoß (4. Obergeschoß)
Office floor plan (4th floor)

2 Südansicht des Hauptgebäudes.
South view of main building.
3 Ostansicht mit Kesselhaus, Pförtnerhaus und
Hauptgebäude.
East view, with boiler house, gate-keeper's lodge
and main building.

Grundriß Versandgeschoß (3. Obergeschoß)
Mail-order floor plan (3rd floor)

20m
60'

4 Westansicht. Der Beton ist grau gestrichen, die Brüstungen der unteren Geschosse blau, der Bürogeschosse weiß. Die kunststoffbeschichteten Sonnensegel sind gelb.
West view. The concrete is painted grey, the spandrels of the lower floors blue, the office storeys white. The plastic sun blinds are yellow.

5 Verglaster Übergang vom Hauptgebäude zu einem der Treppentürme.
Glazed access ways to one of the stair towers.

6 Innenhof auf dem Niveau des vierten Obergeschosses.
Internal court at 4th floor level.

7 Das Kesselhaus von Norden. Im Kesselhaus sind vier Groß-
kessel für Heißwasser aufgestellt. Brennstoff ist Gaskoks, der
aus dem nahe gelegenen städtischen Gaswerk bezogen wird.
Boiler house (from the North), in which four large boilers for
hot water are installed. The fuel is coke from the municipal
gas works nearby.

8 Blick ins Kesselhaus. Die Ummantelung der Kessel ist blau
emailliert.
Glimpse into boiler house. The boiler casing is enamelled
blue.

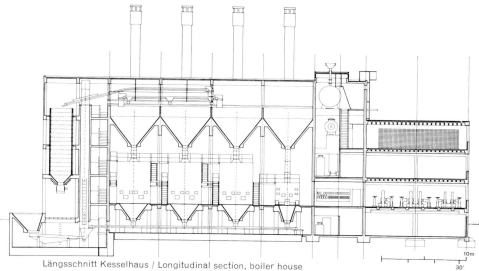

Längsschnitt Kesselhaus / Longitudinal section, boiler house

10m
30'

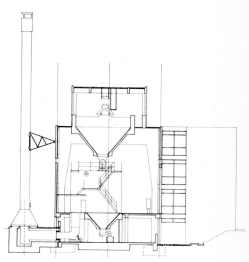

Querschnitt Kesselhaus / Cross-section, boiler house

Verwaltungs- und Betriebsgebäude für das Nordwest-Lotto in Münster – 1960
Architekt: Harald Deilmann, Münster

Offices for North-West Lotteries, Münster – 1960
Architect: Harald Deilmann, Münster

Das Erdgeschoß des Verwaltungstraktes enthält die Eingangshalle und die Räume für den Personalverkehr. Über drei Büroetagen liegen im vierten Obergeschoß Direktion und Sitzungssäle mit einem kleinen Dachgarten. Im Erdgeschoß des niedrigen Betriebsgebäudes sind die Lagerräume für die Spielscheine, Kontrollstellen, Garderoben und die Kantine untergebracht. Im Obergeschoß arbeiten 1500 bis 2000 Mitarbeiter in vier Sälen an der Auswertung. Jeweils zwei Säle können durch Zurückschieben einer Faltwand zusammengelegt werden. Die Säle werden von einer einzigen Verteilerzentrale mit Scheinen beschickt und von einer Kabine im Schnittpunkt der Trennwände aus überwacht. Vier Treppenhäuser treten aus den Längswänden heraus; eines von ihnen verbindet das Betriebsgebäude mit dem Verwaltungsbau. Überdachte Zugangswege und ein kleiner Garagenbau, dessen Obergeschoß zwei Wohnungen aufnimmt, ergänzen die Anlage.

The ground floor of the administration block contains the entrance hall and staff rooms. The fourth storey with a small roof garden, above three floors of offices, accommodates the management and board rooms. Storage space for tickets, control points, cloakrooms and a canteen occupy the ground floor of the low operations building. On the upper storey 1,500 to 2,000 employees in four large rooms are engaged in checking tickets. Each pair of rooms can be formed into one by retracting a folding partition. These rooms are fed with tickets from a single distribution centre and are supervised from a cabin straddling the line of the partitions. Four stair towers project from the longitudinal walls, one of them linking the operations building with the administration block. Covered access ways and a small garage building with two flats on the upper floor complete the scheme.

Grundriß Erdgeschoß / Ground floor plan
 1 Eingangshalle / Entrance hall
 2 Wartehalle / Waiting room
 3 Garderobe / Cloakroom
 4 Kantine / Canteen
 5 Anrichte, Ausgabe / Servery
 6 Spüle / Scullery
 7 Tresors / Strong rooms
 8 Adrema / Adrema computers
 9 Druckerei / Printing
10 Auswertungssaal / Ticket-checking room
11 Garagen / Garages
12 Wasserbecken / Pool

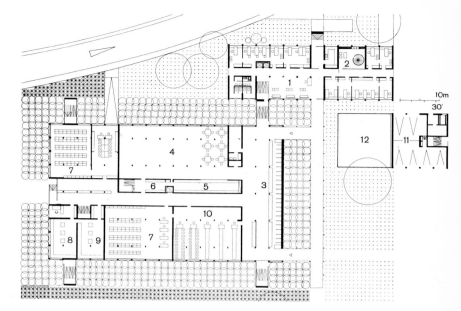

1 Ansicht von Osten. Links das Betriebsgebäude, rechts der
  Garagenbau, dahinter der fünfgeschossige Verwaltungstrakt.
  View from the East. Left, the operations building; right, the
  garage block; behind the 5-storey administration wing.
2 Modellaufnahme von der Ostseite.
  Photo of model, seen from the East.
3 Betriebsgebäude von Südosten mit den herausgezogenen
  Treppenhäusern.
  South-East view of the operations building with its prominent
  stair towers.

173

4 Zugang von der Ostseite. Sichtbeton, schwarz glasierte Ziegelverblendung und das Aluminium der Fenster, Jalousien und Dächer bestimmen die farbige Erscheinung des Äußeren. In dem rechteckigen Wasserbecken zwischen Vordach und Garagenbau steht eine Plastik von Bernhard Heiliger.
Entrance from the East. Exposed concrete, the black glazed brick skin, and the aluminium of the window frames, sunblinds and roofs characterize the external colour effect. A sculpture by Bernhard Heiliger stands in the rectangular pool between the canopy and garage building.
5 Wendeltreppe im Verwaltungsgebäude.
Spiral staircase in the administration block.

Schnitt durch Verwaltungstrakt und Betriebsgebäude
Section through the administration and operations blocks

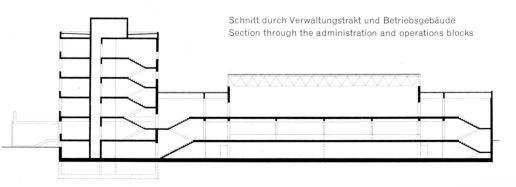

6 Zwei Auswertungssäle im Betriebsgebäude, durch Zurück-
klappen der mittleren Faltwand zusammengelegt. Die Säle
sind mit einem Tragwerk aus geschweißten Stahlrohren
überspannt und durch seitliche Oberlichtstreifen erhellt.
Two ticket-checking rooms in the operations block combined
by retracting the central folding partition. The rooms are
spanned by a framework of welded steel tubes and lit by
ribbon windows along the top of the side walls.

7 Sitzungssaal.
Board room.

Verwaltungsgebäude der Unterharzer Berg- und Hüttenwerke in Goslar – 1957–58
Architekt: Friedrich Wilhelm Kraemer, Braunschweig

Office building for the Unterharzer Berg- und Hüttenwerke, Goslar – 1957–58
Architect: Friedrich Wilhelm Kraemer, Brunswick

1 Eingangsfassade des Haupttraktes.
Entrance front of the principal block.

Als Gewinner des im Jahre 1951 ausgeschriebenen Wettbewerbes wurde F. W. Kraemer mit der weiteren Bearbeitung beauftragt. Die Schwierigkeit der Aufgabe lag in der Eingliederung des Gebäudes in die Grünzone am Rande der im Krieg unzerstört gebliebenen Altstadt von Goslar. Der hohe Haupttrakt wurde auf Stützen gestellt. Ein erdgeschossiger, um zwei Innenhöfe gruppierter Atriumflügel mit dem großen Sitzungssaal ist auf der Westseite an die verglaste Eingangshalle angeschlossen. Damit wurde eine Abriegelung der Parklandschaft durch die großen Baumassen vermieden. Über den fünf dreibündig angelegten Bürogeschossen ist das verglaste Dachgeschoß zurückgesetzt. Es enthält einen Erfrischungsraum und ein Sitzungszimmer. Alle konstruktiven Teile, das Dachgeschoß ausgenommen, bestehen aus Stahlbeton. An den Fassaden sind zwischen die Pendelstützen aus Betonwerkstein wandhohe Fensterelemente mit emaillierten Brüstungspaneelen gesetzt.

Winner of the competition held in 1951, F. W. Kraemer was commissioned to carry out the scheme. The difficulty lay in fitting the building into the green belt on the periphery of the old town of Goslar, which was not damaged during the war. The high, principal, block was placed on stilts. At ground level, a wing grouped about two internal courts, containing the large conference room, is linked on the West side to the glazed entrance hall. By this arrangement it was possible to avoid obscuring the country side by large building masses. Stepped back, above the five office floors, a glass walled roof storey is constructed, comprising a canteen and small conference room. All structural members, except those of the roof storey, are of reinforced concrete. The façades have storey-high window units with enamelled panels between the hinged stanchions.

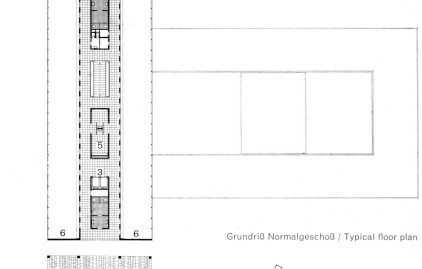

Grundriß Normalgeschoß / Typical floor plan

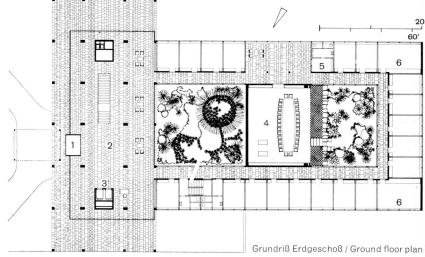

1 Windfang / Porch
2 Eingangshalle / Entrance hall
3 Aufzüge / Lifts
4 Sitzungssaal / Conference room
5 Garderoben / Cloakrooms
6 Büros / Offices

Grundriß Erdgeschoß / Ground floor plan

2 Gesamtansicht der Anlage im Modell.
General view (model).

3 Die verglasten Wände des Erfrischungsraumes im Dachgeschoß geben den Blick auf die Altstadt frei.
The glazed walls of the canteen on the roof offer an uninter-
rupted view of the old town.

4 Ansicht von Südwesten. Über dem niedrigen Atriumflügel
erhebt sich der Haupttrakt. Die geschlossenen Fassadenteile
sind in Betonwerkstein ausgeführt.
View from the South-West, with the main block rising above
the low "court" wing. The solid elements of the façades are
composed of a crushed stone and concrete aggregate.

5 Eingangsvordach und Windfang.
Entrance canopy and porch.

6 Blick vom Windfang in die Eingangshalle und zum Innenhof,
der von eingeschossigen Bauten umschlossen ist.
View into entrance hall and internal court, which is enclosed
by a single-storey structure.

7 Ansicht von Nordwesten.
View from North-West.

8 Blick aus dem großen Sitzungssaal in den Gartenhof.
View from the large conference room into the garden court.

Zentralamt des Deutschen Wetterdienstes in Offenbach am Main – 1955–57
Architekt: Paulfriedrich Posenenske, Offenbach am Main

Central Office of the German meteorological service, Offenbach–on–Main – 1955–57
Architect: Paulfriedrich Posenenske, Offenbach-on-Main

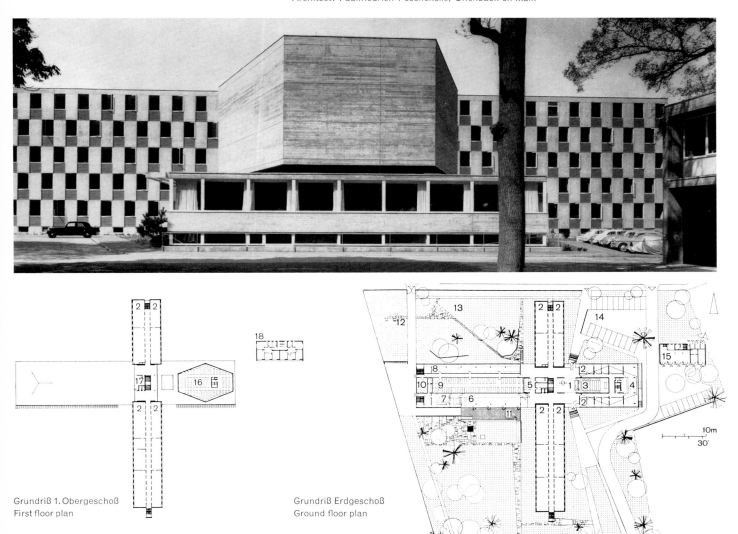

Grundriß 1. Obergeschoß
First floor plan

Grundriß Erdgeschoß
Ground floor plan

Ein fünfgeschossiger Haupttrakt wird von einem eingeschossigen breiteren Querflügel durchdrungen. Im Schnittpunkt liegen Eingangshalle und Haupttreppenhaus, Aufzüge und Toiletten. Der Haupttrakt enthält Büros sowie im vierten Obergeschoß die Wetternachrichten- und Sendezentrale. Der niedrige, dreibündige Querflügel nimmt Lesesaal, Hollerithabteilung, Speisesaal und Küche auf. Im mittleren Bund dieses Flügels liegen vollklimatisierte Archivräume und ein Hörsaal für 100 Personen. Über dem östlichen Flachbau erhebt sich der dreigeschossige, sechseckige Bücherspeicher. Die Stahlfenster des Haupttraktes sind in der armierten Außenwand von Geschoß zu Geschoß versetzt. Der farbig gestrichene Sichtbeton ist auf der Innenseite mit Ytongplatten isoliert. Im verglasten Haupttreppenhaus sind die Stützen nach innen gelegt. Die gleiche Konstruktion ermöglicht im Flachbau eine durchgehende Fensterfront.

A five-storey main building is pierced at right angles by a wider, single-floor, cross-wing. The entrance hall, main staircase, lifts and lavatories are grouped at the place of intersection. The main building contains offices, the weather information and broadcasting centre being on the fourth floor; the lower cross-wing houses the reading room, computer department, the canteen, and kitchens. Fully air-conditioned record rooms and an auditorium for 100 people occupy the middle area. Above the low structure on the East side rises a three-storey, hexagonal, book stack. Steel-framed windows alternate with the reinforced concrete external cladding from floor to floor. The exposed, colourwashed, concrete is insulated on the inside by ytong panels. The stanchions of the glass-fronted main staircase block are placed inside, and similar methods of construction in the low wing make possible continuous ribbon windows.

180

1 Eingangshalle / Entrance hall
2 Büroräume / Office space
3 Hörsaal / Auditorium
4 Lesesaal / Reading room
5 Garderobe / Cloakrooms
6 Speisesaal / Canteen
7 Küche / Kitchen
8 Hollerithabteilung / Computer department
9 Lochkartenarchiv / Punched card records
10 Klimaanlage / Ventilation plant
11 Terrasse / Terrace
12 Wetterstation / Weather station
13 Beobachtungswiese / Observation field
14 Parkplatz / Parking
15 Garagen / Garages
16 Büchermagazin / Book stack
17 Toiletten / Lavatories
18 Wohnungen / Two flats

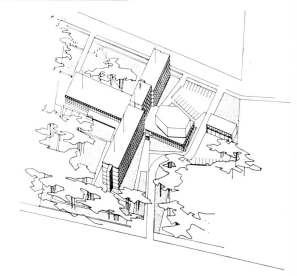

1 Ansicht von Osten. Im Vordergrund das Büchermagazin über dem Lesesaal.
  East view. In the foreground, the book stack over the reading room.
2 Der Haupttrakt von Südwesten.
  The main building from the South-West.
3 Die verglaste Südwand des Speisesaales mit festen Sonnenschutzlamellen. Dahinter das Haupttreppenhaus.
  The glazed wall of the canteen with fixed sun-protection device. Behind, the main staircase.
4 Blick von Süden auf das Büchermagazin. Links der Haupttrakt.
  View from the South to the book stack. Left, the main building.

Mannesmann-Hochhaus, Düsseldorf – 1956–58
Architekten: Paul Schneider-Esleben, Düsseldorf, und Herbert Knothe, Düsseldorf

Tower office block for the Mannesmann Company, Düsseldorf – 1956–58
Architects: Paul Schneider-Esleben, Düsseldorf, and Herbert Knothe, Düsseldorf

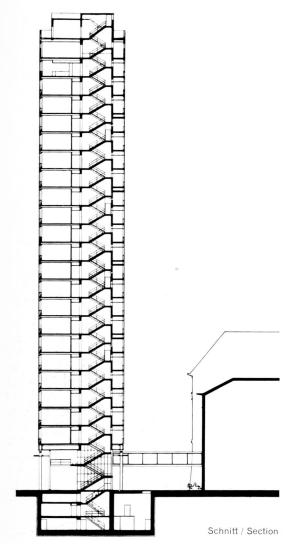

Schnitt / Section

Das Projekt wurde bei einem Ideenwettbewerb im Jahre 1954 mit dem ersten Preis ausgezeichnet. Der schmale Grundriß und die Orientierung ermöglichten es, die Lücke zwischen älteren Bauten als Verbindung der östlich gelegenen Parkanlage mit der Rheinuferstraße auf der Westseite zu erhalten. Die gesamte Ost-, West- und Südseite der 22 Obergeschosse wird als Bürofläche genutzt. Der durch alle Geschosse gehende Stahlbetonkern auf der Nordseite, in dem die vertikale Verkehrsführung mit den Installations- und Nebenräumen zusammengefaßt ist, steift das Gebäude gegen die Windkräfte aus. An den Außenwänden stehen in einem Abstand von 1,80 m (zugleich Büroachsmaß) Pendelstützen aus Mannesmann-Stahlrohren. Davor sind als Außenhautelemente Aluminiumrahmen mit emaillierten Stahlblechpanels und fester Verglasung gehängt. Ein Randträger verteilt die senkrechten Kräfte auf die freistehenden Erdgeschoßstützen.

The scheme was awarded first prize in a competition held in 1954. The narrow plan and skilful siting made it possible to retain the area between the old buildings as a link between the parkland to the East and the road along the Rhine bank. The entire East, West and South sides of the 22 upper storeys are used as office space. The reinforced concrete core on the North side, which rises through every floor and contains the vertical traffic ways, service installations and ancillary rooms, strengthens the building against wind stresses. Along the outside walls hinged stanchions of Mannesmann steel tubing are set at intervals of 6 feet (which is also the axial measurement of the offices). In front of these are hung, as an external skin, aluminium frames with enamelled pressed steel panels and sealed windows. A perimeter beam distributes the vertical forces on to the free-standing ground floor piers.

182

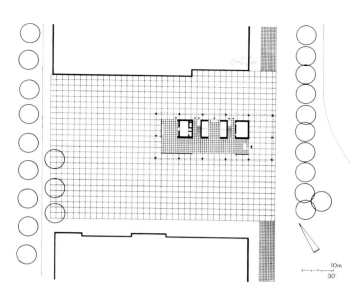

Lageplan mit Erdgeschoßgrundriß
Site and ground floor plan

1 Ansicht von Süden.
  South View.
2 Ostansicht.
  East view.
3 Fassadendetail. Zwischen den Erdgeschoßstützen Regen-
  rinne. Die weißen Deckenverkleidungen sind von den blauen
  Brüstungsplatten abgesetzt und verdeutlichen den struktu-
  rellen Aufbau des Gebäudes.
  Detail of façade. Rainwater gutters between the ground floor
  stanchions. The white floor cladding contrasts with the blue
  panels below the windows, emphasizing the structural arti-
  culation of the building.

Grundriß Normalgeschoß / Typical floor plan

4 Zweigeschossige Eingangshalle im zurückgesetzten Erd- und
  Zwischengeschoß.
  The entrance hall, two storeys high, on the ground floor and
  mezzanine, which are set back.
5 Direktionszimmer. Die Fenster sind mit innenliegenden
  Lamellenstores versehen.
  Manager's room. The windows have internal blinds.

6 Gang in einem Normalgeschoß.
   Passage on a typical floor.
7 Büro in einem Normalgeschoß. Die Fenster sind fest verglast,
   da die Klimatisierung nur bei völlig geschlossenen Räumen
   wirksam arbeitet. Sie werden von einem Putzwagen aus gereinigt, der an der Fassade auf- und abgleiten kann.
   Office on a typical floor. The windows are sealed, since air-
   conditioning can only be completely effective if direct external ventilation is excluded. They are cleaned from a cradle
   which can be moved up and down the face of the building.

Hochhaus für die Phoenix-Rheinrohr AG, Düsseldorf – 1957–60
Architekten: Helmut Hentrich und Hubert Petschnigg, Düsseldorf

Multi-storey block for the Phoenix-Rheinrohr Company, Düsseldorf – 1957–60
Architects: Helmut Hentrich and Hubert Petschnigg, Düsseldorf

1 Die Schmalseiten der drei Scheiben sind völlig geschlossen.
The narrow sides of the three blocks have no openings.
2 Ansicht der Längsfassade. Das Haus ist voll klimatisiert. Die geschlossenen Fensterflächen werden von außen durch Putzwagen gereinigt.
General view. The building is fully air-conditioned. The sealed windows are cleaned from two external travelling cradles.

Diesem Bau liegt eine Variante zu einem mit dem ersten Preis prämiierten Wettbewerbsentwurf zugrunde. Der Baukörper ist in drei gegeneinander versetzte Scheiben gegliedert, von denen die mittlere die beiden äußeren um drei Geschosse überragt. Sie enthält den zentralen Festpunkt, der die Aufzüge und die sanitären Anlagen aufnimmt und die doppelbündig angelegten Büroräume erschließt. Diese Anordnung ermöglicht es, die Verkehrsfläche gegenüber der Bürofläche zu reduzieren und die verhältnismäßig kurzen Flure von der Kopfseite her direkt zu belichten. Die Nottreppen sind so an die Enden des Kerns gesetzt, daß sie in unmittelbarer Verbindung mit dem Freien stehen. Die Stahlskelettkonstruktion ist über einem unterirdischen, drei Kellergeschosse umfassenden Gründungskörper aus Stahlbeton errichtet. An den Außenseiten ist ein Curtain-Wall aus Nirosta, Aluminium und Glas vorgehängt, die Schmalseiten sind völlig geschlossen.

In principle, this building is a variant of a scheme which won first prize in a competition. It is divided into three blocks placed side by side. The middle one, being three floors higher than the other two, contains the central structural core, which houses the lifts and services and opens on the two ranges of offices. This arrangement makes it possible to reduce circulation ways in relation to office space and to provide direct lighting for the comparatively short passages from either end. The emergency stairs are placed at the ends of the central core, so that they are in immediate contact with the open air. The steel skeleton frame is erected upon deep reinforced concrete foundations, which incorporate three basement storeys. The façades carry an external skin of stainless steel, aluminium and glass, the narrow end walls have no openings.

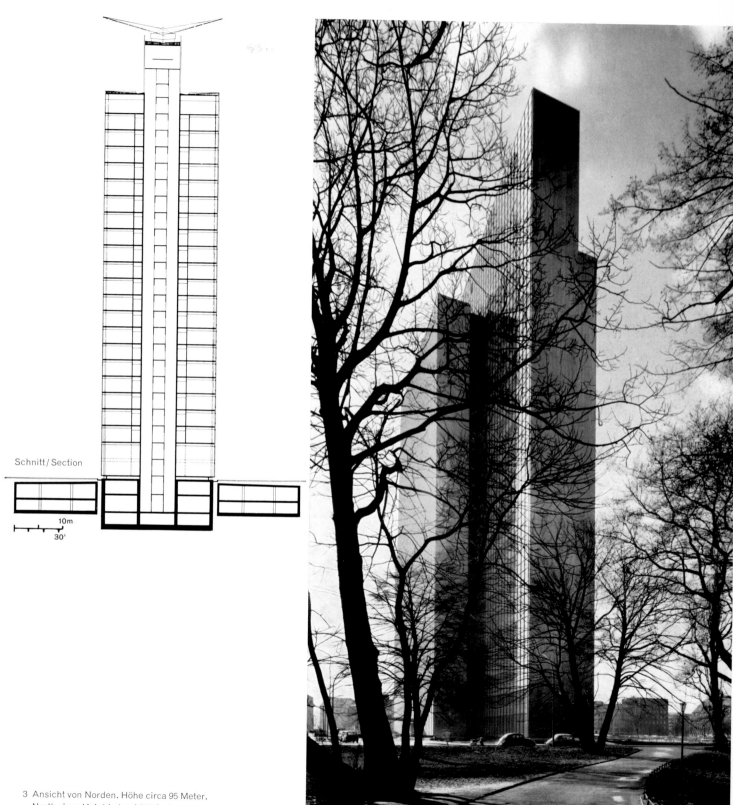

Schnitt / Section

10 m.
30'

3 Ansicht von Norden. Höhe circa 95 Meter.
   North view. Height about 310 feet.

4 Direktionsraum.
Executive's office.

5 Bürogroßraum. Die Stützen sind hinter die vorgehängte
Fassade zurückgesetzt. Sonnenschutz durch innenlaufende
Lamellenstores.
Large office. The stanchions are placed behind the curtain-
walled façade. Internal louvred blinds provide sun protection.

Grundriß Normalgeschoß / Typical floor plan

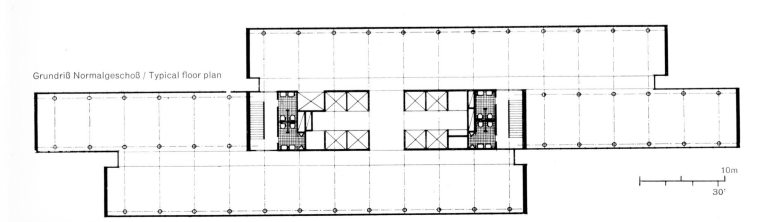

10m

30'

Fleischerei-Innung in Heidelberg – 1957
Architekten: Lothar Götz, Heidelberg/Karlsruhe, und Gerhard Hauss, Heidelberg

Meat-processing plant, Heidelberg – 1957
Architects: Lothar Götz, Heidelberg/Karlsruhe, and Gerhard Hauss, Heidelberg

Das Raumprogramm umfaßt die verschiedenartigsten Funktionen. Den Straßen zugewandt liegen, zum Teil im Untergeschoß angeordnet, die Büros und Geschäftsräume der Fleischerei-Innung, die Depositenstelle einer Bank, Verkaufs- und Ausstellungsräume für Fleischereimaschinen. Die Betriebsräume – Häuteannahme, Klimareifeanlage und Verkauf – sind zum Hof orientiert. Da der Hauptbau an allen vier Seiten umfahren werden kann, ist das Anfahren der Lastwagen an die Verladerampe ohne Zurückstoßen möglich. Die Kühlräume nehmen die Mitte des Gebäudes ein. Im Kellergeschoß befinden sich Räume für die Aufbereitung und die Lagerung der Häute. Für die Konstruktion durften nur Baustoffe verwendet werden, die widerstandsfähig gegen die Salzhaltigkeit der Luft sind. Sämtliche Wände und Decken bestehen aus unverputztem, weiß und schwarz gestrichenem Beton. Installationsleitungen und Strahlungsheizung sind in der Schalung verlegt und einbetoniert.

The programme embraces widely differing activities. Facing the roads, and partly accommodated in the basement, are the offices and business rooms of the meat-processing concern, a deposit branch of a bank, and sales and exhibition space for butchers' machines. Technical operations – reception of skins, maturing (preserving) procedures and sales – take place in rooms facing the yard. As vehicles can drive round all four sides of the main building, vans reach the loading bay without reversing. Cold storage rooms occupy the middle of the block. Rooms for preparing and storing skins are located in the cellars. Structural materials capable of withstanding the high saline content of the air are exclusively used. All walls and ceilings are of unfinished concrete, painted white and black. Service ducts and heating coils are imbedded in the concrete floors.

Erdgeschoßgrundriß / Ground floor plan

1 Sitzungszimmer / Board room
2 Geschäftsführung / Management
3 Depositenstelle der Bank / Deposit-bank
4 Verkaufs- und Ausstellungsraum für Maschinen
  Sales and exhibition space for machines
5 Verkaufsbüro / Sales office
6 Verkaufsraum für Fleischereiprodukte
  Sales room for meat-products
7 Kühlräume / Cold storage
8 Häuteannahme / Skins reception
9 Klimareifeanlage / Preserving (maturing) room
10 Hof / Yard
11 Garage
12 Personalräume / Staff rooms
13 Rampe zum Keller / Ramp to cellar
14 Verladerampe / Loading bay

2 Vogelschau der Gesamtanlage.
  Bird's eye view of the general layout.

Kellergrundriß / Basement floor plan

15 Büros / Offices
16 Heizung / Heating
17 Häutewaschraum / Skin-washing room
18 Aufsalzflächen für die Häute / Processing area for skins
19 Häutelager / Skins store
20 Rampe zum Hof / Ramp to yard
21 Vorratskeller für die Verkaufsräume / Stock for sales rooms

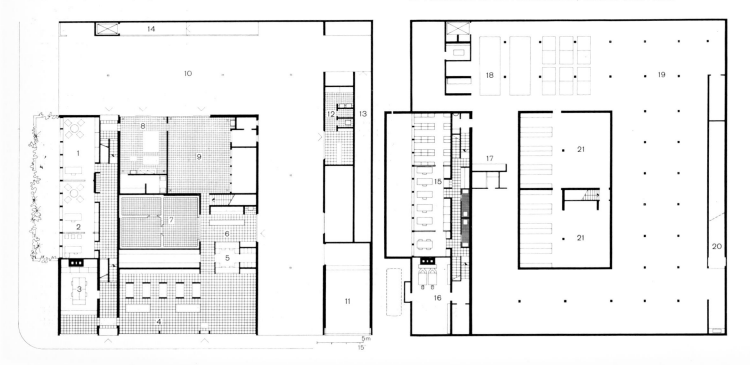

5m
15'

190

3 Bepflanzter Lichtschacht vor den Büros des Untergeschosses.
Plants in the light well, in front of the offices of the ground
floor.
4 Straßenansicht mit den Schaufenstern des Bankraumes und
des Ausstellungs- und Verkaufsraumes.
Street view, showing the windows of the bank and of the
display and sales area.

Schallplattenfabrik in Langenargen – 1958
Architekten: Hans Maurer, München, und Siemens-Bauabteilung

Gramophone record factory, Langenargen – 1958
Architects: Hans Maurer, Munich, and Siemens Building Department

Die fertiggestellten Teile bilden den ersten Bauabschnitt einer großen Fabrikanlage, die später auch einen sechsgeschossigen Verwaltungsbau und ein Kasino erhalten soll. Die Raumgruppen sind ihrer funktionellen Zusammengehörigkeit entsprechend in Zonen aufgeteilt, deren Abfolge von Osten nach Westen bei der späteren Erweiterung nach Norden beibehalten wird. Die Nebenbetriebszone, in der bis jetzt die Halle für Musikschrankbau, Schlosserei, ein kleines Kasino und das Kesselhaus ausgeführt sind, soll im endgültigen Zustand zur Mittelachse eines symmetrischen Betriebes werden. Die Arbeitsvorbereitungszone enthält Büros, kleine Werkstätten und Materialzwischenlager. Zwischen die Shedhalle, in der die Schallplatten in Spritzgußmaschinen hergestellt werden, und das Fertiglager ist eine Sozialzone mit Garderoben, Waschräumen und Meisterbüros eingeschoben. Am westlichen Abschluß der Halle liegt eine Auslieferungsrampe für Lastwagen.

The completed parts represent the first stage of a large factory building scheme, which will later include a six-storey office block and a club. Spatial groups are divided into zones according to their functional relationship, the sequence proceeding from East to West and, in subsequent extensions, Northward. The zone for subsidiary operations, in which up till now the radiogram construction hall, the machine shop, a small staff club and a boiler house are located, will ultimately form the middle axis of a symmetrically organized layout. The zone for preparatory work includes offices, small workshops and materials stores. Between the main factory, in which the records are turned out by injection moulding machines, and the store for finished goods, there is a "social" zone with cloak- and washrooms, and foreman's offices. At the West end of the factory is a dispatch ramp for lorries.

1 Gesamtansicht von Südwesten.
  General view from the South-West.
2 Modellansicht der geplanten Gesamtanlage von Nordwesten.
  Rechts Verwaltungsbau und Sozialgebäude mit Kasino.
  Model of the whole proposed scheme from the North-West.
  Right, office block and "social" building with club rooms.

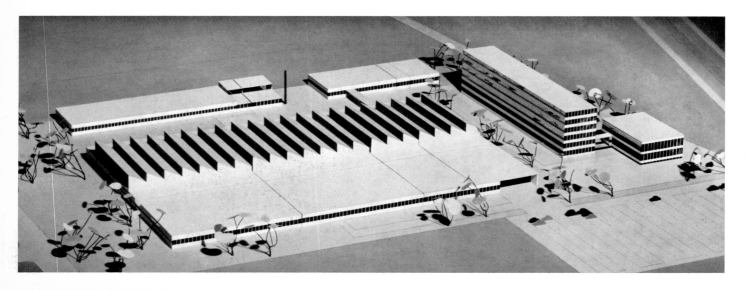

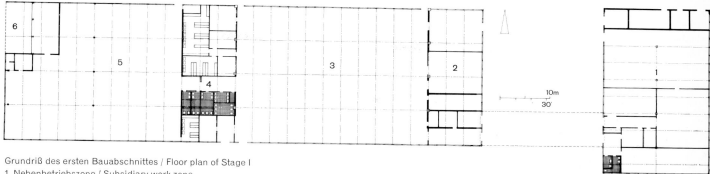

Grundriß des ersten Bauabschnittes / Floor plan of Stage I
1 Nebenbetriebszone / Subsidiary work zone
2 Arbeitsvorbereitungszone / Preparatory work zone
3 Werkhalle / Factory
4 Sozialzone / "Social" zone
5 Lagerhalle / Storage for finished goods
6 Auslieferung / Dispatch

3 Verbindungsdach zwischen Nebenbetriebsräumen und Werkhalle. Im Hintergrund das Kesselhaus.
   Canopy linking the factory with the subsidiary work shops. In
   the background the boiler house.
4 Ansicht der Werkhalle von Nordosten. Alle Gebäude sind in
   Stahl konstruiert. Durisolplatten und Stahlfenster schließen
   die Außenwände zwischen den Stahlstützen.
   View of the factory from the North-East. All buildings are
   steel, with Durisol slabs and steel-frame windows set between
   the stanchions.

Fabrikationshalle und Bürogebäude der Phönix-Elektrizitäts-GmbH, Blomberg – 1957
Architekten: Eckhardt Schulze-Fielitz, Ulrich S. von Altenstadt und Ernst von Rudloff, Essen

Production shops and office building for the Phönix-Elektrizitäts-GmbH, Blomberg – 1957
Architects: Eckhardt Schulze-Fielitz, Ulrich S. von Altenstadt and Ernst von Rudloff, Essen

1 Ansicht des Verwaltungsgebäudes von Norden. Links die Fabrikationshalle.
View of the office building from the North. Left, the production shops.

Das am Stadtrand gelegene Zweigwerk der Firma umfaßt eine Fabrikations- und Lagerhalle, eine Kantine und ein Bürogebäude. Die dreischiffig angelegte Halle enthält in ihren Seitenschiffen die Produktion, im Mittelschiff Lager und Versandabteilung. An der südlichen Schmalseite erlaubt das abfallende Gelände das Ein- und Ausladen über eine Rampe. Dem Personaleingang an der Nordseite gegenüber liegt der Zugang zum Kantinenbau mit den Personalräumen. Im Kern des Verwaltungsbaues ist die Ölheizung untergebracht, deren Kamine mit mechanischem Zug südlich vor dem Gebäude stehen. Die Stahlskelettkonstruktionen der drei Bauteile tragen ebene, nach innen entwässerte Dächer aus Siporex-Platten. Die Längswände der Fabrikationshalle sind mit fünf Meter langen Siporex-Wandplatten und Fensterelementen aus Holz, die von innen gegen die Stahlstützen geschraubt sind, ausgefacht. Ihre Giebelwände sind aus Siporex-Bausteinen gemauert.

The branch works of the firm, which lie on the outskirts of the town, comprise a production and storage building, a canteen and an office block. The three-aisled structure contains production shops in the side aisles and a stores and dispatch department in the middle. At the narrow South end the sloping site permits loading and unloading over a ramp. Opposite the employees' entrance at the North end stands the entrance to the canteen block with staff rooms. The oil-heating plant is placed inside the administration building, at the South front of which rise the chimneys, which have a mechanical draught device. The steel skeleton construction of this tripartite group has flat roofs of Siporex (light concrete) slabs with internal drainage ducts. The long sides of the production building consist of 16' long Siporex wall panels and wood-framed window units, which are screwed on the inside to the steel stanchions. The end walls are constructed with Siporex blocks.

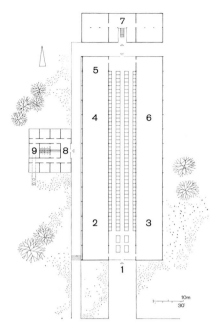

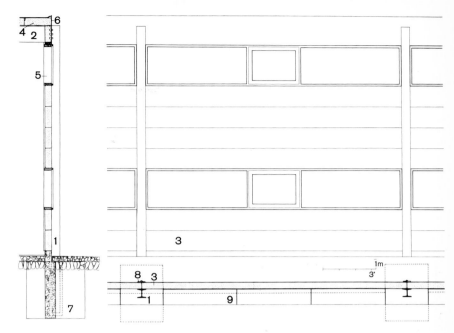

Grundriß / Floor plan
1 Eingang Versandraum und Lager
  Entrance to dispatch and stores
2 Tablettiermaschinen / Machine shop
3 Dreherei, Schrauben / Turnery, screws
4 Kunststoffpressen / Plastic moulding presses
5 Werkzeugmacherei / Switch gear shop
6 Montage / Assembly
7 Kantine, Personalräume / Canteen, staff rooms
8 Verwaltung / Administration
9 Heizung / Heating

Fassadendetail / Detail of façade
1 I 14 / 5¹/₂″ steel stanchion
2 I 32 / 12³/₅″ steel beam
3 Siporex-Wandplatte 40/500/12 cm
  Siporex wall panel
4 Siporex-Dachplatte 50/500/12 cm / Siporex roof unit
5 Holzfenster 500/80 cm / Wood/framed window
6 Blechverkleidung / Thin metal skin
7 Fundament / Foundations
8 Halteleiste aus Holz / Wood cleat
9 Betonplatten / Concrete slabs

3 Ansicht von Westen mit den freistehenden Kaminen. Die
  Außenwände der Kantine und des Verwaltungsbaues bestehen aus wandhohen, verglasten Holzelementen.
  West view, showing the free-standing chimneys. The external
  walls of canteen and office building comprise storey-high,
  glazed, timber units.

2 Eingangsfassade der Kantine.
  Canteen entrance façade.

Werkstattgebäude 9 der Firma Franke & Heidecke, Braunschweig – 1957–58
Architekt: Friedrich Wilhelm Kraemer, Braunschweig

Production building 9 of the Franke & Heidecke Company, Brunswick – 1957–58
Architect: Friedrich Wilhelm Kraemer, Brunswick

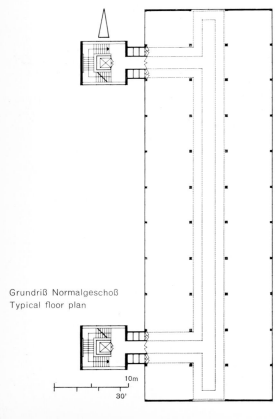

Grundriß Normalgeschoß
Typical floor plan

Dieses Gebäude sollte nach dem Wunsch des Bauherrn die gleiche formale und technische Folgerichtigkeit und Präzision zeigen, wie sie für die Kameras, die darin hergestellt werden, bezeichnend sind. Eine solche Forderung wurde durch stereometrisch knappe Baukörper, Durchsichtigkeit, klaren Grundriß, Exaktheit und Dauerhaftigkeit der Ausführung erfüllt. Die Arbeitsflächen (insgesamt 4500 qm) im Erdgeschoß und in den vier Obergeschossen mit ihren unterzuglosen Decken können beliebig zusammengefaßt oder unterteilt werden. In den Nordwest- und Südwestecken jedes Geschosses liegen jeweils die WC-Räume, Wasch- und Umkleideräume. Heizung und Klimaanlage sind im Keller untergebracht. Zwei quadratische, an zwei Seiten verglaste Treppentürme wurden aus dem Baukörper herausgestellt, zwischen ihnen und dem Hauptbau verlaufen Lüftungs- und Leitungsschächte.

The clients wanted this building to display the formal and technical precision typical of the cameras produced inside it. This requirement was answered by a structure of strict geometrical form, transparent clarity of plan and meticulous accuracy and quality in execution. The unobstructed working areas (some 45,000 sq.ft. in all) on the ground floor and on the four upper storeys can be combined or divided at will. The North-West and South-West corners of each floor contain lavatories, washrooms and changing rooms; the heating and ventilating plants are in the basement. Two square staircase towers, glazed on two sides, jut out from the principal block, and between these and the main building are placed the electrical and ventilation ducts.

196

1 Ansicht von Osten. Feste Verglasung und Klimaanlage ermöglichen die vollständige Abdichtung des Gebäudes gegen Verschmutzung, innenliegende Lamellenstores regulieren das Tageslicht. Das Flachdach wird durch Regenrohre entwässert, die in die Innenstützen einbetoniert sind.

East front. Sealed windows and air-conditioning ensure complete protection from dirt, while inside louvred blinds regulate daylighting. The flat roof is drained of rainwater by pipes set in the internal concrete piers.

2 Ansicht von Westen mit den freistehenden Treppentürmen, deren Stirnwände mit geschliffenen Kunststeinplatten verkleidet sind.

View from the West, with the free-standing staircase towers, the façades of which are clad with polished, artificial stone-panels.

3 Blick auf die Westfassade mit dem verglasten Treppenturm.

View of the West façade with one of the two glazed staircase towers.

4 Fassadenausschnitt. Schalungsrauhes Stahlbetonskelett von größter Präzision der Ausführung (0,5 cm Toleranz), weiß lackierte 4 cm breite Holzrahmen, fest verglaste Scheiben, blau emailliertes Wellblech als Brüstungsfüllung.

Detail of façade. Skeleton frame of exposed reinforced concrete, erected with extreme accuracy ($1/5''$ tolerances); sealed windows with varnished white wooden surrounds ($1^3/5''$ thick); blue-enamelled corrugated panels below the sills.

Parkhaus Breuninger in Stuttgart – 1959
Architekt: Gerd Wiegand, München; Mitarbeiter: H. Hanusch

Parking garage for the Breuninger Company, Stuttgart – 1959
Architect: Gerd Wiegand, Munich; Assistant: H. Hanusch

1 Ansicht von Westen.
View from the West.

Der Mangel an Kundenparkplätzen veranlaßte die Firma Breuninger, trotz der ungünstigen Längen- und Breitenausdehnung der zur Verfügung stehenden Baufläche, gegenüber ihrem Textilkaufhaus am Leonhardsplatz ein Parkhaus zu errichten. Zwei Drittel der Parkstände mußten in den beiden Tiefgeschossen untergebracht werden; zwei offene Oberdecks nehmen die restlichen Stellplätze auf. Aus der geringen Breite des Grundstücks ergab sich die Anordnung der Podestrampen am Kopf der im Einbahnsystem befahrenen Anlage. An den Treppen- und Aufzugsturm vor der Südfront ist ein unterirdischer Fußgängertunnel angeschlossen, der das Parkhaus mit dem Kaufhaus verbindet. Das Erdgeschoß ist entlang der Ein- und Ausfahrtsbahnen mit Tankstationen, Schnellwaschanlage und Kundenraum ausgestattet. Durch die Aufstellung der Fahrzeuge unter 90° und eine spätere Aufstockung kann die Parkkapazität erweitert werden.

Lack of parking space for customers induced the firm of Breuninger to erect a parking garage opposite their textiles store on the Leonhardsplatz, despite the unsuitable dimensions of the site available. Two-thirds of the parking bays had to be arranged on the two basement floors; two open upper decks accommodate the remainder. The placing of the ramp structure at the top end of the building, which is arranged for a one-way system, was due to the restricted width of the site. An underground tunnel for pedestrians linking the parking garage with the Breuninger store, is connected to the stair and lift tower at the South front. Along the entrance and exit lanes at ground level are service and car-washing facilities, and a customers' waiting room. The garage capacity can be extended by parking the cars at 90° and, in the future, by additional floors.

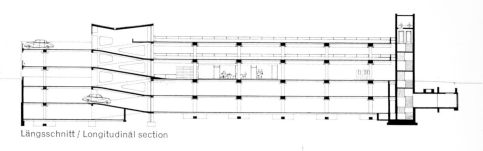

Längsschnitt / Longitudinal section

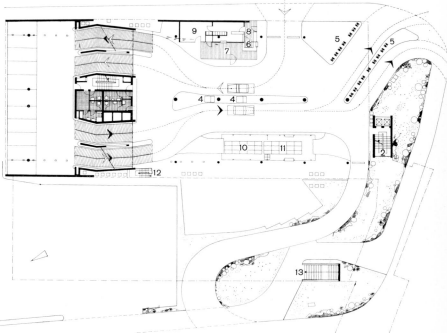

Grundriß Erdgeschoß / Ground floor plan

Legende / Legend

1 Fußgängertunnel / Pedestrians' tunnel
2 Treppen- und Aufzugsturm / Stair and lift tower
3 Treppe zum Gehsteig / Stairs to side walk
4 Kontrollstand / Control cabin
5 Tankinsel / Pumps
6 Kasse / Cashier
7 Kundenraum / Waiting room
8 Tankwarte / Pump attendants
9 Verkaufslager / Stores
10 Waschstand / Washing bay
11 Pflegestand / Lubrication bay
12 Nottreppe / Emergency stairs
13 Treppe zum Fußgängertunnel
Stairs to pedestrians' tunnel

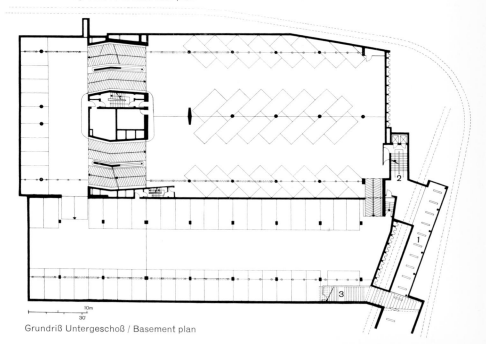

Grundriß Untergeschoß / Basement plan

2 Südwestansicht.
  South-West view.

3 Ansicht von Süden. Der Treppen- und Aufzugsturm ist an zwei Seiten mit schwarzen Schieferplatten verkleidet; die Schmalseiten sind völlig verglast. Die Brüstungsblenden des Oberdecks bestehen aus weiß gestrichenen Betonfertigteilen.
  View from the South. The stair and lift tower is faced on two sides with black slate panels; the narrow ends are completely glazed. The parapets of the upper decks consist of precast concrete components painted white.

4 Einfahrt im Erdgeschoß. Links Kundenraum, rechts Kontrollstände.
  Entrance at ground level. Left, customers' waiting room; right, control cabins.

5 Rampenanlage.
  Ramp structure.

Kirche Heilig Kreuz, Bottrop – 1952–57
Architekten: Rudolf Schwarz und Josef Bernard, Köln

Church of the Holy Cross, Bottrop – 1952–57
Architects: Rudolf Schwarz and Josef Bernard, Cologne

1 Gesamtansicht mit Turm.
  General view (including tower).
2 Innenraum mit Blick zum Altar.
  Interior, looking towards the altar.

Der Bau besteht aus einer hohen, unverputzten Backsteinwand in Form einer Parabel. Da er im Gebiet der Bergbausenkungen errichtet wurde, mußte die Wand in Streifen von vier Meter Breite zerlegt werden, welche auf zwischengelegten Pendelstützen aus Stahlbeton gleiten können. Die Stirnseite, die mittleren Mauerfelder und die Eingangsseite sind steif ausgebildet. Im Scheitel der Kurve ist die Decke steil nach oben abgeknickt. Eine Oberlichtwand aus Glasbausteinen erhellt den Altarbereich. Ihm gegenüber ist an der Eingangsseite zwischen die Schenkel der Parabel eine verglaste Gitterwand aus Stahlbeton gestellt. Neben der Kirche steht die kleine Kreuzkapelle mit einem Altar. Der Vorhof der Kirche wird von einem freistehenden quadratischen Glockenturm gegen die Straße abgegrenzt.

The building, in the form of a parabola, consists of a high walled enclosure in exposed brick. As it was erected in a mining district liable to subsidence, the walls were divided into sections which could be anchored to reinforced concrete hinged stanchions placed at 13' intervals. The front wall, the middle sections of the walls and the entrance front are structurally rigid. The roof swings sharply upwards near the apex of the curve to provide light for the altar by means of a glass brick construction. At the opposite end, a glazed reinforced concrete lattice screen forms the entrance front. The small chapel of the Cross stands at the side of the church. The forecourt is separated from the road by a square, free-standing, bell-tower.

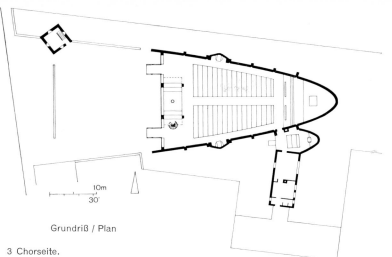

Grundriß / Plan

3 Chorseite.
  Chancel front.
4 Eingangswand von innen. Glasbild von Georg Meistermann.
  Entrance façade from inside. Window design by Georg
  Meistermann.

Kirche Maria Königin, Saarbrücken – 1956–59
Architekt: Rudolf Schwarz, Köln; Mitarbeiter: Hubert Friedl und Maria Schwarz

Church of Mary the Queen, Saarbrücken – 1956–59
Architect: Rudolf Schwarz, Cologne; Assistants: Hubert Friedl and Maria Schwarz

Die Kirche steht auf halber Höhe an einem steilen Hang und beherrscht mit den roten Sandstein-
mauern ihrer vier Konchen das Tal. Man betritt den Bau durch eine niedrige und dunkle Unterkirche
mit einem kleinen Altar und den Beichtstühlen, steigt auf geschwungenen Treppen in die hohe, licht-
durchflutete Oberkirche hinauf, deren Grundriß aus zwei sich durchdringenden Ellipsen geformt ist
In ihrer Mitte steht der Altar. Drei der Kreuzarme nehmen die Gemeindebänke auf. Das Mauerwerk
zieht sich nach oben hin von der Raummitte weg schmal zusammen. Zwei Stahlbetonrahmen, deren
Pfeiler die einspringenden Raumecken bilden, kreuzen sich über dem Altar und tragen die flache
Holzdecke. Im Äußeren treten sie als kräftige Strebepfeiler hervor. Schlanke Stahlbetonstützen
unterteilen die großen Fenster, die die Flächen zwischen Mauerwerk und Pfeiler füllen.

The church stands half way up a steeply sloping site and, with the red sandstone walls of its four
"conches", dominates the valley. The building is entered by a low and dark crypt (containing an altar
and confessionals), from which curved stairs rise to the high, brightly lit, church planned as two intersecting ellipses. The altar stands in the middle, and the congregation sits in three of the cross-arms.
The masonry walls contract as they climb up and away from the middle of the church. Two reinforced
concrete frames, the piers of which mark the angles of the crossing, intersect above the altar and
carry the flat timber roof. Outside, they project like powerful buttresses. Slim reinforced concrete
supporting mullions subdivide the large windows filling the area between the stonework and piers.

1 Längsansicht.
 General view.
2 Stirn des längeren Kreuzarmes, von der Talseite gesehen.
 Façade of the longer cross-arm, seen from the valley side.
3 Innenraum.
 Interior.

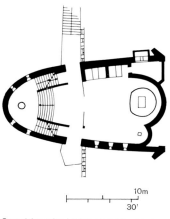

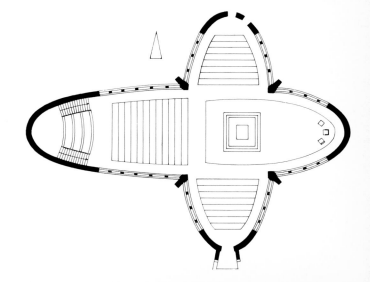

Grundrisse der Unter- und Oberkirche
Plans of the lower and the upper church

1 Hauptschiff mit Blick zum Altar.
  Looking towards the altar.

Eine sechzehn Meter hohe unverputzte Natursteinwand, aufgeführt aus den Mauersteinen der alten, im Kriege zerstörten Kirche, umschließt das gewinkelte Hochschiff, in dessen Knickpunkt der Hauptaltar steht. In den Winkel, den die beiden Hochschiffarme bilden, ist die niedrige Pilgerkirche eingefügt. Zur Hauptkirche in ganzer Länge geöffnet, nach außen durch die Natursteinwand abgeschlossen, von Lichtkuppeln in der Decke erhellt, nimmt sie Taufstein, Beichtstühle und den Reliquienschrein auf. Die über ihr aufsteigende, durch Stahlbetonpfeiler gestützte Glasbausteinwand erleuchtet Haupt- und Querschiff. Diagonal gekreuzte Unterzüge überspannen den Raum und tragen das flach geneigte Betondach. In die Ostwand hinter dem Hauptaltar ist durch die Schichtung der Steine und kleine runde Öffnungen das Zeichen des Lebensbaumes eingearbeitet. In einem späteren Bauabschnitt sollen an der Nordseite eine Sakristei und vor dem Haupteingang ein Turm angefügt werden.

A fifty-foot high wall in exposed natural stone, constructed from the masonry of the war-damaged church, encloses the rectangular nave, with the altar standing in a slight recess. The angle formed by transept and nave, accommodates the low-roofed pilgrims' church. Open to the main church throughout its length, separated from the outside by a natural stone wall, and with domed roof lights, it contains a font, confessionals and the reliquary. Above it, supported on reinforced concrete piers, rises a glass-brick wall, which lights the nave and transept. Beams, intersecting diagonally, span the interior and carry the slightly pitched, reinforced concrete, roof. By laying the stones in patterned courses and by leaving small round openings, the symbol of the Tree of Life has been worked into the East wall behind the high altar. At a later stage a sacristy will be added on the North side, and a tower in front of the principal entrance.

2 Ansicht von Nordosten. In die Wand sind Skulpturen von
  Franz Gutmann und Günther Haese eingefügt.
  View from North-East. The walls carry sculptures by Franz
  Gutmann and Günther Haese.
3 Ansicht von Südwesten. Über der niedrigen Pilgerkirche die
  Glasbausteinwände der Hochschiffe.
  View from South-West. Above the low pilgrims' church rise
  the glass-brick walls of the nave.
4 Pilgerkirche. Vor den Öffnungen zum Querschiff der Reliquienschrein. Der Fußboden besteht aus dunklen Schieferplatten.
  Pilgrims' church. The reliquary stands in front of the openings
  towards the transept. The floor consists of dark slate slabs.

Grundriß / Plan
 1 Windfang / Porch
 2 Pilgerkirche / Pilgrims' church
 3 Querschiff / Transept
 4 Altar
 5 Kanzel / Pulpit
 6 Hauptschiff / Nave
 7 Sänger, Orgel / Choir, organ
 8 Weihwasser / Holy water
 9 Taufstein / Font
10 Annaaltar und Schrein / St. Anne's altar and shrine
11 Beichtstühle / Confessionals
12 Turm (geplant) / Tower (proposed)
13 Sakristei (geplant) / Sacristy (proposed)

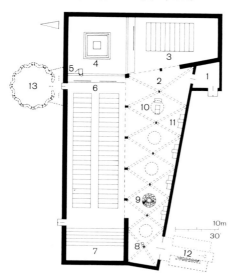

Pfarrkirche Maria in den Benden, Düsseldorf-Wersten – 1958
Architekten: Emil Steffann und Nikolaus Rosiny, Mehlem; Mitarbeiter: Paul Hopmann

Parish church of St. Mary, Düsseldorf-Wersten – 1958
Architects: Emil Steffann and Nikolaus Rosiny, Mehlem; Assistant: Paul Hopmann

1 Ansicht von Südosten. Rechts der Chor, links das Hauptportal.
View from the South-East. Right, the choir; left, the main
entrance.
2 Innenhof.
Internal court.

Die geschlossene Backsteinmauer und das gemeinsame Satteldach fassen die Kirche mit dem Pfarrhaus zusammen und heben sie aus der mit kleinen Wohnhäusern bebauten Umgebung, einem Vorort
im Südosten von Düsseldorf, heraus. Kirche, Sakristei, Pfarrhaus, Kindergarten, Gemeindesaal und
Küsterwohnung umschließen einen quadratischen Innenhof. Über dem querrechteckigen Kirchenraum fällt die holzverschalte Decke zum Altar hin ab, hinter dem die Außenwand zu einer weiten
Konche ausschwingt. Die Kirchenbänke umgreifen den Altar von drei Seiten. Der Raum erhält sein
Licht durch die hohe Glaswand zum Innenhof. Der untere Teil der Glaswand kann hochgeschoben
werden; der Innenhof dient dann als erweiterter Gemeinderaum für hohe Feste. Die Taufkapelle ist
als Vorraum zwischen Portal und Kirchenraum eingeschoben. Seitlich neben dem Eingang liegt eine
Werktagskapelle.

Plain brick walls and a common pitched roof link church and parsonage to form a prominent feature of
a built-up area of small homes in a South-Eastern suburb of Düsseldorf. Church, sacristy, parsonage,
infants' school, meeting hall and verger's flat enclose a square internal court. A timber-lined roof
slopes downwards over the rectangular church interior to the altar, behind which the wall bends
outwards in a wide apse. The pews surround the altar on three sides. The interior is lit from the internal
quadrangle by a glass partition, the lower section of which slides upwards. Thus the quadrangle
can serve as an extension to the church for important occasions. The baptistry forms a passage between porch and church. To the side close to the entrance is a chapel for week-day use.

Grundriß / Plan

1 Hauptportal / Main porch
2 Innenhof / Internal court
3 Kapelle / Chapel
4 Taufbrunnen / Font
5 Kirche / Church
6 Sakristei / Sacristy
7 Pfarrhaus / Parsonage
8 Kindergarten / Infants' school
9 Küsterwohnung / Verger's flat
10 Treppe zum Pfarrsaal / Stairs to parish room

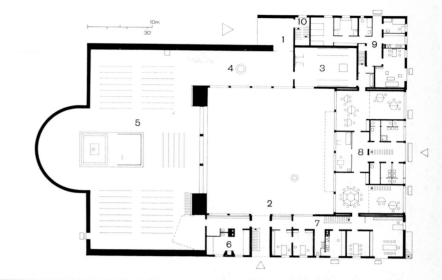

3 Innenraum der Kirche. Fußboden in Kirche und Hof aus
Waschbeton, Altarinsel aus Naturstein.
Church interior. Church floor and courtyard are concrete. The
altar dais is natural stone.

209

Heilig-Kreuz-Kirche in Düsseldorf-Rath – 1957–58
Architekt: Josef Lehmbrock

Church of the Holy Cross, Düsseldorf-Rath – 1957–58
Architect: Josef Lehmbrock

1 Im Innenraum ist das einfallende Licht auf den Altarbereich
  konzentriert.
  In the interior light is concentrated on the area of the altar.
2 Modell der Dachkonstruktion.
  Model of the roof construction.

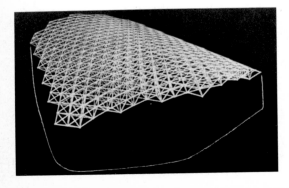

Der Innenraum wird von einem in der Mitte leicht nach oben gewölbten, vom Eingang zum Altar ansteigenden räumlichen Tragwerk aus dünnen Stahlrohren überspannt. Die umschließende Wand ist
aus lauter gleichen Elementen, rhythmisch vor- und zurückgesetzten, flammenförmig gefertigten
Betonteilen, die als verlorene Schalung mit Beton ausgegossen wurden, doppelwandig aufgerichtet.
Sie sind zum Teil als Rahmensteine ausgebildet und mit Dickglas versehen. Diese in wechselnder
Dichte in der oberen Wandzone verteilten Öffnungen sind die einzigen Lichtquellen des Raumes. Sie
bilden über dem Altar eine farbig differenzierte Kreuzgestalt, in der Dornenkrone, Herzwunde, Hände
und Füße hervorgehoben sind. Die Dichte der Öffnungen ist – vom Kreuz ausgehend – beiderseits des
Altars am größten. Sie vermindert sich mehr und mehr bis zur Eingangswand, die durch trauben-
ähnliche Gruppen nochmals betont wird. Der Taufstein steht in der Nähe des Haupteingangs. Die
Sakristei ist seitlich angebaut.

The interior is spanned by a space framework of thin steel tubes, slightly vaulted in the middle and
gradually rising from the entrance towards the altar. The enclosing walls consist entirely of similar,
prefabricated, flamelike concrete elements, rhythmically projecting and recessed, erected as two
partitions of permanent shuttering with concrete filling the cavity between. Some are formed into
frames and provided with glass, and these openings, spread over the upper part of the walls in
varying densities, are the sole source of light for the interior. Above the altar they form a coloured representation of the cross, in which the crown of thorns, the stigmata, and the hands and feet are con-
spicuously indicated. The density of these openings, starting from the cross, is thickest on either side
of the altar. It steadily declines towards the entrance façade, which is adorned with clusterlike groups.
The font is placed close to the main entrance. The sacristy is built to one side.

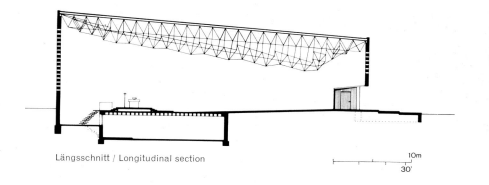

Längsschnitt / Longitudinal section

10m
30'

Grundriß / Plan

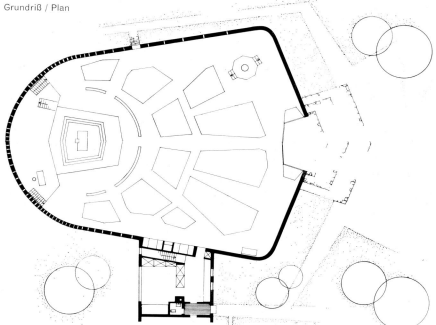

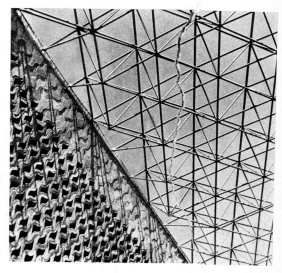

3 Rohbauaufnahme. Anschluß des räumlichen Tragwerkes an die Umfassungswand.
   Detail of the method of joining the space-framework to the enclosing wall.
4 Außenansicht der Eingangswand.
   View of entrance front.

St. Albertus Magnus in Leverkusen-Schlebusch – 1958–59
Architekt: Josef Lehmbrock, Düsseldorf

Church of St. Albertus Magnus, Leverkusen-Schlebusch – 1958–59
Architect: Josef Lehmbrock, Düsseldorf

Die Weite des ovalen Innenraumes ist stützenfrei von einem einzigen zum durchlaufenden First hin gewölbten Dach überspannt, dessen sichtbare Konstruktion wie ein Netz über Altar und Gemeinde ausgeworfen ist. Die Außenwand ist in einen von teleskopartig angeordneten Betonpfeilern gegliederten Lichtmantel aufgelöst. Der Altarbereich wird durch die ansteigende Traufe und zunehmende Helligkeit hervorgehoben. Das Dach besteht aus einem Flächentragwerk, das sich aus einzelnen, rautenförmig aufeinanderstoßenden Holzlamellen mit Bolzenverbindung zusammensetzt und von einem Ortbetonringbalken ausgesteift wird. Über dem Windfang des Hauptportals ist eine Orgelempore aufgesetzt. Seitlich ist dem Hauptschiff eine kleine Kapelle als Werktagskirche und die Sakristei angefügt. Die gegenüber geplante achteckige Taufkapelle ist noch nicht ausgeführt.

The unobstructed oval interior is spanned by a single roof curving upwards to the continuous ridge, the exposed construction being thrown like a net over the altar and congregation. The external wall is a translucent envelope sustained by a seemingly telescopic arrangement of concrete piers. The altar area is emphasized by the rising roof line and intensified light. The roof consists of a shallow framework of rhomboid timber sections compressed against one another, bolted, and reinforced by a concrete rim-beam cast in-situ. An organ loft is placed above the porch of the main entrance. A small chapel for week-day services and the sacristy are attached to one side of the nave. The octagonal baptistry, which is planned opposite the church, has not yet been built.

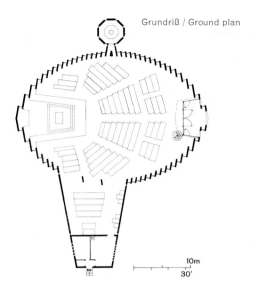

Grundriß / Ground plan

10m
30'

1 Blick zum Altar.
  Looking towards the altar.
2 Außenansicht mit dem Hauptportal.
  External view, showing main portal.
3 Die Dachkonstruktion wird von einem Ringbalken abge-
  fangen und auf die Pfeiler abgestützt.
  The roof structure is carried on a rim-beam, supported by
  piers.
4 Blick vom Altar zum Hauptportal.
  View from the altar towards the main portal.

Evangelische Kirche am Lietzensee in Berlin – 1957
Architekt: Paul G. R. Baumgarten, Berlin

Protestant church on the Lietzensee, Berlin – 1957
Architect: Paul G. R. Baumgarten, Berlin

1 Innenraum. Blick von der Empore zum Altar.
Interior. View from the gallery towards the altar.

Die Kirche steht, abgerückt vom Gemeindehaus an der Straße, in der Parklandschaft am Westufer des Lietzensees. Über einem fünfeckigen Grundriß ist ein aus einzelnen sich gegenseitig abstützenden Stahlbetondreiecken zusammengesetztes Dach entwickelt. Nur an zwei Ecken berührt das Dach die Bodenplatte. Die Glasflächen, die die freibleibenden Außenwände füllen, geben dem Raum überall dort Licht, wo eine Verbindung mit dem umgebenden Grün gewollt ist. Ein Teil der 700 Sitzplätze ist auf der rückwärtigen Orgelempore angeordnet. An der Eingangsseite sind die Sichtbetonwände über der Empore hochgeführt. Sie tragen einen offenen Glockenstuhl, der die ganze Breite der Kirche einnimmt und den in der großstädtischen Bebauung Berlins städtebaulich unwirksamen Turm ersetzt. Das nach Osten abfallende Gelände ermöglichte es, Sakristei, Küsterei und zwei Konfirmandenräume in das Sockelgeschoß zu verlegen.

The church stands in a park setting on the West bank of the Lietzensee, and is set back from the parish hall on the road. Over a pentagonal plan rises a roof composed of separate reinforced concrete triangles braced one against the other, and touching the floor slab at only two points. The glazed partitions, which form the external walls, provide light for the interior, wherever a link with the surrounding green landscape is wanted. Some of the 700 seats are arranged in the organ gallery (loft) at the back. On the entrance side the exposed concrete walls are extended above the gallery, and carry an open belfry, occupying the entire width of the church and replacing the tower, which would conflict with Berlin city planning recommendations. The site, falling away to the East, made it possible to place sacristy, vestry, and two confirmation classrooms in the crypt.

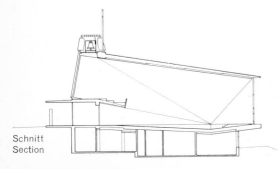

Schnitt
Section

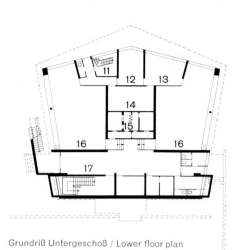

Grundriß Untergeschoß / Lower floor plan

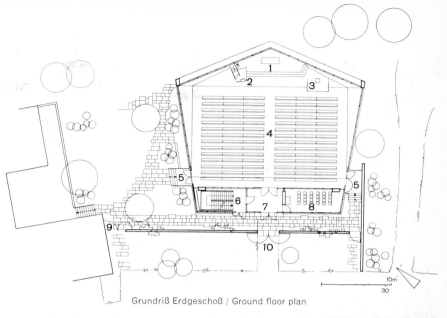

Grundriß Erdgeschoß / Ground floor plan

1 Altar
2 Kanzel / Pulpit
3 Taufstein / Font
4 Kirchenraum / Interior (congregation)
5 Notausgang / Emergency exit
6 Treppenhaus / Stairs
7 Windfang / Porch
8 Andachtsraum / Devotional room
9 Seitentor, links davon das alte Gemeindehaus
   Side gate. Left, the old parish hall
10 Haupteingang / Main entrance
11 Sakristei / Sacristy
12 Küsterei / Vestry
13 Rendantur / Church accounts
14 Archiv / Parish records
15 Lüftung / Ventilation
16 Konfirmandensäle / Confirmation classrooms
17 Flur und Garderoben / Vestibule

2 Eingangsfront.
  Entrance front.
3 Seitenansicht von Süden.
  Side view from the South.

4 Ansicht vom Lietzensee aus.
  View from the lake.
5 Die Stahlbetondreiecke des Daches sind im Inneren mit Holz
  verschalt.
  The reinforced concrete triangles of the roof are lined on the
  inside with timber.

Christuskirche, Bochum – 1957–59
Architekt: Dieter Oesterlen, Hannover; Mitarbeiter: W. Schumann, P. G. Wieschemann, W. Fleck

Christchurch, Bochum – 1957–59
Architect: Dieter Oesterlen, Hanover; Assistants: W. Schumann, P. G. Wieschemann, W. Fleck

1 Blick vom Eingang zum Altar.
View from the entrance towards the altar.

Der von der zerstörten neugotischen Kirche erhalten gebliebene Turm steht nun als Campanile frei neben der Eingangsseite, da die neue Kirche etwas aus der Achse der alten gedreht ist. Sie ist nicht nur die evangelische Hauptkirche der Stadt Bochum, sondern dient auch als Ort größerer kirchenmusikalischer Veranstaltungen. Die Forderungen, die sich daraus für den Innenraum ergaben – gleichwertige Stellung von Altar und Kanzel in einem nicht von der Gemeinde gesonderten Chorraum, gute Sicht von allen Plätzen aus, Mittelgang für festliche Anlässe –, wurden durch eine Verbindung von Zentralraum und Langraum gelöst. Das Faltwerk des Daches wird in den senkrechten Wänden von gestaffelten Wandscheiben aufgenommen. Sie sind so ausgerichtet, daß das Licht der großen farbigen Fenster auf den Altar fällt, ohne die Gemeinde zu blenden. Ein niedriger Anbau an der Nordseite enthält Sakristei und Nebenräume und verbindet den Turm mit der Kirche.

The surviving tower of the destroyed Neo-Gothic church now stands as an independent campanile close to the entrance front of the new church, which is turned slightly away from the axis of its predecessor. This is not only the principal protestant church of the town of Bochum, but also the focal point of important occasions in the world of church music. The conditions laid down for the interior – an equal value to be allotted to the placing of the altar and pulpit in a choir which should not be segregated from the congregation, an unobstructed view from every seat, a central aisle for processions – were met by a combination of a long and central type of nave. The folds of the roof are absorbed into a perpendicular design of stepped slab walls, so arranged that the light from the large stained glass windows falls on the altar without dazzling the congregation. A low annexe to the North contains the sacristy and adjoining rooms and links the tower to the church.

Querschnitt
Section

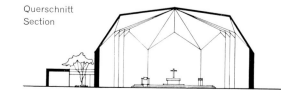

1 Vorplatz / Forecourt
2 Windfang / Porch
3 Kirchenraum, 700 Sitzplätze / Interior, with seating for 700
4 Altar
5 Kanzel / Pulpit
6 Lesepult / Lectern
7 Taufstein / Font
8 Sakristei / Sacristy
9 Feierraum / Community room
10 Besprechungsraum / Conference room
11 Innenhof / Yard
12 Vorraum / Anteroom
13 Turm / Tower

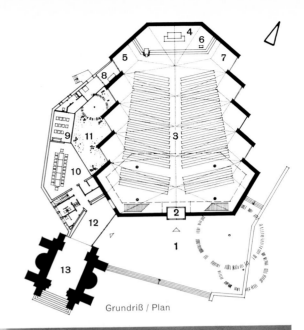

Grundriß / Plan

2 Ansicht von Osten. Schräggestellte Wandscheiben, verbunden durch farbige Glasflächen, nehmen die Faltung des Daches auf.
East view. Slab walls, placed obliquely and connected by
stained glass windows, absorb the folds of the roof.

218

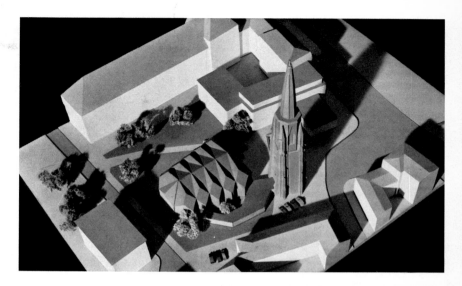

3 Modellansicht von Nordwesten. Der neugotische Turm wird durch die symmetrische Geschlossenheit des Kirchenbaues und die leichte Drehung der Achse zu einem selbständigen Campanile.
Model seen from the North-West. The Neo-Gothic tower becomes a free-standing campanile, thanks to the self-contained plan of the church and its slight deviation from the original axis.

4 Eingangsseite. Der alte Turm ist mit einem eingeschossigen Verbindungsbau, der Sakristei und Nebenräume enthält, an die Kirche angeschlossen. Der Vorplatz vor dem Portal wurde um einige Stufen angehoben.
Entrance front. The old tower is joined to the church by a single-storey structure. Steps lead to the forecourt.

5 Blick von der Empore. Die gefaltete Decke ist mit Holz verschalt, die seitlichen Betonwände mit Backstein verblendet. Die großen Fenster sind von Helmut Lander, Darmstadt, entworfen.
View from the gallery. The folded roof is lined with timber; the concrete lateral walls are brick-faced. The large windows were designed by Helmut Lander of Darmstadt.

Industriesiedlung in Nienburg an der Weser – 1955–56

Architekten: Peter Hübotter, Bert Ledeboer, Rolf Romero und Egon Busch, Hannover

Housing for industrial workers, Nienburg an der Weser – 1955–56

Architects: Peter Hübotter, Bert Ledeboer, Rolf Romero and Egon Busch, Hanover

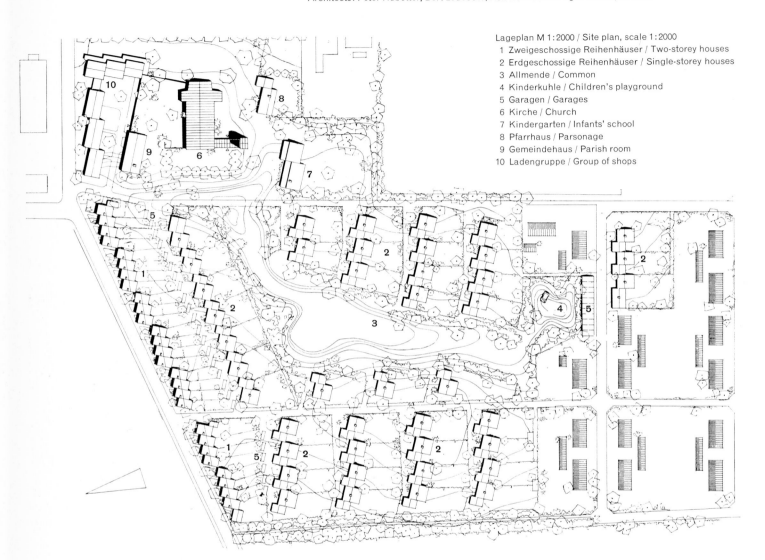

Lageplan M 1:2000 / Site plan, scale 1:2000
1 Zweigeschossige Reihenhäuser / Two-storey houses
2 Erdgeschossige Reihenhäuser / Single-storey houses
3 Allmende / Common
4 Kinderkuhle / Children's playground
5 Garagen / Garages
6 Kirche / Church
7 Kindergarten / Infants' school
8 Pfarrhaus / Parsonage
9 Gemeindehaus / Parish room
10 Ladengruppe / Group of shops

42 ebenerdige und 27 zweigeschossige Reiheneigenheime sind locker um eine von der Bebauung frei-gehaltene Grünzone gruppiert, die den tiefer gelegenen Teil des leicht gewellten Geländes ein-nimmt. Im Bereich dieser Allmende befindet sich eine Spielkuhle für Kinder. Alle Häuser sind gegen-einander versetzt, die niederen durch eingeschobene Nebenräume voneinander getrennt. Vor den nach Südwesten ausgerichteten Wohnräumen entstehen gegen Einblick geschützte Freiräume. Die Grundstücke der eingeschossigen Häuser sind 250 bis 450 qm groß. Das Wohngebiet ist durch schmale Durchfahrten und Wohnwege sparsam erschlossen. Zusammen mit der Siedlung wurde auf einem benachbarten Grundstück ein Gemeindezentrum mit Kirche, Gemeindehaus, Pfarrhof und Kindergarten gebaut. An der Einmündung der Aufschließungsstraße in die Durchgangsstraße ist eine Ladengruppe mit Waschküche geplant.

42 single-storey and 27 two-storey terrace homes are grouped informally about a green space, which has been kept free of buildings and occupies the lower part of a gently undulating site. This "common" includes a children's playground. The houses are in staggered rows, those of the one-storey type being separated from one another by utility rooms sandwiched between. In front of the living rooms, facing South-West, there is an open-air space, which cannot be overlooked by neighbours. The plots for the single-floor dwellings vary in area from 2,700 to 4,800 sq. ft. The whole estate is economically served by a system of drives and footpaths. A community centre, with church, parish room, parsonage and infants' school has been built, in conjunction with the housing scheme, on a neighbouring site. A group of shops and a laundry are planned where the road from the estate meets the main highway.

1 Blick aus einem Wohngarten über die ebenerdigen Reihenhäuser zum Kirchturm.
  Looking from a garden towards the church tower over the
  single-storey terrace houses.
2 Ansicht einer zweigeschossigen Häuserreihe von Süden.
  View of a row of two-storey houses from the South.
3 Kindergarten und Kirche von Süden gesehen.
  Infants' school and church from the South.

Grundriß eines ebenerdigen Hauses
Floor plan of a single-storey house
1 Eingang / Entrance
2 Diele mit Heizung / Hall with heating plant
3 Küche / Kitchen
4 Bad / Bath
5 Wohnraum / Sitting room
6 Schlafräume / Bedrooms
7 Überdeckter Sitzplatz / Sheltered sitting space
8 Hobbyraum / Games room
9 Abstell- und Trockenraum / Storage and drying room

Wettbewerb Montanunion in Luxemburg, Erster Preis – 1959
Architekten: Walter Schwagenscheidt und Tassilo Sittmann, Kronberg

Montanunion competition, Luxemburg, First prize – 1959
Architects: Walter Schwagenscheidt and Tassilo Sittmann, Kronberg

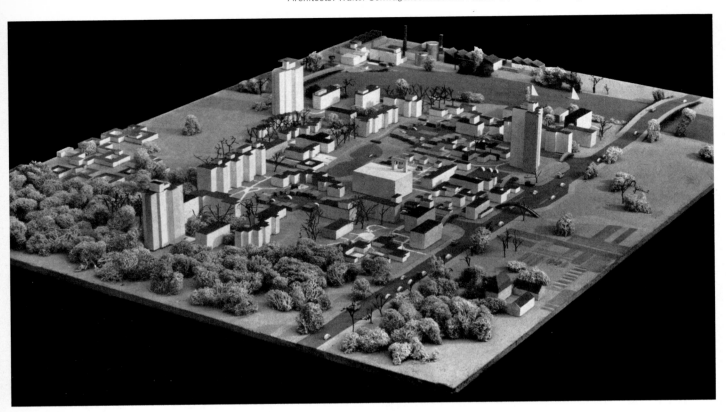

Das Stadtviertel ist in stark differenzierte, aber leicht überschaubare Gebäudegruppen unterteilt. Wohnhäuser von unterschiedlicher Größe und Stockwerkszahl – vom ebenerdigen Atriumhaus über zwei- bis siebengeschossige Stockwerksbauten bis zu elfstöckigen Punkthäusern – sind um intime, individuell gestaltete Gemeinschaftshöfe gestellt, die gegen den umgebenden Grünraum um einige Stufen gehoben oder abgesenkt sind. Hier gibt es Kinderspielplätze, Ruhebänke für die Alten, Planschbecken und Freiraum, wo die Jugend zum Spiel zusammenkommen kann und wo nachbarliche Gemeinschaft gepflegt wird. Eine Kirche steht im Zentrum der Anlage. Zwei Stichstraßen, die in zweigeschossigen Parkplätzen enden, erschließen die Siedlung für den Autoverkehr. Die Wohnwege, von den Fahrstraßen streng getrennt, sind so geführt, daß der Fußgänger zwangsläufig durch das Einkaufszentrum geleitet wird. Bei der Ladengruppe liegt die Omnibushaltestelle.

The proposed new quarter is divided into strikingly varied groups of buildings which are however easy to survey. Dwellings, differing in size and number of floors from single-storey patio houses and two-to seven-storey blocks of flats to eleven-storey towers, are disposed round garden courts, intimate in scale and individual in design, which are raised above, or sunk below, their green surroundings by a few steps. Here are to be found children's playgrounds, seats for old people, paddling pools and playgrounds, where the young can meet for play and a neighbourly atmosphere be cultivated. A church stands in the centre of the scheme. Two service roads, terminating in two-storey parking lots, provide for motor traffic. The footpaths, strictly segregated from the roads, are so arranged that the pedestrian is bound to pass through the shopping centre. The bus stop is close to the shops.

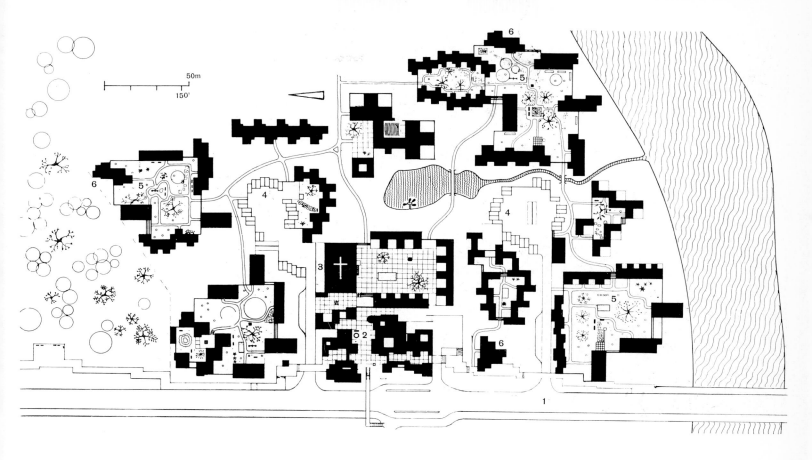

50m
150'

1 Modellansicht von Nordwesten.
  View (model) from the North-West.
2 Modellansicht von Westen. Leichte Fußgängerbrücken über-
  queren Hauptverkehrs- und Erschließungsstraßen.
  View (model) from the West. Light footbridges span the main
  and service roads.

Gesamtplan / General plan
1 Hauptverkehrsstraße / Main road
2 Ladenzentrum / Shopping centre
3 Kirche / Church
4 Garagen / Garages
5 Gemeinschaftshöfe / Communal gardens
6 Hochhäuser / Tower blocks

Neues Verwaltungszentrum in Hamburg – 1958–59
Architekt: Werner Hebebrand, Hamburg

Proposed new Civic (and business) centre for Hamburg – 1958–59
Architect: Werner Hebebrand, Hamburg

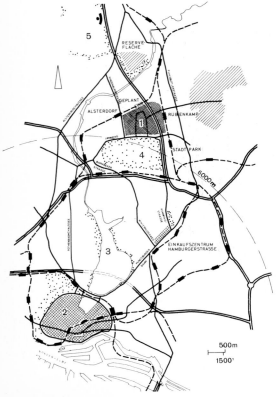

Um eine zu dichte Bebauung der Altstadt und ein willkürliches Auswuchern der City in die Wohngebiete zu verhindern, ist am Nordrand der Kernstadt auf einem 117 ha großen Gelände die Anlage eines zweiten Verwaltungszentrums geplant. Das in städtischem Besitz befindliche Gebiet war bisher durch Behelfsheime, Kleingärten und Sportanlagen genutzt. Es wird im Nordwesten von der U-Bahn, im Osten von der S-Bahn tangiert. Straßenzüge beiderseits der Alster, der an der südlichen Begrenzung vorbeiführende Jahnring und die projektierte Stadtschnellstraße stellen die Verbindung zur City und den übrigen Stadtteilen her. Eine große Straßenschleife, östlich an die Schnellstraße angebunden, erschließt das Gebiet vom Jahnring her für den Autoverkehr. Unabhängig davon ist das Fußgängernetz an die U- und S-Bahnhöfe angeknüpft. Im Anschluß an den südlich gelegenen Stadtpark bleibt die Mitte des Planungsgebietes als Grünzone ausgespart.

To prevent too dense development in the Old Town and unregulated expansion of the "City" into residential districts, a scheme for a second civic and business centre is proposed on the Northern perimeter on a 289-acre site. This area, which falls within the municipal limits, has hitherto been used for temporary housing, allotments and sports grounds. It is served on the North-West and East by suburban railways. Roads on both sides of the Alster, the "Jahnring" skirting the Southern boundary, and the proposed motorway, provide access to the "City" and to other parts of the town. Motor traffic from the Jahnring reaches the area via a wide loop road, connected on the East to the motorway. There is an independent system of footpaths to the railway stations. The middle of the planned zone is preserved as a green space, and is linked to the town park to the South.

1 Modellansicht von Nordosten.
  View (model) from the North-East.
2 Lage des neuen Verwaltungszentrums (1) zur Altstadt (2);
  Alster (3), Stadtpark (4), Flughafen (5).
  Site of the new civic centre (1), Old Town (2), Alster (3), town
  park (4), airport (5).

3 Modell. Für die Bebauung wurde eine Geschoßflächenzahl von 1,5 festgelegt. Wegen des nahen Flughafens wird die Gebäudehöhe auf 50 m begrenzt. Die Anordnung der einzelnen Bauten soll durch Wettbewerbe geklärt werden.

Model. For the built-up areas a floor space index of 1.5 was laid down; and, because of the adjacent airport, the height of buildings was limited to 160 feet. The siting of individual buildings will be decided by competitions.

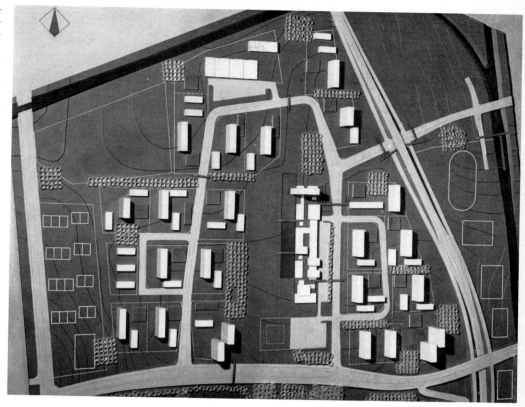

Lageplan / Site plan
1 S-Bahnstation
   Station (streetcars)
2 U-Bahnstation
   Station (underground)
3 Schnellstraße / Motorway
4 Jahnring
5 Stadtpark / Town park
6 Bestehendes Wohngebiet
   Existing residential areas
7 Sportanlage / Sports grounds
8 Bauschule / School of building
9 Zentrale Bauten (Hotel, Kino, Bankfilialen, Restaurants, Bar, Warenhaus) / Central buildings (hotel, cinema, banks, restaurants, bar, department store)
10 Wasserbecken / Water
11 Versorgungsbetriebe
    Services and supplies
12 Geschäftsgebiet, in 22 Grundstücke aufgeteilt
    Businesszone, divided into 22 plots

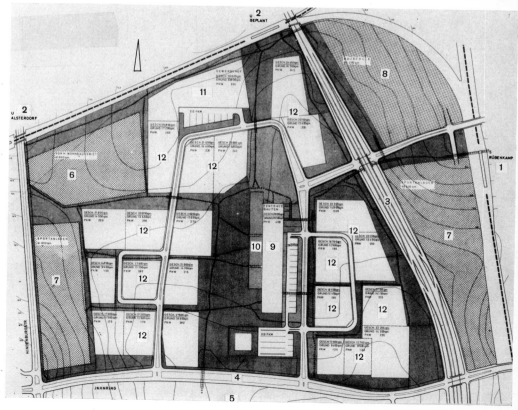

Wettbewerb Hauptstadt Berlin – 1958
Architekten: Friedrich Spengelin, Fritz Eggeling und Gerd Pempelfort, Hamburg und Hannover

Capital City Competition for Berlin – 1958
Architects: Friedrich Spengelin, Fritz Eggeling and Gerd Pempelfort, Hamburg and Hanover

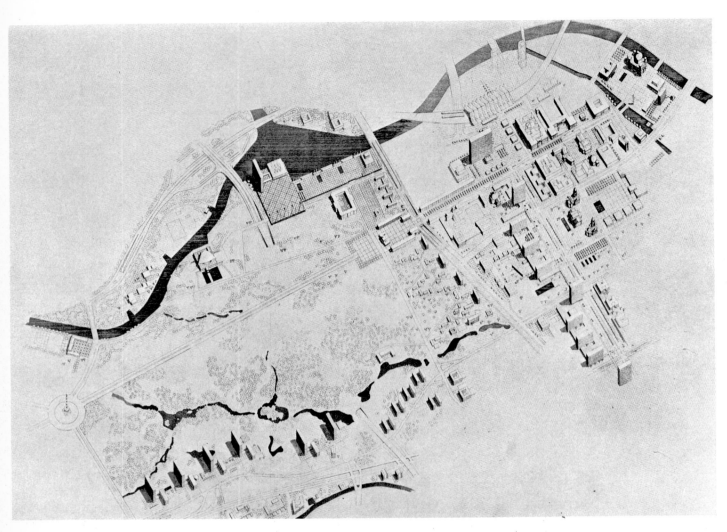

Isometrie / Isometric

Der Entwurf erhielt bei dem Wettbewerb für die Neugestaltung des Berliner Stadtkerns den ersten Preis. Innerhalb des tangentialen Schnellverkehrsstraßenvierecks ist ein Verteilerring vorgesehen, der die City vom Durchgangsverkehr frei hält. Die Regierungsgebäude sind rings um das Grün des Tiergartens gruppiert. Die erhöhte Plattform des Parlamentforums ist zwischen das alte Reichstagsgebäude und die seeartig erweiterte Spree gestellt, die Ministerien stehen frei im Südteil des Parks. Die Verwaltung von Stadt und Land Berlin ist um das erhaltene Rathaus zusammengezogen. Die kulturellen Einrichtungen und die kirchlichen Hauptbauten reichen von der Museumsinsel bis zum Kern der City. Dem als Kauf- und Vergnügungszentrum geplanten Gebiet um die Friedrichstraße sind die Verwaltungsgebäude der Wirtschaft zugeordnet. Zusammenhängende Grünflächen ziehen sich, vom Tiergarten ausgehend, quer durch die City und entlang der Spree.

This scheme won first prize in the competition for renovating the central area of Berlin. Inside the quadrilateral of perimeter highways a ring of roads is provided to serve the city, which will thus be undisturbed by through traffic. Government buildings will be grouped about the green area of the Tiergarten. The raised platform of the Parliament Forum is placed between the old Reichstag building and the Spree, widened here to form a lake, the freestanding ministries being placed in the Southern part of the park. The administration of Berlin city and province (Land) is concentrated around the old, preserved, City Hall. Cultural institutions and the principal churches extend from the museums island into the heart of the city. The commercial zone borders the Friedrichstrasse, which is designated as a shopping and amusement centre. Interconnected green spaces are spread across the city and along the Spree.

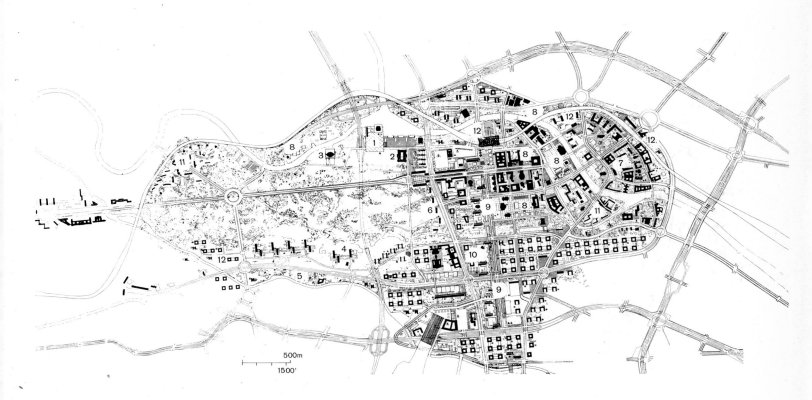

500m
1500'

Lageplan / General layout
1 Legislative: Parlament und Länderkammer
  Legislative: parliament and provincial chambers
2 Reichstagsgebäude / Reichstag building
3 Kongreßhalle / Congress hall
4 Exekutive: Ministerien / Executive: ministries
5 Vertretungen der Länder / Provincial representatives
6 Diplomatische Vertretung des Auslandes
  Foreign diplomatic representatives
7 Verwaltung von Stadt und Land Berlin
  Berlin Municipal and Provincial Government
8 Bischofskirchen und kulturelle Bauten (Universität, Aka-
  demien, Bibliotheken, Museen, Theater, Konzerthäuser)
  Cathedrals and cultural buildings (university, academies,
  libraries, museums, theatres, concert halls)
9 Kauf- und Vergnügungszentrum an der Friedrichstraße
  Shops and places of amusement on the Friedrichstrasse
10 Banken und Versicherungen / Banking and insurance
11 Wohngebiete / Residential areas
12 Hotels

Wettbewerb Hauptstadt Berlin – 1958
Architekt: Hans Scharoun, Berlin; Mitarbeiter: Wils Ebert, Berlin

Capital City Competition for Berlin – 1958
Architect: Hans Scharoun, Berlin; Assistant: Wils Ebert, Berlin

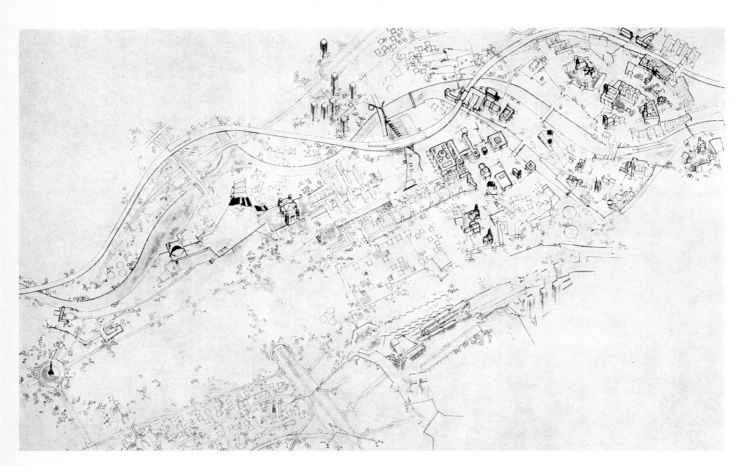

Isometrie / Isometric

Der bei dem Wettbewerb Hauptstadt Berlin mit einem zweiten Preis ausgezeichnete Vorschlag ergänzt die vier Tangentialstraßen durch ein Begleitstraßensystem. Die Erschließungsstraßen im Inneren und der größte Teil der Parkplätze sind unter die Erde gelegt. Das Regierungszentrum ist um das Reichstagsgebäude, die Stadtverwaltung um das alte Rathaus konzentriert. Der geschlossene Komplex der Wirtschaftsbauten im Südteil der City ist in seiner Struktur auf intensive Kommunikation und Flexibilität abgestellt. Die Hauptverkehrsadern des alten Berlin – Unter den Linden, Leipziger Straße und Teile der Friedrichstraße – werden als Zentren öffentlichen Lebens in die neue Konzeption aufgenommen. Hier finden Ausstellungsbauten, Kauf- und Vergnügungsstätten ihren Platz. In der vom Tiergarten nach Osten bis zur Spree reichenden Grünzone sind das Banken- und Versicherungsviertel und die kulturellen Institutionen inselartig angeordnet.

In the "Berlin as a Capital City Competition", this project, awarded a second prize, complements the four perimeter trunk roads, with a secondary road system. The feeder roads in the inner area and most of the parking places are underground. The centre of the federal government is concentrated about the Reichstag building, the municipal government around the old City Hall. The enclave of industrial and commercial buildings in the Southern section of the city is essentially flexible in its structure and adapted to rapid communications. The main traffic arteries of old Berlin – Unter den Linden, Leipziger Strasse and parts of Friedrichstrasse – are incorporated into the new conception as centres of community life. Here will be found exhibition buildings, shops and places of amusement. In the green belt stretching Eastwards from the Tiergarten to the Spree, the banking and insurance quarter and cultural institutions form islands.

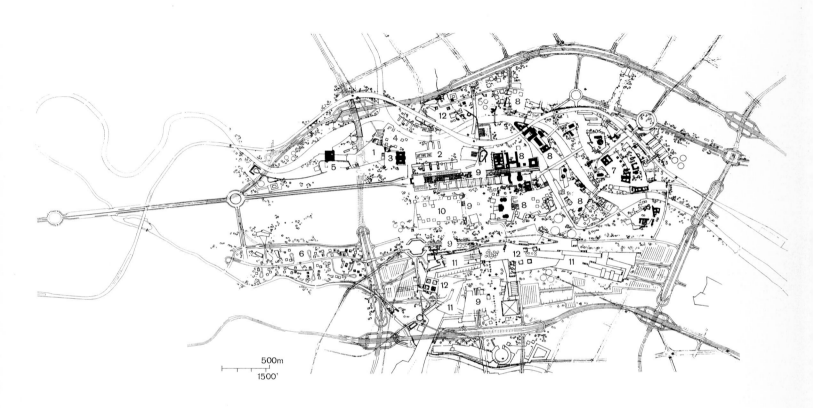

Lageplan / General layout

1 Legislative: Parlament und Länderkammer
  Legislative: parliament and provincial chambers
2 Exekutive: Ministerien / Executive: ministries
3 Reichstagsgebäude / Reichstag building
4 Vertretungen der Länder
  Provincial (Länder) representatives
5 Kongreßhalle / Congress hall
6 Diplomatische Vertretungen des Auslands
  Foreign diplomatic representatives
7 Verwaltung von Stadt und Land Berlin
  Berlin Municipal and Provincial Government
8 Bischofskirchen und kulturelle Bauten (Universität, Akade-
  mien, Bibliotheken, Museen, Theater, Konzerthäuser)
  Cathedrals and cultural buildings (university, academies,
  libraries, museums, theatres, concert halls)
9 Kauf- und Vergnügungsstätten
  Shops and places of amusement
10 Banken und Versicherungen / Banking and insurance
11 Bauten der Wirtschaft
  Commercial and industrial buildings
12 Hotels

Verzeichnis der Architekten und Mitarbeiter
List of Architects and Assistants

Verzeichnis der Fotografen
Acknowledgements to Photographers

Erich Angenendt, Dortmund, Poststraße 14: 90 (2)
Baubehörde, Hamburg, Stadthausbrücke 8: 224, 225
Martin Botsch, Karlsruhe-Hagsfeld, An der Bahn 15: 27
Deutsche Presse-Agentur, Frankfurt/Main: 128
Walter Ehmann, Köln-Klettenberg, Gottesweg 104: 39 (1), 40, 41, 44
I.+W. Faigle, Stuttgart-O, Gänsheide 26: 108, 109, 110, 111
Paul Förster, Offenbach/Main, Bernardstraße 105: 76, 77, 99 (2), 162, 163, 180
Inge Goertz-Bauer, Düsseldorf, Uhlandstraße 17: 182, 183, 184, 185, 211 (4), 213 (4)
Grieshaber, Frankfurt/Main, Vatterstraße 7: 99 (3, 4)
Grimm-Foto, Feucht bei Nürnberg, Pfinzingstraße 301: 80, 81
Hans-Dieter Haren: 181 (3)
Robert Häusser, Mannheim-Käfertal, Ladenburger Straße 23: 118 (3), 119
Atelier Heidersberger, Braunschweig, Wilhelmstraße 5: 42, 43, 90 (1), 92, 93, 100,
    101, 102, 103, 142, 143 (2), 144, 145, 176, 177, 178, 179, 196, 197, 217, 218, 219
Aenne Heise, Isernhagen, Am Rotdorn 20: 221
Karl E. Jacobs, Berlin-Lichterfelde, Finckenstein-Allee 76: 48, 49, 50, 64, 133 (3)
Foto-Kessler, Berlin-Wilmersdorf, Offenbacher Straße 7: 51 (5), 63, 65, 66, 67, 82, 83,
    112, 114 (3, 4), 115, 117, 135, 151, 214, 215, 216
Ernst Knorr, Gelsenkirchen: 120 (1), 121
Rolf Koehler, Berlin-Charlottenburg, Leibnizstraße 101: 54, 55, 62
Arthur Köster, Berlin-Lichterfelde, Potsdamer Straße 59 a: 56, 57, 68, 69, 84, 85 (2),
    140, 141
Foto-Kramer, Lünen in Westfalen: 87, 89
Mahnert-Prawit, Essen-Rüttenscheid, Zweigerstraße 33: 194, 195
Konrad Mahns, Köln-Merheim, Am Krausen Baum 7: 208, 209
Klaus Meier-Ude, Frankfurt/Main, Merianstraße 40: 34, 35
Horstheinz Neuendorff, Baden-Baden, Friedrich-Ludwig-Jahn-Straße 2: 164, 165,
    168, 169, 170, 171 (7)
Foto-Atelier Obigt, Berlin-Friedenau, Bundesallee 131: 148, 149
Orgel-Köhne, Berlin-Charlottenburg 9, Ahornallee 38: 150, 152
Gudula Petz, Frankfurt/Main, Berliner Straße 27: 146, 147
Artur Pfau, Mannheim, Schützenstraße 15: 70–75, 117, 118 (5), 153, 154, 155, 189,
    190, 191, 202–207
Gottfried Planck, Stuttgart, Ludwigstraße 63: 198, 201
Karl-Heinz Riek, Offenbach/Main, Bernardstraße 105: 94, 96, 97
H. J. Röse, Berlin-Spandau, Breite Straße 10: 58, 59, 60 (2), 61
De Sandalo, Frankfurt/Main, Ravensteiner Straße 2: 181 (2, 4)
Ilse Schmall, Berlin-Zehlendorf, Teltower Damm 208: 136 (1)
Hugo Schmölz, Köln, Klingelpütz 29: 28, 29
Schubert, Stuttgart, Gänsheidestraße 26: 37, 38 (5)
Ernst G. Schwab, Stuttgart, Wagenburgstraße 22: 30, 31
Herbert Schwöbel, Tübingen, Katharinenstraße 9: 38 (4)
Senator für Bau- und Wohnungswesen, Berlin: 52, 53
Stadtbildstelle Remscheid: 106 (3)
Dieter Storp, Düsseldorf, Lindemannstraße 1: 158 (4)
Gregor Stühler, Bochum, Kortumstraße 75: 120 (2), 122
Friedhelm Thomas, Hamburg: 78, 79, 106 (4, 5), 172, 173 (3), 174, 175
Eberhard Troeger, Hamburg-Großflottbeck: 166, 167
H. Urbschat, Berlin-Charlottenburg, Mommsenstraße 6: 85 (3), 130, 131
USIS, American Embassy, Bad Godesberg: 132, 133 (2), 134
Hans Wagner, Hannover, Wolfenbüttler Straße 14: 192 (1), 193
Waldthausen, Berlin-Schmargendorf, Weinheimer Straße 23 b: 51 (6, 7)
Foto-Wimmer, Berlin W 15, Uhlandstraße 167: 60 (1)
Ludwig Windstosser, Stuttgart, Christophstraße 6: 45, 46, 47 (5), 124, 126, 127,
    171 (8), 200 (2)
Foto Woscidlo, Frankfurt/Main, Dehmhardtstraße 49 A: 98
Arno Wrubel, Düsseldorf, Friedingstraße 1: Umschlag / Jacket, 186 (2), 187, 188
Friedrich Zieker, Stuttgart, Heinrich-Baumann-Straße 28: 159, 160, 161
Foto Zwietasch, Kornwestheim bei Stuttgart, Jahnstraße 50: 24, 25